T0302094

Replacing GDP by 2030

How did Gross Domestic Product (GDP) become the world's most influential indicator? Why does it still remain the primary measure of societal progress despite being widely criticised for not considering well-being or sustainability? Why have the many Beyond-GDP alternatives not managed to effectively challenge GDP's dominance?

The success of GDP and failure of Beyond-GDP lies in their underlying communities. The macroeconomic community emerged in the aftermath of the Great Depression and the Second World War. This community formalised their "language" in the System of National Accounts (SNA) which provided the global terminology with which to communicate. On the other hand, Beyond-GDP is a heterogeneous community which speaks in many dialects, accents and languages.

Unless this changes, the "Beyond-GDP cottage industry" will never beat the "GDP multinational". This book proposes a new roadmap to 2030, detailing how to create a multidisciplinary Well-being and Sustainability Science (WSS) with a common language, the System of Global and National Accounts (SGNA).

RUTGER HOEKSTRA is the owner of MetricsForTheFuture.com which provides consultancy services to governments, international institutes and companies on Beyond-GDP and Beyond-Profit. He has worked on well-being and sustainability from an academic, governmental and business perspective. He has worked with the United Nations, OECD, World Bank, European Commission, European Central Bank and other international organisations. He was the co-chair of the UNECE/OECD/Eurostat Task Force which developed the *Conference of European Statisticians Recommendations on Measuring Sustainable Development*. He has lectured at various universities and authored numerous publications on sustainable development, globalisation, circular economy and big data applications. He was also Scientific Director of the KPMG True Value methodology at KPMG Sustainability.

Advance Praise for Replacing GDP by 2030

'There are many publications criticising, for the right or for the wrong reasons, GDP and national accounts. But hardly anyone comes up with a valid way out. Rutger Hoekstra not only puts forward a well-thought-out alternative, but also provides a strategy for replacing the hegemony of GDP. Will it work?'

Peter van de Ven
Head of National Accounts, OECD

'This is a powerful and timely contribution to the debate about how to move beyond GDP – and what to use instead – in seeking to understand the economy and bring about improvements in people's lives. There is no question that the conventional economic statistics have outlived their use; they obscure rather than enlighten. The importance of this book is in its thoughtful and detailed proposals for change.'

Diane Coyle
Bennett Professor of Public Policy, University of Cambridge
Author of *GDP: A Brief but Affectionate History*

'The Beyond-GDP discussion has been raging on for decades, and progress has been slow. Drawing upon years of experience as a high-level international statistician, Rutger Hoekstra offers an original and highly informed view from the trenches on the why and how. His innovative and ambitious proposal for a way out deserves to be widely read and discussed.'

Marcel Timmer
Professor of Economic growth and development and Director of the
Groningen Growth and Development Centre (GGDC), University of
Groningen

'This book shows why a "Beyond-GDP world" is needed and how it can be built. A must-read contribution to the move towards a sustainable future.'

Enrico Giovannini
Professor of Economic Statistics at University of Rome Tor Vergata
Former Italian Minister of Labor and Social Policies

'In crisp prose, Rutger Hoekstra conveys an important message. We won't convince policy makers to look beyond GDP simply by multiplying the production of well-being indicators. Something more is clearly needed.'

Marco Mira d'Ercole
Head of Household Statistics, OECD

'This book by environmental economist Hoekstra not only offers a good read and an excellent introduction to the big debate about GDP and Beyond-GDP. It also provides a clear strategy to make Beyond-GDP much more effective and to learn from the success of GDP as an indicator and language.'

Frits Bos
CPB Netherlands Bureau for Economics Policy Analysis
Author of *The National Accounts as a Tool for Analysis and Policy*

Replacing GDP by 2030

Towards a Common Language for the Well-being and Sustainability Community

RUTGER HOEKSTRA

MetricsForTheFuture.com

CAMBRIDGE
UNIVERSITY PRESS

CAMBRIDGE
UNIVERSITY PRESS

University Printing House, Cambridge CB2 8BS, United Kingdom

One Liberty Plaza, 20th Floor, New York, NY 10006, USA

477 Williamstown Road, Port Melbourne, VIC 3207, Australia

314–321, 3rd Floor, Plot 3, Splendor Forum, Jasola District Centre,
New Delhi – 110025, India

79 Anson Road, #06–04/06, Singapore 079906

Cambridge University Press is part of the University of Cambridge.

It furthers the University's mission by disseminating knowledge in the pursuit of
education, learning, and research at the highest international levels of excellence.

www.cambridge.org
Information on this title: www.cambridge.org/9781108497336
DOI: 10.1017/9781108608558

First published 2019

A catalogue record for this publication is available from the British Library.

Library of Congress Cataloging-in-Publication Data
Names: Hoekstra, Rutger, 1974– author.
Title: Replacing GDP by 2030 : towards a common language for the well-being
    and sustainability community / Rutger Hoekstra.
Description: First Edition. | New York : Cambridge University Press, 2019.
Identifiers: LCCN 2018049980 | ISBN 9781108497336 (hardback) |
    ISBN 9781108739870 (paperback)
Subjects: LCSH: Social indicators. | Well-being–Measurement. | Resilience
    (Ecology)–Measurement. | Sustainable development–Measurement. | BISAC:
    BUSINESS & ECONOMICS / Development / Economic Development.
Classification: LCC HN25 .H64 2019 | DDC 339.3/1–dc23
    LC record available at https://lccn.loc.gov/2018049980

ISBN 978-1-108-49733-6 Hardback
ISBN 978-1-108-73987-0 Paperback

This book is dedicated to Tjeerd, Cas and Suzanne for ... everything

I also dedicate this book to Jan Pieter Smits who has been my cherished companion on this intellectual and personal journey

Contents

Figures

Tables

Boxes

Preface

This book was born out of frustration. Since 2007 I have worked in the area of measuring well-being and sustainability, initially with great enthusiasm. It felt like an important task to provide information which went beyond our current dominant economic indicators. Around that time there was a reinvigorated debate about creating a better "compass" for society to navigate towards a future based on human well-being and sustainability. I started to work on the issue with great zeal and sense of purpose. Yet a couple of years later I became disheartened and later still my disenchantment grew to the point that I wanted to write down my thoughts in a book. This personal evolution is rather important to understand the motivation of the book, so I will briefly expand on it.

My interest in this topic started in the 1990s when I was studying for an MSc in environmental economics and later a PhD in ecological economics. I was taught that Gross Domestic Product (GDP), the way we measure the economy, is a flawed metric. GDP is fine if you want to measure economic activity but totally inadequate for measuring societal progress. Yet I did not fully grasp the complexity underlying these statements. I can distinctly remember a friend of mine, a student of geosciences, asking me to explain a simple paradox of economic thinking. Why do economists think that economies should keep on growing indefinitely while at the same time acknowledging that GDP does not measure well-being? Why not strive for a society in which the population becomes happier but the economic activity remains constant or even diminishes? In hindsight I might be forgiven for not having a response in my first year of university, but I can remember feeling rather embarrassed that I could not answer this seemingly simple, but rather fundamental, question.

In the early 2000s I got a front-row seat to the GDP issue as
I started to work in the Department of National Accounts at Statistics
Netherlands. This gave me an opportunity to see the enormous media
interest and societal impact of GDP firsthand. Statistics Netherlands
produces many other statistics, including excellent environmental
accounts and social data, but the societal impact of GDP growth
figures are in a different league. To paraphrase George Orwell,
"all statistics are equal but some statistics are more equal than
others". GDP is the headliner of the statistical world. I couldn't
help but wonder why society craves this information above all
other data.

As fate would have it, I got a life-changing opportunity to
contribute to "Beyond-GDP", the quest to look for alternatives to
GDP, in 2007. Together with my close colleague and friend, Jan Pieter
Smits, I started working on the *Sustainability Monitor for the
Netherlands* in the summer of 2007. The Dutch government
commissioned Statistics Netherlands and three other policy institutes
to create a measurement system for sustainable development.

Jan Pieter and I eagerly accepted the role of project manager. In
the beginning, we spent quite some time going over the literature and
reviewing the many alternatives to measure well-being and
sustainable development. Despite our academic background in this
field, we were overwhelmed by the plethora of measurement systems
that were available. There were simply too many to review
comprehensively. We plodded on enthusiastically because we learned
every day about the enormous range of interesting and clever
methods. Perhaps more importantly, we spoke to many inspiring and
motivated people who were all working towards better measurement
of societal progress. Hearing the energetic speeches at the various
conferences confirmed to us that we were working on something
interesting and important.

One of the most inspiring gatherings that we attended was the
presentation of the Stiglitz-Sen-Fitoussi report on 14 September 2009.
This report was commissioned by the French President Nicholas

Sarkozy because he wanted better measures of societal progress, and he asked Joseph Stiglitz and Amartya Sen (both Nobel Prize winners) and Jean Paul Fitoussi to lead a group of prominent thinkers to advise him. We were, naturally, very impressed by the grandeur of the Sorbonne auditorium, the quality of the report and the stellar speakers. But what struck us most was the "inclusive" philosophy of the report. The report was respectful of many strands of economic literature which had previously been given little attention by mainstream economists. These concepts, such as subjective well-being and social capital, were endorsed by the Stiglitz Report and synthesised into a coherent framework.

The Stiglitz Report was also crucial in our next project. In 2009, Jan Pieter and I were asked to be the co-chairs of the Joint UN–ECE/OECD/Eurostat Task Force on Measuring Sustainable Development (TFSD). The TFSD was tasked to creating greater harmonisation in the measurement of sustainable development in developed countries. This was a daunting goal because the three lead institutions (UN-ECE, OECD and Eurostat), the World Bank and the ten developed countries already had their own frameworks to measure sustainable development. After five years of meetings a compromise was reached which synthesised many of the insights from the various countries' experiences. The TFSD was based heavily on the Stiglitz report and it is probably fair to say that without this conceptual basis it would have been nearly impossible to achieve a compromise.

In the end, the TFSD reached agreement and proposed a "suggested list of sustainable development indicators". In 2014, Jan Pieter and I had a proud moment when the report was endorsed by the Conference of European Statisticians (CES) – an organisation which has statistical representatives at the highest level from over fifty countries. Subsequently, the *CES Recommendations on Measuring Sustainable Development*, as the report is formally called, has been adopted by a couple of countries. There was however no pressure on the CES members to adopt the system and the subsequent adoption has been slow.

Overall, the 2007–2014 period was very fulfilling. It was a time when I learned a great deal and worked with many fine colleagues, both nationally and internationally. We spoke at many conferences and gatherings. Jan Pieter and I became close friends. Yet as time went on, I felt a growing frustration about the Beyond-GDP scene. Around 2012, I had come across an (incomplete) database on the internet which showed that there were over 900 systems to measure sustainable development. Up to that point I knew that there were many measurement systems, but I had not expected it to be as high as 1,000![1]

Jan Pieter and I had also started to become more critical of conferences in which the enthusiastic creators were advertising the benefits and achievements of their indicator systems. In 2007 we thought this was inspiring, but by 2012 it started to look somewhat pointless to try to keep up with all the new initiatives. Every couple of weeks my email and Twitter account would alert me to yet another index that had been launched by a researcher or institute. Press conferences were held to promote the index and argue its superiority over other approaches. Fancy websites and slick web presentations would be made to convince everyone of the virtue of the new measurement system. And the number of alternatives to GDP just keeps on growing. Where is this leading?

The enormous enthusiasm and energy of the Beyond-GDP community is admirable and the past decades have resulted some excellent proposals. Yet at the same time "our" common goal of replacing GDP does not seem to be coming any closer. The number of alternatives is expanding at a staggering rate, but the societal impact is not. If a fairly experienced researcher like myself is having trouble keeping up with all the new initiatives, how confusing must this be to the general public? The Beyond-GDP community seems to be suggesting new indexes in the hope that one day one will hit the jackpot. But even after hundreds of attempts this strategy has not yet yielded the "golden index" – none has ever come close to replacing the role of GDP in society. Certainly there are success stories, such as the Human Development Index, Genuine Progress Indicator, Happy Planet Index, Adjusted Savings, the Better Life Index, Inclusive Wealth Index and Ecological Footprint, but these pale in comparison to GDP. Apparently there is hope in the community that one of these indexes will achieve a breakthrough or that someone, somewhere, is currently working on an amazing project which is so clever that someday soon the GDP hegemony will be broken. Over the years I have become increasingly convinced that this is wishful thinking. Something else is needed.

To channel our energy, Jan Pieter and I agreed to work only on projects that helped to reduce the number of measurement systems rather than expand it. Harmonisation efforts became our focus. The *CES recommendations* was an example that contributed to convergence. In our private conversations, we jokingly speculated about how to achieve more harmonisation. My favourite draconic rule was: "if you want to propose the 1001st indicator system you first have to explain what is wrong with the 1,000 others".

We started focusing on the commonalities of the various measurement initiatives rather than their differences. It turned out that if you look at the systems closely, there is a surprising degree of overlap. For the European Commission we wrote *The Convergence Report* in which we argued for more harmonisation of Beyond-GDP measures and more cooperation of the Beyond-GDP community.[2] We also started to work with the Global Reporting Initiative (GRI) to see whether there was common ground with the leading framework to measure Corporate Social Responsibility (CSR).

Ironically, the disarray of the Beyond-GDP scene made my respect for GDP grow enormously. Not for GDP as an indicator but rather GDP as a process. I started reading about the history of national accounts and GDP.[3] I remember reading a PhD thesis by Frits Bos which said that by 1900 only nine countries had ever attempted to measure national income.[4] Nine! Up to the 1930s, national income was an obscure, ad hoc and fairly inconsequential metric, known only by a niche group of academics and statisticians. There were many different methodological approaches promoted by various researchers and institutes. In that period researchers would argue their definition of national income at economic conferences and gatherings. This sounded familiar to the situation that Beyond-GDP is currently in!

I became interested to know what happened after the 1930s to set GDP off on this amazing "rags to riches" success story. How did GDP become the superstar indicator that it is today? Does that story provide any insights into why Beyond-GDP is currently failing? Perhaps more importantly, does it provide clues about how Beyond-GDP might succeed?

My curiosity and frustration eventually led to the finalisation of this manuscript. In the process, my pessimism has made way for reasoned optimism: there is a way out of this situation.

There are two important messages in the book. Part I argues that Beyond-GDP is not doing well and will probably never succeed if this uncontrolled ever-expanding proliferation of initiatives continues. A new strategy is needed. In Part II it is argued that the main problem is that Beyond-GDP is a loosely connected set of theories and methodologies. It does not have a coherent community such as macro-economics. The strategy proposed in this book is to create a similar community for well-being and sustainability by 2030. It is this community which will create the new indicators, accounting framework and policies.

So despite the fact that this book was driven by frustration, it ends on a hopeful note. The optimism lies in the fact that there is more than enough scientific knowledge and data. The many decades of research have provided enough insights to offer a solid basis for the community. The well-being and sustainability research has more commonalities than differences. In addition, the big data revolution provides opportunities to create data at a lower cost or produce data on phenomena that are not yet measured. The only real challenge is how to get this community-building process institutionalised at the global level. International institutes will be vital to supporting these efforts.

My worst nightmare is that the strategy is not changed and that this unfocused explosion of Beyond-GDP initiatives continues. By 2030, there might be hundreds, perhaps thousands, of additional indicator systems without having any meaningful impact on the hegemony of GDP.

Acknowledgements

This book was written in the period September 2016–May 2018 but some of the ideas have been brewing for much longer. A decade earlier, in August 2007, I received a phone call from Onno van Sandick of the Ministry of the Environment asking whether Statistics Netherlands would be willing to lead the "Sustainability Monitor for the Netherlands". As fate would have it, one month later Jan Pieter Smits came to work at Statistics Netherlands. Together we embarked on a tumultuous journey which included the UN-ECE/OECD/Eurostat Task Force for Measuring Sustainable Development (TFSD), the European Union's "e-Frame-project" and the Dutch Parliamentary Commission for Broader Welfare Measures.

In these projects, Jan Pieter and I worked together intensely. We spent many hours talking about conceptual issues as well as tactical moves on how to get support for the ideas. It is hard to imagine that I will ever learn as much and work as closely together with a colleague. Without this basis I am convinced that this book would never have come about. Although our careers have now diverged, our friendship endures.

Along the way, I have been given many opportunities by my former employer Statistics Netherlands. Peter van de Ven, Brugt Kazemier, Marleen Verbruggen and Bert Kroese were particularly important during the initial phases. We collaborated with many great colleagues such as Ruben van der Helm, Anna Kulig, Hans Kolfoort, Marieke Rensman and Remco Kaashoek, who laboured tirelessly to make the various sustainability projects successful. Although I have not worked with them, I am also grateful to Karin van de Ven and Edwin Horlings for their dedication to the follow-up work on "Broader Welfare Measures".

At Statistics Netherlands, I am greatly indebted to my manager, Egon Dietz, who made it possible for me to take my initial six-month sabbatical. The narrative of the book evolved so much during this period. I am convinced that this is only possible if one takes a dedicated period for writing and reading, and I am extremely grateful to Egon for this opportunity. He did also make me promise to dedicate an entire paragraph to him in the acknowledgements. You're welcome!

Over the years we have also worked with many colleagues at Dutch and international institutes. Interinstitutional cooperation is sometimes cooperative and sometimes adversarial. Although the former is definitely more pleasant than the latter, it is often the disagreements from which you learn the most. They help stimulate ideas and bring discussions to a higher level. I would like to thank colleagues at the economic, environmental and social policy institutes of the Netherlands as well as our colleagues at the OECD, Eurostat and the World Bank for this cooperation. In particular, I would like to thank Lidia Bratanova of the UN-ECE for giving Jan Pieter and myself the opportunity to lead the TFSD. The support of Tiine Luigi and Vania Etropolska was also invaluable in making it a success. The Task Force meetings were always a guarantee for stimulating discussions in a cooperative atmosphere, which is a credit to the many dedicated members of the TFSD.

I am grateful for the feedback I received from my colleagues at Statistics Netherlands and from the participants of my lectures at various institutes, workshops and universities. Your compliments and criticisms stimulated me to keep on refining the arguments in the book. I am also grateful to my colleagues at KPMG-Sustainability for their tips about my book. In particular, I want to thank Arjan de Draaijer and Frits Klaver for stressing that the utimate aim of metrics is that they must lead to better decisions. I am also grateful for the inspiring brainstorm sessions with I had with Janne Dietz which helped me to sharpen my thoughts on the social dimension of well-being.

In the writing process, I have received written comments
or verbal advice from many people, for which I am very thankful:
Barteld Braaksma, Bernhard Michel, Bram Edens, Brent Bleys, Brugt
Kazemier, Carl Obst, Dirk Hoekstra, Edwin Horlings, Faye Duchin,
Frits Bos, Marieke Rensman, Hans Opschoor, Jan de Haan, Jan Pieter
Smits, Jeroen van den Bergh, Karin van de Ven, Kees Zeelenberg,
Marcel Timmer, Marco Mira D'Ercole, Marianne Paasi, Mark de
Haan, Peter van de Ven, Piet Verbiest, Rachael Milicich, Robert
Kornfeld, Robert Went, Ruut Veenhoven, Sangwon Suh, Sjoerd
Schenau, Viveka Palm, Ton Bastein, Dirk van den Bergen, Leendert
Hoven, Lars Hein, Kees Baldé, Sanjeev Majahan, Arjen Siegman,
Elmer Rietveld, Mattheus van der Pol, Jeroen Boelhouwer and
Pim Claassen. This feedback really helped the narrative to evolve
to its current state. I am extremely grateful for your time, effort,
thought-provoking ideas and enthusiasm.

Special thanks go to Jeroen van den Bergh, my PhD supervisor,
who has always remained interested in my work. When you heard
about this project you were immediately supportive. Your detailed
review of the preliminary version was reminiscent of the time we
spent on my PhD thesis. Thanks for your insightful and honest
feedback.

I would also like to thank the team at Cambridge University
Press for their professional management and feedback. Phil Good,
Matt Sweeney, Toby Ginsberg, Sri Krishnamurthy Ilangovan and
Joan Dale Lace smoothed the finalisation of the manuscript.

The support of friends, family, neighbours and colleagues has
been important in this entire process. At get-togethers and parties
people were always curious about the book and disappointed to hear
that the deadline had been moved forward once more. Initially I had
said that the six-month sabbatical would be sufficient... Some
friendly advice to prospective authors: never communicate a deadline.

Special thanks go to my wife Suzanne for enduring the many
weekends and evenings which I spent working on the book. From
the start you supported me on this journey despite knowing that it

would be a long and unpredictable process. I am grateful that our life makes this type of project possible. Thanks for everything. Finally, a note to my children Cas and Tjeerd, who will turn twenty-five and twenty-three in 2030. I hope that this book makes a small contribution to the society and environment in which you will live.

PART I Why a New Strategy Is Needed

I Replacing the Most Influential Indicator in the World

FOUR TIMES A YEAR . . .

. . . a group of civil servants go into the "lock-up" procedure in a secure room at 4600 Silver Hill Road, Maryland, USA. In the afternoon they enter an office where their name and time of arrival are recorded. They are not allowed to leave until they are officially dismissed, no earlier than 18:00. Contact with people outside the room is heavily restricted. All computers have been disabled for outside communication. There is only one telephone, which is controlled by the lock-up manager, who logs all conversations. Worksheets, notes, rough drafts, unused copies, single-strike ribbons or laser cartridges are collected when the lock-up ends. "Shredder Bins" are provided for office trash. If someone leaves the room to verify necessary information, this has to be authorised by the Director and/or Deputy Director. In case of family emergency or personal illness, participants need official permission to leave. During the lock-up the civil servants review the information and the executive staff write a press release. When all analysis has been done, the document is approved by a group of top management officials. The report is transmitted to the adviser of the President of the United States, who may brief the President before the general public is notified.[1]

The above procedures may seem appropriate for an intelligence agency, but these civil servants are far from secret agents: they are statisticians. They work for the Bureau of Economic Analysis (BEA). The adviser to the President is the Chairman of the Council of Economic Advisers (CEA). This procedure is followed every quarter. The report includes a key indicator called Gross Domestic Product (GDP), which is a measure of the economic activity of the United States.

3

More importantly, it shows whether GDP is growing ("economic growth") or shrinking.

The following morning the report is made public. The contents are transmitted all over the United States and all over the world. The media report the results almost instantly, politicians comment, stock markets rise or fall, economic pundits interpret the results and investment decisions are (re)considered. If the economic growth is high, the media will qualify the developments as "healthy", "buoyant" or "strong". If the figure is stable, the economy is said to be "anaemic" or "sluggish". If GDP diminishes significantly, words such as "slowdown" and "recession" start to be used. If economic growth is below stock market expectations, share prices and bond markets are affected.

When GDP growth is disappointing, the ruling party gets anxious and the opposition starts to question the abilities of the government. Voters start to lose confidence. George Bush enjoyed good approval ratings in 1991 but was still defeated a year later. His opponent, Bill Clinton, capitalised on the poor economic figures and his campaign team famously used the phrase "It's the economy, stupid" to keep on-message. The way that incumbents and challengers deal with economic issues has been an important predictor of US elections since at least 1952.[2]

THE GDP MULTINATIONAL

At the same time as the BEA officials in Maryland are calculating quarterly GDP growth for the United States, statisticians in many countries in the world are doing exactly the same. The countries of the European Union and the Organisation for Economic Co-operation and Development (OECD) all release their quarterly GDP figures within a period of around 30–45 days after the end of the quarter. Although not all countries produce quarterly GDP data, there are annual GDP figures for 200 countries and regions in the United Nations statistical database.

GDP figures are collected and disseminated by all the major international institutions, such as the World Bank, International

---

BOX 1.1   **Terminology: National Income, GNP, GDP and Other SNA Aggregates**

In this book, the term GDP is used to refer to the headline indicator of the national accounts. In reality the name and definition of the key indicator have changed over the course of history. Before the 1950s the term most commonly used was "national income". The first two official versions of the System of National Accounts (1953 and 1968) used the indicator Gross National Product (GNP). Later on, in the SNA 1993, GDP was adopted and GNP was sidelined.

It would be correct to use each term for the periods in which they were employed. However, using so many different terms will be confusing and it is also impossible to pinpoint an exact year when terminology changed. The term GDP is used most, although I sometimes also use the generic term "national income" for the periods around the Second World War.

The SNA includes other macroeconomic aggregates such as Gross National Income (GNI). For Official Development Assistance (ODA), for example, country contributions are based on GNI. The same holds for the contributions which EU member states have to pay to the European Union. The technical differences between the various macroeconomic aggregates do not contribute to the narrative of this book and therefore are not explained further.

Monetary Fund, OECD and the European Commission. These institutions use the data to project economic developments of individual countries and the global economy. International agreements such as the contributions to Official Development Assistance (ODA) or the contribution to the United Nations are made on the basis of macroeconomic figures (see Box 1.1). Geopolitical bodies such as the G7 or G20 are organised on the basis of GDP ranking. GDP data is also used by economists for academic research, stock brokers for investment decisions, as well as a host of other users and applications.

There is a vast national and global infrastructure underlying the calculation, dissemination and use of GDP data. This includes the methodological guidelines which govern the calculation of GDP. These are recorded in an international handbook called the *System of National Accounts* (SNA), which was last updated in 2008. It is a 722-page manual on how to record the economic transactions and resources of a society.[3] Adherence to the SNA is not legally binding on the global level but there is significant pressure to conform. In some regions, such as the European Union, there are legal requirements for member states to deliver the data according to the handbook.[4]

GDP is without question the superstar of indicators. The global logistical, legal and communications infrastructure is like no other statistic. National Statistical Institutes and international organisations have created an efficient machine that is churning out new numbers all the time. In the current media landscape, with twenty-four-hour news networks and business reporting, GDP figures are very welcome. Quarterly GDP figures are produced by all major economies so the headlines basically write themselves: "New growth figures for the US (or China, Germany, France or the UK) show economy is growing/stabilizing/in recession."

In addition there are growth projections of the major economies and world GDP by institutes such as the IMF and OECD, which guarantee even more news stories. Simply insert the country and growth percentage in the following sentence "GDP growth for [country] projected to be [percentage]"; then ask a couple of economist talking heads to comment and a quarter of an hour of television is filled.

It is easy to argue that GDP has a lot in common with a multinational company. It has a worldwide presence and vast logistical infrastructure. There is a structure in which international organisations such as the UN, IMF, World Bank and OECD cooperate with the statistical bodies of all countries in the world. The "product" is created using globally harmonised SNA methodology. Quality control procedures are in place, to ensure consistent delivery.

People all over the world recognise the GDP "brand", which has become the proxy indicator for the "success" of a country. This

REPLACING THE MOST INFLUENTIAL INDICATOR IN THE WORLD 7

indicates that GDP has obtained a meaning which transcends its objective "product specifications". GDP measures the size of the economy yet the perception is that it measures whether a society is doing well or not.

These positive associations are common for other global brands as well. Global sneaker companies want their shoes to be associated with qualities such as freedom or an independent way of life. These emotions are important for product sales, which is why advertising rarely stresses the objective characteristics of a product but rather tries to appeal to these deeper emotions.

Society is unaware of the product characteristics of GDP (what it actually measures) but has a basic feeling that "high GDP is good and low GDP is bad". This has real-world implications because if a government or political party advocates lower economic growth it is likely to be ridiculed in the media and suffer in the polls. It is only fringe political parties or small isolated countries (e.g., Bhutan[5]) that have challenged the GDP multinational.[6]

Multinationals have drawbacks, however. The larger they become the more difficult it becomes to innovate. The GDP multinational is no different. Altering the "product specifications" of GDP requires years of laborious negotiations between many parties. The SNA has only been revised four times in the last seventy years (1953, 1968, 1993, 2008), despite the fact that society and the economy have changed radically.

For the first two editions of the SNA the number of active countries/experts was small and was led only by the UN. In the last revision, the SNA 2008, all countries and all the international institutes were involved. New guidelines are therefore slow to adapt because all countries have to agree and implement changes, which are sometimes very costly. Given that many developing countries still have poor statistical infrastructures this is a major barrier to innovation. As a result, the SNA is slow to react to changes in the economy and scientific knowledge and has changed little in the past seventy years.

THE BEYOND-GDP COTTAGE INDUSTRY

GDP is a measure of economic activity but not, as is the general perception, a measure of societal success. This has been known for a long time. Simon Kuznets, one of the pioneers of national accounting, famously wrote in 1934 that "the welfare of a nation ... can scarcely be inferred from a measurement of national income".[7] Even the SNA, the worldwide handbook, explicitly warns: "GDP is often taken as a measure of welfare, but the SNA makes no claim that this is so and indeed there are several conventions in the SNA that argue against the welfare interpretation of the accounts."[8] Issues such as well-being, sustainability and inequality are not measured by GDP. As a result of these shortcomings many alternatives to GDP have been proposed. These are known under the collective term "Beyond-GDP" but defining the boundaries of this field are difficult.

Among economists, the best known are "green accounting" indicators. This approach includes indicators such as the Measure of Economic Well-being (MEW), Sustainable National Income (SNI), Index of Sustainable Economic Welfare (ISEW), Genuine Progress Indicator (GPI), Genuine/Adjusted Net Savings or Wealth Index. These are usually based on GDP (or other SNA aggregates) which are adjusted by subtracting welfare-reducing impacts such as environmental damage (measured in monetary terms) and adding a monetary value for welfare-enhancing dimensions such as leisure time. Economists use neoclassical welfare economics or the capital theory to create these green accounting aggregates.

There are other approaches too. The field of subjective well-being (SWB) includes approaches which provide data on the "life satisfaction" or "happiness" of a population. This is done by asking respondents to score their life situation on a scale of 1 to 10 or some other range. The confrontation of GDP and SWB is often used to argue that GDP is not a good reflection of well-being. It has been argued that beyond a certain threshold, additional growth in GDP does not lead to higher well-being. To put it in layman's terms: money doesn't buy you happiness (at least not beyond a certain point).

The Beyond-GDP debate is more diverse than just green accounting and SWB. In the grey literature and policy documents other approaches are also prevalent. For example, the ecological footprint is cited frequently, including in the *Living Planet Report* of the World Wildlife Fund. There are "composite indicators" such as the Human Development Index (HDI), which aggregates health, education and GDP into a single index. HDI is one of the most visible Beyond-GDP alternatives and is featured every year in the United Nations' Human Development Report.

A popular approach in the grey literature is the use of a "set of indicators". This is also known as a "dashboard" or a "suite" of indicators. Rather than providing a single index, these approaches assume that the multidimensional nature of societal change requires a multidimensional set of indicators. The philosophy is that rather than aggregating economy, health, education, environment, social cohesion, etc. into one figure, these phenomena should be measured separately. This also means that the indicators are measured in various units rather than in terms of a single unit such as money. Indicator sets have become popular amongst governments and statistical offices worldwide. The United Nations' Sustainable Development Goals (SDG), which are a global agreed set of targets for sustainable development, are probably the most famous example of an indicator set.[9]

Thus there is a diversity of approaches, but there is also variety within each approach. There are many types of green accounting, composite indicators, subjective well-being and indicator sets at the national, regional, city and company level. This amounts to hundreds of alternatives. The alternatives are proposed by a highly eclectic group of institutes, researchers, universities and NGOs using a wide range of theories and approaches. All try to measure societal progress but operate in relative isolation, without much coordination.

Some GDP alternatives are one-off efforts whereas others may appear annually. Some have survived for decades while others have been forgotten fairly quickly. Overall, the Beyond-GDP scene is

FIGURE 1.1 GDP multinational versus Beyond-GDP cottage industry

fragmented, with hundreds of different "products" coming from a multitude of small and medium-scale operations – a real cottage industry. This also means that it has all the positive aspects of small business: it is vibrant, full of energy, zeal and enthusiastic people, allowing for innovation to flourish. At the same time it lacks the global power of a multinational.

THE SCHUMPETERIAN DREAM

The previous sections introduced two protagonists to the story: the GDP multinational and the Beyond-GDP cottage industry as depicted in Figure 1.1. The left side of the figure represents the global enterprise with a well-coordinated and harmonised operation, while the right side shows the heterogeneous and chaotic Beyond-GDP situation.

This is a rather static view of the current state of affairs. What happened in the past which has resulted in this situation? And what might happen in the future? For this dynamic view it is useful to look at GDP as an innovation. In fact it was Nobel Prize winner Paul Samuelson who famously said: "While the GDP and the rest of the national income accounts may seem to be arcane concepts, they are truly among the great inventions of the twentieth century."[10] If this is so, how does it stack up to the various phases which are typical of innovation theory? Joseph Schumpeter, one of the pillars of thinking on innovation, defined the stages that innovations go through: early adoption, take-off, saturation and decline.[11]

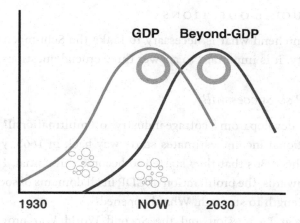

FIGURE 1.2 The Schumpeterian dream

Figure 1.2 is a stylised depiction of these developments. If an innovation is successful it will increase its market share (the y-axis). The blue line shows the ascendance of GDP, which started in the 1930s and has since made a spectacular move up this innovation curve. GDP innovation is now at its peak, or very close to it. At the same time the figure also shows that GDP was not always a multinational; in fact in the 1930s it could also be described as a cottage industry, with many countries and academics having differing views of how to measure national income.

In Schumpeter's theory, a new innovation emerges and replaces the old innovation in a process called "creative destruction".[12] Eventually the old innovation goes into a phase of decline and the new innovation works through the same cycle. The Schumpeterian dream for many researchers is that Beyond-GDP will one day lead to the creative destruction of GDP, as depicted on the right side of Figure 1.2.

Beyond-GDP initiatives have existed for several decades and are definitely on the upward curve of the innovation cycle. However, it is open for debate how high up the curve Beyond-GDP currently is. There can be no doubt however that it is still far from its peak. Why? And what can be done about it? Could creative destruction be a reality by 2030?

THREE CRUCIAL QUESTIONS

To fully comprehend what is necessary to make the Schumpeterian dream a reality, it is important to answer three crucial questions.

Why Is GDP so Successful?

How did GDP develop from a cottage industry to a multinational? The history of national income estimates starts way back in 1665, yet it was only in the 1930s that they started to become influential. From that period onwards, the proliferation of GDP in all domains of society went from strength to strength. What happened?

The Great Depression and the Second World War provided opportunities for economists to contribute to the resolution of two of the most traumatic periods of the twentieth century. Using their national income statistics, economists were able to provide clarity about the crises and also offer policy advice to governments about how to overcome them. Building on this success, the period after the war turned out to be a golden age for economists. It was the era of "big government" and the rise of international institutions such as the UN, IMF, World Bank and OECD.

This national and international governance increasingly relied on economists for advice and as employees. It is impossible to analyse the success of GDP without thinking about the role of economic science and economists in society. The success of GDP is a by-product of the success of macroeconomists. The success of economics and the ascendancy of GDP are two sides of the same coin.

The star of economists continued to rise in the post-war period and even started to expand to "non-economic" fields such as social interactions, politics, time use, education and the environment. This is sometimes referred to as "economic imperialism" by other social sciences that feel that economics is encroaching on their field. Economics started to become increasingly influential in policy areas that were initially the domain of other social sciences like political science or sociology. It also led to many terms from economics becoming commonplace in other fields: human capital, social capital, natural capital, ecosystems services, externalities, etc.

Yet from the 1970s, criticism of economics and GDP increased. Economic turmoil dented trust in economists as the stewards of society. Environmental and social issues were also becoming increasingly important. Similarly, in the wake of the 2008 crisis citizens' mistrust in the models, policies and data advocated by economists started to grow again. Although economics is a catch-all term for a heterogeneous body of research, society seems to hold economists collectively responsible. Perhaps the mistrust was best expressed by Queen Elizabeth II when she asked a group of economists "why did no one see it coming?" Yet despite all the criticism economics has never relinquished its position as the primary social science. Economic thinking and statistics has become so institutionalised that it can weather these storms of criticism.

Thus the success of economic science and GDP are linked. Yet there is another fundamental pillar to the success story. The System of National Accounts is the foundation upon which modern empirical macroeconomics is built. The SNA has, since 1953, prescribed what concepts to use when measuring the economy. Before that time, the calculation of GDP was like a cottage industry with many different methodologies. After the adoption and implementation of the SNA, worldwide national income accounting was harmonised rapidly.

The SNA is not a riveting read. Quite the contrary, it is a boring book of accounting rules. But there is a more romantic and fundamental perspective on the SNA. It can be seen as a "language" because it contains the definitions of macroeconomic terms (dictionary) and also their relationships (grammar). For example, the SNA defines the various words: consumption (C), investment (I), government consumption (G), exports (X) and imports (M). It also defines the relationships between these various "words", its "grammar". The most famous example is John Maynard Keynes' famous formula for national income (Y) which is Y=C+I+G+X–M.

The SNA provides a common language which (macro)econo-
mists all over the world speak. Whether the native language of a
macroeconomist is Swahili, Urdu or Portuguese, they can "speak"
to their fellow (macro)economists using their SNA language. In fact,
many of the terms have gradually percolated into society and media.
Consumption, investment, productivity and capital are just a few
terms which have society-wide use. The situation is similar to the
English language, where a sizeable portion of the world can now speak
a little bit of English although they have had no English lessons. Many
people "speak" a little bit of SNA without ever having taken an
economics course or even knowing of the existence of the SNA. The
development of a common language was crucial in the increased
institutionalisation of economic thought and for creating a macroeconomic community.[13]

This does not mean that the macroeconomic community is a
close-knit happy family. The economic crises of the 1970s and financial crisis of 2008 have led to crises in macroeconomic theorising.
Macroeconomists disagree fundamentally about how to resolve these
types of problems or how to avoid them in the first place. This has
been most visible to the general public in the debate over "austerity
versus stimulation" in the wake of the financial crisis. Despite these
disagreements all these perspectives can still be seen as part of a broad
macroeconomic community. All participants in the debate agree that
the goal is to enhance economic growth and there is no disagreement
about the language to use.[14] They might disagree how to achieve
economic growth, and which policies to implement, but there is an
underlying language which gives the community a coherent and solid
foundation.

What Does GDP Measure (And What Not)?

So what exactly is wrong with this influential indicator? Basically,
there are three lines of argument that are used in the literature.

1) *It doesn't measure the economy very well.* It might be expected that
   criticism of GDP would come from outsiders, but economists are amongst

the most vocal critics. Measuring economic activity and growth is a daunting task for many reasons: the existence of non-market output, price indexes, technological change, globalisation and country comparisons. There are many methodological and empirical challenges when creating national accounts. In addition, the quality of data sources differs significantly worldwide, which is a cause of major concern. In the last few decades the rise of the internet and globalisation have created new challenges to measure the economy.

2) *GDP is not a measure of well-being, inequality or sustainability*... A lot of the arguments against GDP simply point out what GDP does not measure. GDP is not a measure of well-being of society and it provides no information about inequality. Furthermore, GDP does not quantify the future (sustainability). It contains no information about the impact of environmental damage or the accumulation of knowledge and other assets in society.

3) *...but is mistakenly taken as a proxy for welfare.* Many economists will concede that GDP is not a direct measure of welfare, as defined in economic theory. Nevertheless, it is quite often implicitly assumed that the size of the economy is a good proxy. The SNA itself phrases this as follows: "Per capita volumes of major aggregates are often used as a measure of the relative standard of living in countries, despite the misgivings of some social analysts about the adequacy of this measure. Even though the per capita volumes of GDP have some shortcomings, it is clear there is a strong correlation between a country's per capita volume of GDP and its standard of living" (p. 463). In other words, GDP is not theoretically perfect, but in practice it correlates well with other dimensions of social welfare such as education and health. However, in the modern age in developed countries there is a complex relationship between the economy, well-being, inequality and the environment. For some specific periods and countries these developments are correlated, sometimes they are not. It is incorrect to *automatically* take GDP as a proxy for any of these aspects of society.

Why Is Beyond-GDP Not Successful?

Since national income started in the 1930s, there has been criticism from economists and non-economists. As a result, hundreds of alternatives have been proposed which would do a better job as the "compass" for society. They come from an eclectic set of theoretical

---

BOX 1.2   **A selection of Beyond-GDP terminology**

Affect, A-growth, Basic Needs, Beyond-GDP, Capability Approach, Capital
   Approach, Circular Economy, Comprehensive Wealth, Current Well-being,
   Degradation, Depletion, Degrowth, Distribution, Ecological Footprint,
   Economic Welfare, Economic Well-being, Ecosystem Services,
   Environmental Accounts, Footprint, Functionings, Genuine Progress,
   Green Accounting, Green Economy, Green GDP, Green Growth, Human
   Capital, Human Development, Human Well-being, Inclusive Growth,
   Inclusive Wealth, Inequality, Life Satisfaction, Natural Capital, Natural
   Capital Accounting, Needs, Planetary Boundaries, Produced Capital,
   Progress, Quality of Life, Resilience, Subjective Well-being, Social Capital,
   Social Welfare, Societal Progress, Standard of Living, Sustainable
   Development, Sustainable Development Goals, Sustainable National
   Income, Sustainability, Utility, Wealth, Welfare, Well-being.

---

and philosophical traditions (green accounting, subjective well-being,
indicator sets, composite indicators, etc.). Even within each of these
approaches there may be large differences. There have been attempts
to harmonise (parts of) the Beyond-GDP field. Yet few of these are
compulsory and their implementation is limited.

   Despite the fact that the Beyond-GDP cottage industry has
grown, there is still a lot of heterogeneity in the field. The ultimate
problem is that there is no coherent Beyond-GDP community as there
is in macroeconomics. There are various schools of thought, each
with its own methodologies, indicators and terminology. There is no
common language binding the community. The harmonisation efforts
are far removed from the rigour and institutionalisation of the SNA.
The problem for Beyond-GDP is not a shortage of vocabulary. There
are dozens of terms that are used (see Box 1.2 for some examples).
However, these definitions are not clearly defined in a "dictionary".
Meanings will vary from researcher to researcher. What is quality of
life, well-being, welfare, sustainability, progress, development, happiness, etc.? On the "grammatical" side, rules vary from one approach
to the next. Each Beyond-GDP initiative is promoting a different

language, using a different dictionary and grammar book. This is why there is no community. There is no means of communication. How can the general public be expected to understand if the people involved don't even understand each other?[15]

STRATEGY: AN INSTITUTIONALISED COMMUNITY WITH A CLEAR GOAL AND COHERENT STRUCTURE BASED ON A COMMON LANGUAGE

How might the Schumpeterian dream be achieved? Is it possible that the Beyond-GDP cottage industry will be responsible for the creative destruction of the GDP multinational? What would need to be done to achieve this transition by 2030? The history of GDP and of Beyond-GDP suggest that this will not happen automatically. The GDP multinational, despite incessant criticism, has stood the test of time and has become deeply institutionalised. The Beyond-GDP cottage industry has not proven capable of providing a coherent alternative which is strong enough to challenge this dominance. There are no signs that there will be a breakthrough. A new strategy is needed.

Ironically, the history of the GDP success story provides a good template for this strategy. There are four features, shown in Table 1.1, which are crucial features of the GDP multinational. Firstly, each community requires a clear objective. The goal of macroeconomics is to understand the sources of economic growth and create policies by which to enhance it. The second feature is that the community has a clear structure with three layers: an accounting framework (SNA), a key indicator (GDP) and the policy science (macroeconomics).

Probably the most important aspect is the third factor, which is a common language. An effective community requires a language with which to communicate. For macroeconomists this is the SNA. Finally, the success of the GDP multinational is that it has become institutionalised both formally and informally in society. GDP, the SNA and macroeconomic policy have become part of international governance and national governments. Via the media these elements have been institutionalised in society in general.

Table 1.1 *Community features underlying macroeconomics and well-being and sustainability science*

Community features		Macroeconomics (GDP multinational)	Well-being and sustainability science
Goal		Economic Growth	Well-being and Sustainability
Community structure	Policy science	Macroeconomics	Well-being and Sustainability Science
	Accounting framework	System of National Accounts	System of Global and National Accounts
	Key indicator	Gross Domestic Product	System and Quality Indicators
Common language		System of National Accounts	System of Global and National Accounts
Institutionalisation		√	By 2030

Without a coherent community it is unlikely that the field of Beyond-GDP will ever be able to compete in terms of influence on society. The new strategy should therefore be: *to create an institutionalised community with a clearly defined goal, structure and common language.* The next paragraphs will discuss the four features of the community shown in Table 1.1.

Goal

The WSS community's goal is to understand well-being and sustainability and to create policies to enhance them. This is the underlying philosophy of the Brundtland Report which was the seminal publication that led to the institutionalisation of the term sustainable development as "development that meets the needs of the present without compromising the ability of future generations to meet their own needs". This Brundtland definition stresses two dimensions: the well-being of the current generation and the well-being of future generations (sustainability). In essence, it is to understand the current state of humanity ("Here and now") and its future on a finite planet ("Later"). The vast majority of Beyond-GDP initiatives strive to measure current well-being or sustainability, or both.

The advantage of this research goal is that sustainable development is the most institutionalised concept in Beyond-GDP. However, the term sustainable development does not have an unambiguous definition. Its meaning has been debated since the Brundtland Report was published. This book chooses to use the more neutral terms "well-being" and "sustainability", which focuses attention on the temporal dimensions of sustainable development.

Community Structure

Should the community be formed through a political process? If so, a prime candidate would be the Sustainable Development Goals, a list of 169 targets that were adopted by all member states of the UN in 2015. A powerful community already exists around the SDGs and could be enhanced if the entire Beyond-GDP community subscribes to them. However, the SDGs score poorly in terms of scientific underpinnings or accounting, which are so vital in the story of macroeconomics. This book therefore argues that the community should be based on scientific insights rather than a political process.

The scientific community requires three elements: a science (Well-being and Sustainability Science), accounting framework (System of Global and National Accounts) and indicators (Quality and System Indicators). Should economists be in the lead in this process? This book argues that to assess well-being and sustainability requires more scientific insights than mainstream economics offers. It needs the input of heterodox economic literature, such as happiness and behavioural economics, as well as other social sciences such as psychology, sociology and political science. It also requires the input of natural scientists such as geologists, climatologists, ecologists and hydrologists. Rather than creating a common language based on economic terminology, it is better to look for a multidisciplinary language.

As has been argued for macroeconomics, agreeing on a language does not equate to consensus on policy options. Given the breadth of scientific disciplines which would be involved and the current internal disagreements within each discipline, the WSS is more than likely to have a "lively" debate over the right and wrong way to measure and manage society's well-being and sustainability. But having a coherent community with a common language will improve the quality of the debate significantly.

Common Language

There are currently so many languages, dialects and accents in the Beyond-GDP community that researchers are unable to communicate effectively with each other, let alone to society. This book proposes a neutral multidisciplinary measurement framework which should act as a common language: the System of Global and National Accounts (SGNA). The term global requires some explanation. It refers to the scope of the measurement as well as the implementation. The starting point of measurement is a worldwide perspective. The accounting structure does not start from the idea that it is measuring a single country. From the start the accounting framework covers the global environmental, social and economic systems.

Global also refers to the implementation strategy. It should not be implemented in rich developed countries first and then slowly permeate towards developing countries, as was the case for the SNA. Rather, the adoption of the SGNA should be worldwide from the start.

The SGNA is subdivided into four "system accounts":

1. Global Environmental Accounts (GENA)
2. Global Societal Accounts (GSA)
3. Global Economic Accounts (GECA)
4. Global Distribution Accounts (GDA)

In addition, there is a fifth "quality account":

5. Global Quality Accounts (GQA)

The system accounts are based on neutral concepts which exist in many scientific disciplines: stock-flow accounting, networks and limits. The system accounts provide uncontroversial descriptions of the functioning of the environmental, societal and economic systems as well as the distribution within society. They do not assess whether these changes are good or bad, they simply describe the levels and changes in systems. Multidisciplinarity also lies in the use of units in the system accounts. Rather than relying on monetary units only, the SGNA is a multi-unit framework which includes a wide variety of physical and volume units.

The global quality accounts provide quality assessment criteria to understand whether the systems are improving or deteriorating. Each of the quality assessment approaches (welfare economics, capital approach, methods from hedonic psychology/happiness economics/ behavioural/neuro-economics, exergy, resilience, etc.) provide vital criteria with which to judge whether the natural, societal and economic systems are changing for the better or worse. They also provide aggregate quality indicators which can act as an alternative to GDP.

It is conceivable that, over time, there may exist some kind of perfect quality assessment method. However, the underlying premise of this book is that there is currently no perfect approach and that society is best served by looking at the insights from various (imperfect) quality perspectives. Individually, each quality indicator provides only a partial and insufficient depiction of the state of affairs, but taken together the full range of quality indicators provide the best information basis possible.

Institutionalisation by 2030

This book shows that many of the components of the strategy already exist. The many scientific disciplines that underlie well-being and sustainability science have existed for a very long time. Many datasets have already been created on a global scale. All that is needed is that a coherent scientific community is formed from these various pieces of knowledge.

Creating a scientific community might seem difficult but has been done before, and not just by the macroeconomic community. The Intergovernmental Panel on Climate Change (IPCC), which started in the early 1990s, has resulted in a coherent climate science community. The insights are based on an accounting framework for the carbon cycle/energy system of our planet as well as a number of key indicators such as temperature change and carbon dioxide concentration. The many scientific disciplines which were involved in understanding climate change and creating policies now communicate in one voice but also have the language and process with which to discuss points of disagreement.

The IPCC started through a formal process of institutionalisation, and the community has created a narrative which has influenced society. It seems highly likely that climate science would have had less influence on society if it had not created an institutionalised community of scientists who speak a common language.

A similar process is needed for the field of well-being and sustainability. This requires a concerted effort first and foremost by international institutions and national governments. As a deadline for this process this book chooses the year 2030. For some this might be somewhat disappointing – a solution as late as 2030 seems to lack a sense of urgency. Others might be more optimistic about this time frame. A comment in *Nature* by some prominent voices in the Beyond-GDP movement argued in 2014 that "If undertaken with sufficiently broad participation, the hunt for the successor to GDP might be completed by 2015."[16] The thought was that it would take no more than a year to develop the new indicator.

The historical insight provided by this book implies that this type of community building requires a longer time horizon. In fact, there will be others who feel that 2030 is far too ambitious. People who are familiar with the history of the SNA and other initiatives will understand that these processes usually take decades rather than years. Furthermore, 2030 is an appropriate deadline because two important initiatives will be up for renewal around that time:[17]

1) *Revision of the System of National Accounts.* Historically, there has been a new SNA every 1–2 decades. That means that the next one should be expected around 2020–2030.
2) *Renewal of the Sustainable Development Goals.* The SDGs are probably the most institutionalised Beyond-GDP initiative. Since they were chosen through a political process they lack a theoretical basis, but nevertheless they provide a worldwide harmonised set of targets and goals. The current goals should be achieved by 2030. It is likely that by the end of the 2020s they will be discussed, evaluated and (most likely) renewed.

The strategy in this book would ideally be linked to these two processes. This would help to create the necessary institutional momentum to make the strategy a reality.

READING GUIDE/SCOPE AND AUDIENCE

Reading Guide/Scope

Part I of this book covers the three crucial questions which have been briefly introduced: Chapter 2: Why is GDP successful? Chapter 3: What does GDP measure (and what not)? Chapter 4: Why is Beyond-GDP not successful? These questions are important because they substantiate why the current Beyond-GDP situation will not lead to a positive outcome and why a new strategy is needed. The questions also provide guidance on what such a strategy might look like. For people who are new to this topic, these chapters are crucial, but for people who are well informed about Beyond-GDP (or have already been convinced by the brief discussion in the previous sections) one or more of these chapters may be redundant. Readers may skip over them and move directly to Part II.

Part II provides a sketch of the new strategy. It is clearly beyond the scope of this book to provide a full description of the outcome of this long-term process. Remember that the SNA is more than

700 pages long. The accounting framework for the SGNA would therefore probably have thousands of pages. And that is just the accounting framework. Part II provides the overall architecture of the strategy but, by design, this is a long-term process that will only be fully completed by 2030.

Part II starts with an overall description of the strategy in Chapter 5. The subsequent chapters give disproportionately more weight to the common language, the SGNA, because this is the most important feature of a well-functioning community. Chapters 6–9 go into greater detail about this common language: the five sub-accounts of the System of Global and National Accounts (SGNA). For some, these chapters may be too detailed in terms of the discussion of accounting. I have tried to keep the technical terminology to a minimum but for some readers there may be too much detail.

Chapter 10 covers the quality accounts and the (quality) indicators of the SGNA which will replace GDP by 2030. The chapters include broad-brush descriptions of quality assessment approaches from economics and other sciences.

Finally, Chapter 11 discusses the implementation of the strategy, including the crucial aspect of institutionalisation. It also explores the possibilities to use big data in this endeavour. The chapter concludes by asking the important question: "Will it happen?"

This book is based on my training as an environmental economist and my nearly twenty years of experience in national accounts and the measurement of sustainable development. This has given me some expertise to tackle this topic, but at the same time I am acutely aware of the many areas in which my knowledge is lacking.

The strategy I have set out is *a* way of approaching the issue, but I make no claim that it is *the* way to do it. It is a reasoned and logical proposal based on my imperfect experience, knowledge and creativity. The broad-brush character of Part II is therefore not a flaw – it is part of the design. When embarking on such a mission you need to agree on a rough sketch first.

Audience

Who should read this book? Ultimately, the book is aimed at people who are concerned by the importance given to GDP and mainstream economic thinking in society; those who believe that society requires a new compass and policies which are based on well-being and sustainability. This includes a wide range of academics, policy makers, statisticians, journalists and the general public. A basic understanding of economic theory will definitely help, but it is not a requirement.

The book is also aimed at the "Beyond-GDP" audience but I caution beforehand that there might be people in that community who will not like the direction of the book.

First, there is the group that does not believe there is a problem which needs solving. In other words, they do not agree that "Beyond-GDP is not successful" and believe that the situation is not as dire as this book implies. Some might argue that one of the alternatives (green accounting, SDGs, SWB etc.) is on the verge of a breakthrough. Others might cherish the heterogeneity of the Beyond-GDP community and see it as a strength. It is clear that this book argues against these assessments.

A second group of people that will be disappointed are supporters of one of the current Beyond-GDP alternatives. For example, there are many environmental economists that support green accounting. The SDG process also has a lot of institutional support. Alternatively, some might prefer SWB measures, which have garnered a large following. However, those who are expecting an endorsement of their favoured approach will not find it. Also, people that are looking for an outright condemnation of another approach, e.g. welfare economics or the SDGs, will be disappointed. The inclusive philosophy of this book is that each of these approaches is a part in a large jigsaw puzzle. The value lies in creating the entire puzzle, not in choosing one piece and rejecting the others.

The third source of unease is related to the speed of change. Setting a deadline for 2030 will seem far too distant for some. This book argues for a rather ambitious community-building process. That might be viewed as an overly elaborate and time-consuming way of going Beyond-GDP. A narrower focus would also take far less time and lead more quickly to results for this urgent issue.

To each of these groups I would ask for an open mind. This book argues that the situation is indeed dire and that it requires a new, inclusive strategy which will take some time to implement. My hope is that by Chapter 11 the reader will also be convinced that this is a feasible and necessary strategy. Alternatively, I would hope that it will stimulate debate about alternative strategies. The idea behind the book is to provoke others to think about how to make Beyond-GDP a success. It is an open invitation to others to agree, improve or completely reject the ideas in the book. Overall, my aim is to present my view on why Beyond-GDP is failing and what might be done about it. My hope is that this will shift the conversation towards the *process* of creating a post-GDP world and that this is achieved no later than 2030.

2   Why Is GDP Successful?

FROM COTTAGE INDUSTRY TO MULTINATIONAL

GDP was not always as dominant as it is today. Within the last century or so, GDP has transformed from an obscure ad-hoc measure to the most influential indicator in society. To understand how society has come to live an era of "hegemony of growth"[1] it is important to look at historical developments.[2] Recently many books have appeared which deal with GDP and the history of the SNA. Catchy titles such as *GDP: A Brief but Affectionate History*, *The Little Big Number*, *Gross Domestic Problem*, *The Great Invention*, *The Hegemony of Growth*, *The Growth Delusion* and the *Value of Everything* provide ample documentation of the history of GDP and the underlying ideas about "value". These and other more academic publications provide valuable insights about the American school, the British or continental European contributions as well as the perspective of the international institutes such as the OECD and UN. These sources help deconstruct the GDP success story.[3]

The literature usually splits the history of national accounts into two eras: the periods before and after 1930. The first era started more than 350 years ago, when the first national income estimates were published by William Petty in 1665 and William King in 1696 for the United Kingdom.[4] On the opposite side of the English Channel the French also quickly took their first steps in national income measurement.[5] In the centuries that followed, only a handful of countries attempted national income accounting. After England and France came Russia (1790s), the Netherlands (1798), United States (1843), Austria (1861), Germany (1863–1899), Australia (1886) and Norway (1893).[6] In some countries these estimates were followed by new estimates, but in many cases national income estimation was dormant for long periods. For example, after the initial Russian estimates of the 1790s, it took over a century for the next estimates to emerge.[7]

The methods adopted for these early approaches were affected by the reigning economic theories at the time.[8] One of the core questions was which activities in society were deemed to be "productive", i.e. contributing to "the economy". Petty and King's systems included all goods and services, which is known as the comprehensive production system. Later on, the Physiocrats believed that only agriculture was to be seen as a productive sector. Adam Smith, the father of classical economics, expanded the boundary to include all goods but did not include services as part of production. Later, one of the founders of neoclassical economics, Alfred Marshall, reintroduced the comprehensive production concept. His theory was founded on the premise that any good or service that fetched a price was an indication that something of value had been produced. The current national accounts are also based on this production boundary. This brief history of the first era makes clear that "the economy" is not an objective entity but rather that the definition was adapted according to the economic theories of the time.

The second era of national accounting (post-1930) is far more important to this book. Figure 2.1 shows the proliferation of national income estimates since 1900. The two lines in the figure are from two different sources. The first, covering the years 1900 to 1958, is derived from *The Income of Nations* by Studenski (1958), which provides a nearly encyclopaedic overview of national income accounting for the period 1665–1958. The second source is the United Nations, which started to collect national accounts data in 1952. The graph shows the number of countries that submitted data to the UN. Despite some interpretational differences[9] between the two sources, the figure provides a clear picture of the proliferation of national income estimates in the twentieth century. The figure is reminiscent of the Schumpeterian development shown in Figure 1.2. If the "number of countries"

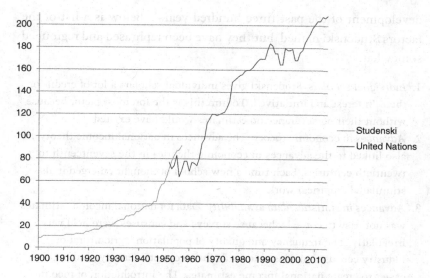

FIGURE 2.1 Number of countries with national income estimates
Source: Studenski (1958); UN (1952, 1957, 1968a, 1982)

is taken as the level of market saturation, it is clear that GDP is at the top of the innovation cycle.

In 1900 only nine countries had attempted national income accounting at some stage in their history. The number of official estimates increased from these nine estimates in 1900 to 209 countries and regions in 2015.[10] Yet up until 1930, the growth was fairly modest. It was only in the 1930s that the number of countries for which national income was calculated started to increase significantly.

STUDENSKI'S PARADOX

What developments contributed to this proliferation of GDP in the world? The earliest analysis of success factors was by Studenski (1958), who analysed the period 1665–1958. He wrote his seminal work in the midst of an explosion of interest and activity in national accounting. Studenski gave thought to the "forces that influenced the development of the past three hundred years". Below is a list of the factors Studenski named, but they have been rephrased and regrouped somewhat:

1. *Individual scholars.* Studenski gives individual scholars a lot of credit for their "interest and initiative". To him this is the foremost factor because without their perseverance no estimates would have existed.
2. *Advances in economic theory.* The advances in national income theory are also linked to the advances in economic theories in the seventeenth to twentieth centuries. Each time a new school of thought emerged it also stimulated empirical work.
3. *Advances in statistics/data availability.* Data for national income estimates was not easy to come by because surveys and censuses were held very irregularly. The frequency and quality of population, agricultural or industry censuses increased towards the twentieth century, making it easier to create national income estimates. The introduction of income taxes was particularly important.
4. *Crises and taxation.* During various crises, kings and governments required information about the amount of taxes that could be raised. Wars, revolutions, technological change, severe economic downturns, breakdowns of fiscal reforms, class or group conflicts stimulated national income estimates.
5. *International commercial and political rivalries.* Throughout history there has been an urge to compare the performance of countries. The English–French rivalry looms large over the first era of national accounting.
6. *Institutionalisation.* Studenski pointed to the important role of the UN and OECD in stimulating research on national income. National income also became a part of normal government policy and planning in the 1930s/1940s in the wake of the Great Depression and the Second World War.

These conclusions were drawn for a period which covered mostly the first era of national income accounting. The remainder of this chapter makes clear that they are still highly relevant for the second era as well. Studenski does however make an intriguing observation: "It is noteworthy that the development of national income estimates has been particularly rapid during periods of political and economic stress and, on the other hand, has been sluggish during periods of tranquillity."[11] In other words, national income estimates emerged when there was a specific need for them but interest soon subsided after the need disappeared. Figure 2.1 shows that this did not happen in the second era: Interest in national income accounting has never waned but has continued to grow and grow. Why? What can explain "Studenski's Paradox"?

This chapter discusses four sub-periods which are crucial to understanding this paradox: 1929–1944, 1944–1973, 1973–2008 and 2008–present. Choosing cut-off points for these periods is of course not an exact science. In this case economic milestones help to demarcate these eras. The year 1929 is chosen because of the Great Depression; 1944 and 1973 are chosen because these symbolise the start and end of the Bretton Woods agreement.[12] Finally, 2008 was the year of the worst financial and economic crisis since the Great Depression.

THE ASCENT (1929–1944)

Statistics are considered an integral part of modern society and of government. In fact the origin of the term statistics is New Latin *statisticum*, which means "of the state". Today statistical evidence is a crucial part of government policy discussions. Society is accustomed to the idea that when there is a problem you first look at the relevant data and use it to model policy options. Once the policies are put in place you need new statistics to see whether the policies are working. This has been the role of statistics for quite a while, although some might argue that populist movements are also threatening this type of reasoning by pointing to "alternative facts", indicative of the "post-truth era".[13]

Trust in statistics by society has not always been so high. A case in point is one of the landmark publications in the history of national accounting: a report by Simon Kuznets on 4 January 1934.[14] This report contained estimates for economic activity which the US Congress requested as a result of the Great Depression. Fortunes were lost, unemployment soared, poverty increased at a dramatic rate and the economy went into a tailspin. Through modern eyes, the Kuznets Report seems like a rather sluggish response to the worst economic crisis of modern times. "Black Tuesday", the day that stock markets plummeted, was on 29 October 1929. Did it really take 1,528 days to get some proper macroeconomic information to Congress? To make matters worse, the Kuznets Report was published when the economy had experienced its first year of growth after successive years of decline. So the Kuznets Report was published when the crisis, or at least the worst of it, was already over. Was Kuznets such a slow worker?

Philipsen (2015) provides a wonderful and detailed overview of what happened in that period. He shows that in the early stages after the Great Depression there was *no desire* to have this statistical information. The Republican President at the time, Herbert Hoover, who had been elected on a laissez-faire platform, had great faith in the economic system's ability to correct itself. Depression and recession were simply part and parcel of the economic cycle. In this line of thinking government intervention was unnecessary, so why spend valuable government resources measuring a problem that will solve itself? The famous business magnate John D. Rockefeller is reputed to have said during the Great Depression: "These are days when many are discouraged. In the ninety-three years of my life, depressions have come and gone. Prosperity has always returned and will again."

As a result of this attitude there was no coherent macroeconomic information when the crisis struck in 1929. This is not to say that there were no statistics at all. There were statistics on agriculture, trade and sometimes information about employment in certain cities, but the macroeconomic indicators that society uses today, particularly unemployment and national income, were not available. As the Depression worsened, and poverty became a major social issue, there was still no information about the size of the problem. Philipsen highlights the efforts of a progressive Republican congressman, Robert La Follette Jr., who throughout the 1920s had tried to convince his colleagues in Congress to start measuring the economy and unemployment.[15] He was defeated on many occasions. There simply was no demand for the data and there was general distrust of government to gather this information from companies and individuals. One might think that when the Depression hit this opinion would change quickly. In reality it took until 8 June 1932 before La Follette could get a majority to vote for resolution 220 which requested national income statistics for the period 1992–1932. That was 953 days after Black Tuesday. More importantly, it was 153 days before Hoover emphatically lost the presidency to Franklin D. Roosevelt, who promised a "New Deal" with a far greater role for government in the recovery and management of the economy. The American attitude towards government and statistics changed significantly in the wake of the Depression.

Resolution 220 was a request to the Department of Commerce, but they did not have the expertise or staff for the job. Another institute was needed to lead the process. The National Bureau of Economic Research (NBER) had been founded in 1920 with the precise aim of promoting statistics in economic decision making. Under the leadership of Wesley Mitchell a lot of empirical experience had been amassed by the institute. The task eventually fell to a young Simon Kuznets, who had fled communist Russia and had started work at the NBER in 1927. He began working on this iconic project in January 1933. So in actuality Kuznets was a very fast worker: it only took him a year to get this landmark report submitted to Congress. The report was definitively noticed by the press and the public. It sold 4,500 copies at $0.20 a copy. No other government report on the economy had ever sold as much.[16]

The Depression and economic turmoil of the 1930s hit other countries as well, and provided an enormous impulse to national income estimates, especially in European countries. Increasingly, governments were relying on this data to track their economies. In many case countries started to create "official" national income measures produced by statistical institutes that were becoming more professional. The success was not just a success of statistics. Economic theory also got a major boost in the 1930s. The Depression had a significant impact on a whole generation of economists and defined many distinguished careers. Economists started to wonder about the origins of the Great Depression and ways to prevent it from happening again.

Take for example a year like 1936, which was an important year from the perspective of economic theory. A hugely influential publication of 1936 was by John Maynard Keynes, one of the defining figures in twentieth-century economics. In *The General Theory of Employment, Interest and Money*, Keynes laid the foundation for macroeconomics and still has great influence today.[17] There were however other economic innovations in 1936. Wassily Leontief published his first paper on input–output economics, in which a model that linked the economic input to the outputs was created for the United States for the year 1919.[18] His thinking would also affect the SNA significantly. In 1936, Jan Tinbergen also published his first work, in which he produced an econometric model for business cycle analysis.[19] Tinbergen shared the first economics Nobel Prize with Ragnar Frisch in 1969 (for econometrics). Leontief won in 1972.

Bos (2009) also stresses other important advances in economic theory related to national accounts. This includes modelling advances from Kuznets (long-term growth), Meade and Stone (public finance analysis and trade balance analysis). All of these names went on to win Nobel prizes except for Keynes, who died before the prize existed.

When the Second World War started, economists had another opportunity to put their statistics and models to use. In the UK and the US there was a belief that the war effort required good economic planning, because it was understood that it could be enormously disruptive to the "real" economy. The production of weapons, the conscription of millions of young men into the military and other resource requirements has a profound impact on markets, labour and prices. The task was to set up a war economy while minimising the damage to the regular economy.

In the UK, this way of thinking was spearheaded by John Maynard Keynes. At the time of the war he was already an influential figure with a long career as an academic and investor. He had already made a name for himself when, after the First World War, he argued that the German economy could not stomach the reparations which the allies wanted to impose. In fact he warned about a second world war resulting from the Versailles treaty.[20] Although he did not manage to convince the British negotiators, his assessment turned out to be on the right side of history.

At the beginning of the Second World War, in 1940, Keynes wrote *How to Pay for the War*. To illustrate his argument, the national accounting figures played a crucial part in his story and he used his influence to make sure that more data was produced during the war. He used his considerable clout to advance the national accounting work of Colin Clark and later Richard Stone and James Meade.

In the United States, Kuznets and Robert Nathan (who had been Kuznets's assistant for the 1934 Congress report) also joined the war planning effort. Using the national accounting information they had amassed in the 1930s, they gave advice about how to manage the war economy. This led to conflicts with the top of the US military, who were not amused that these "bean counters" were telling them what limits there were in terms of spending. Kuznets wrote a report which suggested that military spending could double without creating too much inflationary pressure. In the end, the military wanted to triple spending, to which Kuznets sternly responded, "double does not mean triple". The episode forced the resignation of Kuznets and Nathan from the War Production Board, but the civilian authorities did force the army to adhere to Kuznets's limit.[21] It is testimony to the increase in stature of economists that they could win such a debate against the military in the midst of a world war.[22]

The end result of the 1929–1944 period was that economists had proven their skills to society during some of the most testing crises. Using their national accounts, they had helped provide information about the war and formed theories of how to prevent a Depression happening again. They had also provided insights during the Second World War which ultimately helped the economy to be managed at a time of great consequence.[23] The star of economics and economic statistics was rising fast.

GOLDEN AGE (1944–1973)

Out of every crisis come winners and losers. One of the most important impulses of the Great Depression and the Second World War was the role of government. These crises legitimised the role of government in society and subdued anti-government sentiments. It was not only that national governments grew; international governance also benefited. The international economic order changed significantly at the Bretton Woods meeting in 1944, ushering in a new economic era with the gold standard being replaced by a system in which currencies were pegged to the US dollar. Major international institutes such as the International Monetary Fund (IMF) and World Bank were tasked to oversee this new economic agreement. Another important institute, which will play a significant part in this book, is the Organisation for Economic Co-operation and Development (OECD). Initially called the Organisation for European Economic Co-operation (OEEC), it was founded in 1948 and played an important role in the post-war economic recovery of Europe. But international cooperation also went beyond economic affairs. The ineffective League of Nations was replaced by the United Nations in 1945. In 1949, the North Atlantic Treaty Organization (NATO) was agreed. The European Economic Community, a forerunner of the European Community, was founded in 1957. Government, at both national and international level, turned into "big government".

Economics and economic statistics also came out of the war on a high.[24] Economists had started to climb the ladder of esteem in society and government and had proven their worth in times of great crisis. Their policy recommendations were being listened to by governments and the general public. Society started to crave economic information in a way that was totally different to the period before the Depression.

A real thirst for statistics emerged and governments responded by improving their statistical institutes. International organisations such as the UN and the OEEC/OECD started to coordinate, collect, disseminate and harmonise the statistics from many countries.

The United States had made use of science, government and statistics in a very effective way and had rushed ahead of the pack. On the other hand, the axis countries mismanaged these aspects of society. For example, many of the scientists who worked on the Manhattan Project had fled Nazi Germany, while many economists who played a major role in the US in the decades after the war had come from war-torn Europe (Kuznets, Leontief, Schumpeter, Friedman, Koopmans etc.). The war helped to galvanise the "American century".

Large parts of Europe and Eastern Asia were in ruins and the United States decided that economic development was vital to stabilise Europe. The Marshall Plan, which ran from 1948 to 1952, was a large-scale economic programme designed to put Europe on the road to economic prosperity and peace. It also increased the need for national account estimates. The OEEC was set up to monitor and distribute Marshall Aid. In order to assess where the aid was needed it was important to have information about economic conditions and so the aid recipients had to start producing national accounts on a regular basis. Later the OEEC also oversaw development assistance of southern European countries which led to more national accounts proliferation. The focus then shifted towards former colonies/developing countries, thereby increasing the demand for national accounting even further.[25]

National accounting statistics are also needed to calculate country contributions to international organisations. International organisations require funding from their respective member states and national income estimates became the "taxable income" upon which the contributions were based.

The Second World War was followed by a new conflict: the Cold War. It was a battle between the political systems of the two main victors of the Second World War: communist countries (led by Russia) and the capitalist countries (led by the US). After the war, the geopolitical situation quickly turned to the rivalry between the two superpowers. At that stage, the two blocs of countries were competing to prove to each other, and the rest of the world, which was the superior political system. The United States suffered a harsh blow when, in 1957, the Russians launched the Sputnik satellite, thereby challenging the scientific superiority which the United States had claimed since the Second World War.

It is hard to fathom today, but there was considerable anxiety in the West that they might lose the economic race and that they would be overtaken. This would mean that, in the long run, the communist countries could spend more on their military capacity. Growing the economy became an existential necessity. This was symbolised by the term "Expand or Die". Economic growth became imperative to escape Soviet oppression. There were of course also internal pressures. Communist or socialist sentiments were present in capitalist countries as well, and it was felt that the only way to make sure workers were kept from revolting was by expanding the economy and thereby increasing the income of the workers.

In the meantime academic economists were advancing their knowledge of the determinants of economic growth and employment. After the war the mathematical basis of economics grew progressively stronger.[26] The Harrod–Domar model stressed the importance of economic growth for full employment. The general equilibrium model, published in 1954, is one of the classics in economics.[27] Another classic is the Solow–Swan growth model, which followed a couple of years later.[28]

The post-war period saw a harmonisation of macroeconomic theories. Keynes's theory went largely unchallenged and others simply built on this framework. Curricula in American universities also started to converge. Macroeconomic statistics started to harmonise into the System of National Accounts, with the first edition being published in 1953 (more on the SNA later in this chapter). Overall, the professionalisation of the statistics increased significantly, with a focus on economic statistics. Dissemination, international comparability and methodological advances all proliferated after the war. In fact some authors spoke of a revolution in government which was based on national accounts, the advances in sample survey theory, statistical coordination and computer data processing in the 1960s.[29]

The enhanced esteem of economists and the emergence of "big government" after the war also meant that economists started to work in government in large numbers. Before the war this was rarer, as economists were mostly in academia.[30] One government tool that was increasingly in demand was economic projections. Policy makers wanted to know what the economy of the future might look like for planning purposes. As a result, many national governments and international organisations started to create forecasts of economic growth.

However, economists did not just work in the ministries of finance or economy, they started to work in many non-economic ministries. Schmelzer (2016) describes for example how education and science policy was transformed at the OECD in the 1960s. These policy domains used to be weighed on their own merits, now they were assessed on the basis of how much they contributed to economic growth. Education policy became "human capital" policy. In academic circles this expansion of economic theory towards other fields is exemplified by Gary Becker, Nobel Prize winner of 1992, who applied economic thinking to areas previously thought to be beyond the economic domain: human capital, time, social interactions, advertising, insurance and even marriage.[31]

Margo (2011) summarised these developments succinctly: "The economics profession expanded rapidly after World War II, fuelled by growth in demand for economists in higher education, government, and the private sector." The confidence of society in economics/economists was greatly helped by the historically unprecedented growth rates of the 1950s and 1960s. This period is so extraordinary in terms of economic growth that the French refer to it as the Trente Glorieuses, the Germans call it the Wirtshaftswunder and English speakers refer to it as the Golden Age. All over the western world, and the communist countries, economies were growing rapidly. This of course increased the confidence of the general public in economists. It also boosted the self-confidence of economists because of their apparent ability to manage the economy. In 1970, Van Lennep, the Secretary-General of the OECD, reported that "A major recession would no longer be a *deus ex machina*, but could only result from miscalculation or a deliberate act of government". Prominent economists such as Robert Solow and Paul Samuelson also thought that the instability in capitalist societies had come to an end. And a top US economic adviser thought that recessions were "now ... preventable, like airplane crashes".[32] By 1950 economics had become so important that GDP growth was the number one government priority. It became standard for governments and politicians to start setting growth targets. In 1961, this target setting was elevated to an international goal: the OECD pledged a 50 per cent increase in GDP of OECD countries by 1970.[33] Through the development aid programmes and the Cold War rivalry, growth targets started to spread to countries beyond the OECD.

Before 1950 economic growth was not usually the goal of policy. Up to that point, economists had as their target either employment (Depression), planning the war economy (Second World War) or employment again (after the war). National income data helped in analysing these goals. But after 1950, GDP was no longer descriptive but rather prescriptive. This is perhaps the greatest success of economics in the "Golden Age". The key indicator of macroeconomics had become the most important policy objective of society. This also spread into the media. Business magazines began to emerge and the mainstream media started to include or expand their economics sections. As a result, the general public were increasingly shown GDP figures which quantified the abstract "economy". Economic thinking became an integral part of government policy and societal discourse.

CONTESTED HEGEMONY (1973–2008)

In the 1970s the confidence of economists was seriously tested. Primarily, it was a period of high economic volatility, energy crises and breakdown of the international agreements which had been agreed in

Bretton Woods in 1944. But apart from economic turmoil, there were also concerns such as environmental pressures and social unrest. It alerted society to the fact that the high economic growth did not automatically solve all societal problems.

At the end of the war, the Bretton Woods system had been adopted. The system began to run into trouble at the end of the 1960s because of the United States' financial troubles, which stemmed from the Vietnam War. By 1973 Japan and European countries effectively stopped using the Bretton Woods framework, replacing exchange rates fixed to the dollar with floating currencies. The 1970s also saw periods of high inflation and even the rare phenomenon of stagflation (inflation and unemployment simultaneously). The decade was also marred by two energy crises which exhibited society's vulnerability to external shocks (and reliance on natural resources). The post-war "mixed economy" growth machine started to look fragile. This dented the confidence of the economists in Keynesian policy and invigorated different schools of economic thought, such as the new classical school or the monetarists. This led to different economic policies that looked more at the supply side of the economy and smaller government, increasing deregulation and privatisation. Names like Milton Friedman (Nobel Prize 1976) and Robert Lucas (Nobel Prize 1995) spring to mind.

This economic vision was also adopted by a new generation of politicians such as Ronald Reagan and Margaret Thatcher, who ran on platforms of smaller government and deregulation. One of Ronald Reagan's famous quotes is: "The most terrifying words in the English language are: I'm from the government and I'm here to help." There was a significant shift in economic thinking and government policy in the period 1980–2000.

So the 1970s were an interesting test case for economists. They had failed to predict or resolve economic problems which were affecting society. One outcome could have been that the general public would lose faith in economists. Rather, economics remained the primary social science, but the dominant *type* of economics changed. Most importantly, the central goal of policy remained economic growth. Despite their different perspectives, both Keynesian and new classical economics are based on achieving economic growth. The importance of GDP did not diminish.

The fall of the Berlin Wall and communist system bolstered the idea that capitalist democracies were the superior system of governance. In the 1990s and early 2000s the western economies were characterised by high growth and low inflation. The confidence of the economists again started to grow. Just like at the end of the 1960s and early 1970s economists were confident about their ability to manage the economy. Robert Lucas, Nobel Prize winner and founder of the new classical school, said during his presidential address to the American Economic Association in 2003: "My thesis in this lecture is that macroeconomics in this original sense has succeeded: Its central problem of depression prevention has been solved, for all practical purposes, and has in fact been solved for many decades."[34] In a 2008 paper titled "The State of Macro" Olivier Blanchard, who later was the chief economist at the IMF, declared that "the state of macro is good" and that there was a "broad convergence of vision". One other prominent voice of that period was Alan Greenspan, the Chairman of the Federal Reserve Bank, who was credited with the "Great Moderation", a period which started in the mid-1980s when economic variables such as GDP growth, industrial production, unemployment and inflation began to decline in volatility. When Bob Woodward, famous journalist of Watergate repute, wrote a biography about Alan Greenspan his book was titled *Maestro*.

Aside from economic factors, other fields were also undermining trust in economics and GDP. The criticism from other domains grew significantly in the period of "contested hegemony". Remember that criticism of GDP had existed for a long time. Simon Kuznets himself had been critical of national accounting back in the 1930s. In the 1950s a couple of voices argued against the idea of economic growth. Influential was the *Affluent Society* by John Kenneth Galbraith, which addressed the inequality of "private wealth and public squalor" and the inadequacy of GDP as a measure of welfare.[35] The 1960s were also marred by social unrest, culminating in student

BOX 2.1   **The change in attitude towards GDP in the Kennedy family**

The change in attitude towards GDP in the 1960s can be illustrated by the change in opinion within the Kennedy family. In 1968, Robert Kennedy gave one of the most eloquent of speeches to argue against GDP (or rather GNP at the time):

> Too much and for too long, we seemed to have surrendered personal excellence and community values in the mere accumulation of material things. Our Gross National Product, now, is over $800 billion dollars a year, but that Gross National Product – if we judge the United States of America by that – that Gross National Product counts air pollution and cigarette advertising, and ambulances to clear our highways of carnage. It counts special locks for our doors and the jails for the people who break them. It counts the destruction of the redwood and the loss of our natural wonder in chaotic sprawl. . . . And the television programs which glorify violence in order to sell toys to our children. Yet the gross national product does not allow for the health of our children, the quality of their education or the joy of their play. It does not include the beauty of our poetry or the strength of our marriages, the intelligence of our public debate or the integrity of our public officials. It measures neither our wit nor our courage, neither our wisdom nor our learning, neither our compassion nor our devotion to our country, it measures everything in short, except that which makes life worthwhile. (Robert Kennedy, 1968)

What is usually not mentioned is that this is a complete reversal of the policies adopted by his brother, President John F. Kennedy less than a decade before. John F. Kennedy was instrumental in convincing the OECD to set a growth target for all OECD countries in 1961.[38] In that year, the OECD pledged to increase GDP in OECD countries by 50 per cent in 1970.

protests across the western world in 1968. By the 1970s, organisations such as the OECD, the bastion of post-war economic growth, started programmes to address the "problems of modern society".[36] Box 2.1 illustrates the way in which attitudes towards GDP began to change.

The environmental movement started to gain prominence in the 1950s–1960s. As far back as December 1952, London was confronted by a smog which is estimated to have caused thousands of extra deaths. In the 1960s publications such as *Silent Spring*, *The Tragedy of the Commons* and *The Population Bomb* brought environmental problems and the dangers of population growth to a wider audience.[37]

Over the next couple of decades many new environmental problems emerged and many institutions were created to tackle them. In the 1970s the problem of acid rain in Europe started; in the 1980s the problem of the ozone layer; in the 1990s the emergence of climate change and biodiversity loss were seen as the major problems. Each of these led to further institutionalisation, and in some cases target setting.

There were also scientific advances such as the emergence of environmental economics as a separate field in economics in the 1970s.[39] Not only did the field start to look at effective environmental policies, but also modelling and scenario studies advanced during this period. For example, the RAINS (Regional Acidification Information and Simulation) model played an integral part in facilitating the acid rain negotiations in Europe.[40]

By the end of the 1980s a new concept which linked economic, environmental and social issues emerged. The term "sustainable development", which was popularised by the Brundtland Report,[41] has become ubiquitous ever since. Chapter 4 provides more context about the significance of environmental and sustainable development discussion.

DEMISE? (2008–2030)

Did the role of economists in society change after the financial crisis of 2008? What role will economics and GDP play in 2030? Clearly, the financial crisis of 2008 had a major impact on the faith of society in economists. This event was the single worst recession since the Great Depression. In 2007 there was a big problem in the "subprime mortgage market" in the United States. Banks had been lending to households that were high risk because of unemployment, divorce, medical emergencies or other factors. The securities that backed these mortgages started to devalue at a rapid rate and financial institutions started to get into trouble. A real shock wave went through society when Lehman Brothers filed for bankruptcy on 15 September 2008. To avoid a financial domino effect governments all over the world were forced to bail out financial institutions, spending trillions of dollars in taxpayers' money. Stock markets and housing markets collapsed and economic growth dropped in many countries.

Up to that point, economists had (again) been growing in confidence about their ability to manage the economy. The financial crisis clearly dented the (self-)image of economists and also led to a crisis in economic theory. It reopened old debates which showed that there was a big divide separating various factions in macroeconomics. In the *New York Times*, a year after the Lehmann Brothers' collapse, Paul Krugman explained the rift in his op-ed "How Did Economists Get It So Wrong?"[42] To the general public it was clear that there were vastly differing views on how to manage the aftermath of the crisis. Some economists favoured a return to demand stimulation (post-Keynesians) while the new classical economics supported austerity measures. Krugman terms this rift freshwater versus saltwater economists, referring to the proximity of the universities of the two factions to the Great Lakes versus the East/West coasts of the United States.[43]

The crisis also diminished society's confidence in economists. The trust of society in economists is not regularly measured but Sapienza and Zingales conducted an interesting survey to see whether there was difference in opinion between economic experts and average Americans.[44] They concluded that "Economists' opinions differ greatly from those of other ordinary Americans: on average the percentage of agreement with a statement differs 35 percentage points between the two groups". They also found that

> The topics most covered in the economics literature, where
> economists agree among themselves the most, are also the topics
> in which their opinions are most distant from those of average
> Americans. This difference does not seem to be driven by
> knowledge, since informing people of the expert opinions does
> not have much impact on the responses of ordinary America.

Based on their survey, Sapienza and Zingales speculate that "The explanation most consistent with our limited evidence is that people do not trust many of the implicit assumptions embedded into the economists' answers and that economists take them for granted".

Popular discontent with policies such as deregulation and globalisation is growing in the wake of the 2008 crisis. Many economists have been promoting these policies for quite some time. It is seen almost as a natural law that free trade is automatically good for society. Yet popular protest against the Transatlantic Trade and Investment Partnership (TTIP) and other free trade agreements shows that society's trust in this economic rationale is no longer automatic. Donald Trump ran on an isolationist platform that wants to limit trade ("America first") and won. He withdrew from the Trans-Pacific Partnership (TPP) soon after he was elected, which was a major break in US policy. Some economists have also been vocal critics of the idea that free trade is always good. Dani Rodrik, in *The Globalisation Paradox*, shows that although additional free trade might boost the economy a little, it also leads to less democratic control and societal disenchantment.

Thus there are signs that mainstream economists are viewed with some scepticism. At the same time, there is little evidence that there is a viable alternative which might replace economics as the dominant policy science. But before I discuss Beyond-GDP, I will explore three other reasons why the importance of GDP might diminish: the reducing importance of statistics, low growth rates and big data.

The historical overview has shown that confidence in statistics is not automatic. The importance which society attaches to quantitative information has varied over time. At the moment, the rise of populism in many developed countries is often coupled with a disdain for science, experts and statistics. Since the middle of the 2000s, populist parties have been gaining ground in many nations. In Europe, these parties have started overtaking the traditional parties in terms of electoral appeal. In the United States, the Republican Donald Trump ran on an anti-establishment and populist platform. Trump has taken this "post-truth" narrative to new levels. An adviser to the president famously referred to the existence of "alternative facts". It might be easy to dismiss the Trump presidency but there has been criticism from more mainstream quarters. Nicolas Sarkozy was interviewed about the Stiglitz Report and addressed the lack of faith in statistics. He linked this scepticism to the dominance of economic ("market") thinking in an interview with the *Financial Times*: "The world over, citizens think we are lying to them, that the figures are wrong, that they are manipulated. And they have reasons to think like that. Behind the cult of figures, behind all these statistical and accounting structures, there is also the cult of the market that is always right."[45]

Conceivably, if these sentiments continue and society loses its appetite for statistics, then this information will become less important and funding will reduce. Interest in indicators such as GDP might diminish. Overall, this scenario does not seem highly likely, given that modern governance and the media news cycles are hungry for new data. Perhaps certain portions of the population will lose faith in statistics but it seems unlikely, for the moment, that statistical facts will be rejected by the majority in society.

An issue which might diminish the importance of GDP is the prospect of low growth figures. Quite a few economists have warned that society needs to start getting used to the idea that growth rates could be close to zero in the coming decades. Economists such as Robert Gordon in his book *The Rise and Fall of American Growth* argue that high growth rates are behind us for the foreseeable future.[46] This slowing down of growth in developed countries is already occurring. Even countries such as China, which saw spectacular growth rates from the 1990s, is seeing a slowing down. Assuming that these predictions for the developed world come true, and growth rates drop, it is easy to see how GDP would lose its status as a media darling. If all GDP growth rates (both quarterly and annual) and GDP predictions are zero or very small, how much longer will the media be interested?

By far the biggest unknown for GDP is the emergence of "big data". This is a generic term which refers to the widespread availability of electronic data which has come about because of automation of registers and the internet. The national income estimates after the Second World War were helped by the fact that survey theory was greatly improved around that time. The consequence of big data for GDP and other official statistics is yet to be seen. Electronic data might have a tremendous influence on the speed at which economic data emerges. Getting GDP data 30–45 days after the end of a quarter might seem impressive now but by 2030 it is highly conceivable that there will be a variety of daily indicators of economic activity.[47] The quarterly GDP estimate might still be produced, but only to confirm what the daily indicators had already revealed weeks before. In fact, such developments are already a reality for another economic indicator, inflation. The "billion prices project" of MIT collects data from websites using webcrawlers to calculate daily inflation rates for many countries.

Therefore a loss of faith in economists and statistics, low growth rates and big data might lead to lower interest in GDP data. The final reasons that interest in GDP might diminish is because of "Beyond-GDP" alternatives. This is covered in Chapter 4.

A COMMON LANGUAGE: THE SYSTEM OF NATIONAL ACCOUNTS

There is a really important component of this history: the System of National Accounts (SNA).[48] It is so crucial to our story that it is discussed separately. Remember that up to the Second World War, all the way back to Petty in 1665, there had been a wide range of methods to create national income estimates. Depending on the reigning economic theories and ideas of the principal researcher, decisions were made as to the production boundary and classification of income, intermediate, final use, capital, depreciation and consumption.

In April 1939, the Committee of Statistical Experts of the League of Nations included in its programme the measurement of national income. Work was delayed by the war, but afterwards the newly founded Statistical Office of the UN started to work on two initial tasks: survey sampling theory and national income accounting. In the autumn of 1945, a subcommittee was initiated under the chairmanship of Richard Stone. Stone had worked in Great Britain on national income accounts together with James Meade and was supported by John Maynard Keynes. Members of the subcommittee hailed from Australia, the Netherlands, Canada, the United States, Mexico, Norway and Switzerland. They met at Princeton in December 1945 to discuss a memorandum written by Richard Stone. The subcommittee produced a report two years later which can be seen as the start of the harmonisation process of the system of national accounts.[49] The 1947 report still has many accounting features which have endured to the present day.

It is easy to think that there was free market of ideas on national income accounting and that in the end the "best idea" on national accounts won. Yet Stone's ideas were also helped by institutional and political factors. Notably, many ideas of Simon Kuznets on national income were ignored in the SNA. After the 1934 report to Congress and his work in the war, Kuznets started to grow increasingly uncomfortable about the direction of national accounts. The Department of Commerce, which had started regular production of the accounts in the 1930s, slowly distanced itself from his ideas.[50]

In the UK such tensions were far less evident. Based on the conceptual work of Keynes, and with his significant public support, his protégés Meade and Stone produced a system which included all government expenditures. In 1942, Stone published a paper in which he estimated a US national account based on the British system.[51] Crucially, Stone coordinated with the United States: not with Kuznets but rather with the Department of Commerce. During a meeting in September 1944, Richard Stone and Milton Gilbert of the Department of Commerce met, also in the presence of the Canadian George Luxton. It was at this "tripartite meeting" that the United States shifted position towards the Keynes–Stone accounting structure.[52]

Building on the 1947 report, Stone again made some excellent choices. He led the work on two OEEC handbooks on national income accounting (1951 and 1952) which were used in the administration of the Marshall Plan. The British/American system thereby became entrenched in European statistics. Then, in 1953, Stone was the principal author of the first ever UN handbook, which is considered the first "official" SNA.[53] This document provided a global harmonised system of national accounts. Its scope was far more modest than the 1947 report, because it had to take into account its practical applicability in countries all over the world.

Overall it might be said that Stone operated well in the political and institutional setting while Kuznets was not cut out for these types of processes. Kuznets preferred to move on to other academic topics such as inequality and business cycles. This is also not to say that the Stone system does not have considerable merit. There is ample reason why he was awarded the Nobel Prize for economics in 1984. Yet the support of Lord Keynes and his ability to forge an agreement with the US Department of Commerce and international organisations such as the OEEC and UN played a significant role. Other schools of thought in continental Europe were also overruled by the SNA process. For example, various Scandinavian countries and countries such as the Netherlands had their own systems which were, in the end, replaced by the SNA. So when it comes to the content of the SNA it is important to realise it is too simplistic to think that "the best idea" prevailed. Institutional and political factors played a major role in arriving at a single system.

After the SNA 1953, the SNA went from strength to strength. This was also the era of official estimates, produced by government agencies.[54] This professionalisation of statistical offices grew significantly. The SNA handbook was subsequently updated in 1968, 1993 and 2008.[55] The SNA 1993 was the first time that all major international institutes and all countries of the world fully agreed to a single system.

Even within the UN there was an alternative accounting framework, the Material Product System (MPS), which was used in over a dozen centrally planned communist countries. As the SNA was being revised at the end of the 1980s, the MPS system was also being updated. The fall of the Berlin Wall in 1989 put an end to this process. De facto, the SNA 1993 was then the only internationally agreed method to measure the economy.[56] Taking the report of the 1947 sub-committee as the starting point of the harmonisation process, it took forty-six years to reach full worldwide harmonisation. In fact, some might argue that the harmonisation is still not complete because of differences in the way that countries apply the SNA.[57]

Achieving this level of harmonisation was truly a Herculean task. Although in the beginning it was conceived by a small group of people, it turned into a global force with input from around the world. It is no exaggeration to call the SNA one of the biggest achievements in the history of the international statistical community.

From a technical point of view the SNA is important because it makes macroeconomic figures comparable between countries. Just imagine if each country used a different approach to measure its economy. This would be a major drawback in economic research. But the significance of the SNA goes much further. By agreeing to the SNA, macroeconomists suddenly had a benchmark publication which formalised their thinking. It created a "language" with which to discuss macroeconomic matters. It contains a dictionary of the definitions of the words that are used in macroeconomics. It specifies, for example, terms like consumption and domestic product so that economists all over the world know what they are talking about.

It also provides terminology such as gross/net and domestic/national, which have very precise meanings. The SNA not only has the vocabulary but it also provides the "grammar rules" which specify the relationships between the terms.

The SNA is thus the formalisation of the "language of macroeconomics". Just as in real languages, a dictionary and book on grammatical rules are exceedingly boring, yet no one contests their importance as a basis for communication. It makes communication between economic academics, policy makers and statisticians possible wherever they live in the world. The fact that economists developed this language made their communication and coordination efficient and effective. In fact, the SNA language has also percolated into society and people all over the planet, without realising it, speak a bit of "SNA".

The language has stood the test of time. When Keynes's theory became heavily criticised in the 1970s or when the 2008 financial crisis led to disagreements between macroeconomists, it did not undermine the underlying language of the community: the SNA. The various schools might disagree on the way in which growth should be achieved, but they do not dispute that the SNA provides the language with which to conduct the debate.

A SUCCESSFUL COMMUNITY

In the first era of national income accounting (1665–1930) there was an ebb and flow of interest in this data. The demand for these figures increased and decreased because of wars or other crises. The second era (1930–now) displayed a different pattern: there has been an unrelenting expansion of the use of national income aggregates. This chapter has referred to this as the "Studenski paradox". What explains this paradox? The bottom line is that in the period after the war, the GDP multinational was created.

The GDP multinational is a scientific community which has four important features. Firstly, it has a clear goal, which is to understand the sources of economic growth and to create policies to stimulate growth. Second, the community is structured around a science (macroeconomics), a statistical framework (SNA) and a key indicator (GDP). Successes in each of these domains are mutually reinforcing. Thirdly, macroeconomists have agreed on a formal macroeconomic language: the System of National Accounts. The language has proven to be versatile and has survived shifts in macroeconomic theory. Finally, the community has become heavily institutionalised. The SNA and GDP have grown to become worldwide standards with a vast statistical infrastructure. In addition, economic thinking has increasingly become entrenched in governments, international institutes and society.

Together these factors help to explain "Studenski paradox", and the increase in influence of macroeconomics and its main indicator GDP starting from the 1930s–1940s to the present. Despite external criticism and internal disagreement on economic policies, this power has endured. It will take something very special to replace this powerful community.

3   What Does GDP Measure (And What Not)?

The GDP is the most influential indicator in society, but has been criticised since it was conceived. For decades, critics have been pointing to the flaws of this indicator yet GDP figures are still used regularly. In "The GDP Paradox", Jeroen van den Bergh refers to this as the "the greatest information failure" in the world.[1] Overviews of the problems related to GDP have been written dozens of times, summing up various issues related to the measurement and interpretation of GDP.[2] There are basically three areas of criticism to cover.

Firstly, there is the criticism that GDP does a poor job of measuring economic activity. This is perhaps surprising to some people who are unfamiliar with economic statistics, but there are countless methodological, practical and data problems related to GDP estimates. Measuring an economy is not easy. The rapid expansion of Information and Communications Technology (ICT) and globalisation in the last couple of decades have only made these problems bigger.

Secondly, GDP does not measure well-being, inequality, environmental damage or future impacts (sustainability of well-being). These are traditional criticisms which have been discussed for many decades.

Economists tend to concede that GDP is, theoretically speaking, not a measure of welfare/well-being but use national accounting data anyway. The argument which is often implicit is that GDP might not be a very good *direct* measure of welfare, but it is still a pretty good *proxy* because it strongly correlates with important dimensions such as health and education. The third line of criticism questions this rationale and points to the evidence that GDP cannot be taken to automatically correlate with social welfare.

IT IS DIFFICULT TO MEASURE "THE ECONOMY"

"The Economy" Is What You Define It to Be

What is "an economy"? Probably the most fundamental question, which has been debated for a long time, is the question of the production boundary of the economic system. The answer to this question has varied as economic theories have shifted. Due to the success of the SNA process, there is only one remaining definition of the economy. As a result, when people talk about the economy, it is synonymous with the system described in the SNA, and the size of the economy is measured by GDP. It would be tempting to say that there is now an objective definition of the economy, but convergence towards a common definition does mean that this is the only interpretation of this abstract concept.

In the early days of modern national accounting there were people who argued that it was not necessary or even desirable to have one single definition of an economy. The Swede Ingvar Ohlsson, for example, wrote back in 1953 that different applications required different datasets. In other words, the national income accounts should be tailor-made to suit the object of research. He found that if you are studying either the results of economic developments or the behavioural aspects of a macroeconomy, certain categories of income should be recorded differently. Ohlsson concluded that there were three options:

1) The construction of a general-purpose national accounts system from which to extract the special-purpose system.
2) The construction of different national accounts systems for different purposes.
3) The construction of one special-purpose national accounts system with a list of corrections for the main items for which the different treatment for different purposes is required.

Ohlssen himself preferred option two but his idea never really caught on, probably because it was costly.[3] Kuznets had a similarly nuanced idea about the use of national accounts. He felt, for example, that in a time of war, for the purposes of war planning, it was justified to include government spending in the national accounts. Nevertheless, after the war he felt that many government expenditures were actually intermediate inputs, which contributed little to nothing to welfare. Especially expenditures on the military and general planning activities did not seem to contribute to welfare gains in peacetime.

Another classic debate is whether the production boundary should include household production. Household production refers to services that can be performed by the market but can also be done at home. For example, you can clean the house yourself or you can hire a cleaner. You can eat out, have a meal delivered or you can cook yourself. Yet doing your own cleaning or cooking is not part of the economic production boundary. Many have argued that these activities should be considered economy production. Some of the proponents come from a feminist perspective which stressed that even though women were not taking part in formal employment they were nevertheless making an important contribution to the economy.

Some proponents also point to the large differences between developed and developing countries in this respect. The home production (but also other areas of the non-observed economy[4]) in developing countries is much greater and these are things that are missed in the current SNA. So if you wanted a better comparison of economies it could be good to measure these components. However, it does very much depend on the application at hand. If you want to decide how much each country should contribute to the United Nations you need GDP to be a good proxy for "taxable income". If you added home production to the calculations, African countries would probably need to contribute more than they do today. Also, there would be an implicit assumption that it is possible to raise taxes from these activities. The reality is, of course, that taxes on cooking your own meals or cleaning your own house are not viable or desirable in practice.

Note that not all aspects of home production are excluded from the national accounts. There is one significant exception, which is the provision of "housing services" to oneself.[5] There are, in essence, two ways of obtaining housing services. Either you can rent a house from someone or you can buy a house and live in it yourself. In the first case it is part of a market transaction because you pay the owner of the house. If you live in your own dwelling then no rent transaction takes place. Nevertheless, the SNA assumes that a housing service has been delivered to you (by yourself). A rental price is "imputed" as an estimate for the services that are rendered. It is the only durable good that is treated in this way. The transportation services that you provide to yourself with your car or the airline services provided by a private airplane are not treated in this way.

Thus the discussion about the boundaries of the economy is not set in stone. Society has simply converged on a definition. It took from 1665 to 1993 before the entire world reached this consensus about where the boundaries of "the economy" were. Despite this agreement it seems prudent to leave open the possibility that the current SNA is just one of the ways in which to define the economy. Ohlsson's long-forgotten idea that the definition of the economy could vary according to the macroeconomic question remains important.

Measuring Output and Value Added

The size of the economy is heavily affected by the definition of the production boundary. But even if the boundary is defined, it is not always clear how to measure the output of certain sectors. Estimating the level of the output of market goods is considered to be least problematic because there is a clearly defined tangible product with a market price. Later on, this section will show that this does not mean that there are no problems in estimating growth of these products.

For services, the value is not always self-evident. For example, the insurance sector output was defined in the SNA 1993 as the difference between the premiums and the amount paid out. In other words, the value which insurance adds to the economy is the difference in the income and outlays. This rule led to some strange problems. In the 2001 German national accounts (old SNA 1993 series) *negative* exports of insurance services were recorded to the US. The reason was that the attacks of 11 September led to a lot of insurance claims and many US companies were reinsured by German companies. As a result, more claims were paid out than the premiums received, which turned the exports negative. This was of course a rather odd result so the SNA 2008 has created a far more complicated method which should make this type of situation impossible. However, the real question is, of course, what exactly is the value of the service which is provided by the insurance sector?

One of the big problems in market services is defining the output of the banking services. This has been an issue for national accounting even long before the financial crisis of 2008. What are the services that banks provide? What is the share of the financial sector in the total economy? The SNA has always treated banking as a productive activity but the way it has been recorded and how it has contributed to value added has varied. The most problematic category has been Financial Intermediation Services Indirectly Measured (FISIM). When people put money into a bank, they pay a fee for the account. This fee is clearly a banking service and is recorded in the SNA as such. However, the bank makes more money from the money in a current or savings account. The bank makes a profit because it can lend money to borrowers at a higher rate than it gives on a savings or current account. This margin is seen as the implicit value of the intermediation services provided. This is called FISIM and there has been a long debate on how to record this in the national accounts and how to calculate it. Changing the way FISIM is recorded has significant impact on countries with large financial sectors. It is also used by the financial sector to point to its size in the economy. Yet the importance of the sector is very much a matter of definition of the SNA.

These are all examples of market services, but the biggest imputation of all is in the non-market sector: the valuation of government output. There is no "market" for government services and so it is impossible to estimate what the value of the output would have been if there was no government. National accountants have reverted to the only feasible solution: the output is measured as the sum of costs incurred to supply the service. This is unsatisfactory for productivity analysis because it requires inputs and outputs to be measured independently. Given the large government sectors in developing countries, this means that a sizeable portion of the economy cannot be included in these productivity analyses.[6]

These discussions show that the "value added" of sectors is not always obvious or uncontroversial. Marianne Mazzucato, in *The Value of Everything*, advocates a renewed debate about the concept of value.[7] She argues that big technology, banking and pharmaceutical companies might seem to be adding value because they are making large profits but they are actually extracting value from society through monopolies and market power. At the same time she argues that the value which governments add to society is underestimated. She eloquently reasons that the narrative that "businesses are the risk takers/value creators and government only spend money" is seriously flawed. The way in which the SNA measures the value added of the private and government sectors perpetuates this incorrect narrative, which is why she argues for a fundamental rethink of what "value" really is and which sectors are contributing to it.

Country Comparisons

One of the primary applications of GDP has been for between-country comparisons. Which country has a bigger economy? Even in the first English estimate by Petty in 1665, calculations for France and the Netherlands were also included. However, country comparisons open up another set of methodological and practical issues. How do you compare countries that have different currencies? Although you might have an exchange rate it will not always be a good reflection of the differences in an economy. In fact, even in countries which share the same currency, such as the euro area, the amount of goods and services that you can buy will vary. The famous Big Mac index of *The Economist* magazine tracks the price of this famous hamburger in all countries that have a McDonald's restaurant. In the Eurozone, in January 2017, a Big Mac cost €4.55 in Finland while in Portugal it was €3.05.[8] A whopper of a difference.

These differences exist for all products, not just hamburgers. For this reason, statistics are collected in order to compare the absolute price levels between countries. One of the primary sources is the International Comparison Program (ICP), which is a worldwide statistical partnership led by the World Bank. It collects comparative price data, detailed expenditure values of countries' gross domestic products (GDP) and estimates purchasing power parities (PPPs).[9] Despite the enormous importance of measuring these prices it is a costly affair and is only done every couple of years.

On the webpage of the ICP the following historical overview is provided: "Comparisons of final expenditure on GDP have been completed for 1970, 1973, 1975, 1980, 1985, 1993, 2005, and 2011. They covered 10, 16, 34, 60, 64, 117, 146, and 199 countries respectively." So, although the country coverage is now much better, there have only been two rounds in the last twenty years. The importance of these statistics in comparing countries is great, but it is clear that the empirical quantification is a major challenge.

Measuring Economic Growth and Productivity

Economists tend to analyse the *growth* of the economy rather than the absolute size. This leads to new measurement problems because you need to compare two different years and define the "growth" in the goods and services provided. For a single product there are three things that can change over time: the quantity, quality and price of a product. In reality, all three of these will change simultaneously. But not all three are considered as contributing to growth.

Just imagine that in one year a million apples of a certain quality are sold at $2. The next year a million apples (with the same quality) are sold for $2.2 million. In current prices, the sale of apples has increased by $0.2 million because the price of apples has increased from $2 dollar to $2.20. However, there is no economic growth because the volume (both quantity and quality) of apples has stayed constant. "Real" growth was zero but "nominal" growth was 10 per cent.

In principle the quality of apples remains constant, but this is not the case for Apples, with a capital "A". In fact, the quality of electronic goods changes very rapidly. This also happens in discrete steps, so when Apple introduces a new iPhone, the product specifications change from one year to the next. In this case the quantity, quality and price might change simultaneously, making it much harder to estimate economic growth. "Hedonic methods" are used to decompose the total nominal change into changes in price, quality and quantity but these require significantly more data on the specifications of the products.

Thus growth in goods which have a constant quality requires information about the price and quantity only. It is therefore fairly straightforward to estimate. For products which change quickly but are mass-produced it is more difficult but still possible if the specifications can be obtained. However, increasingly there are tailor-made products. In the field of services this is even more prevalent. Business services or consulting services are geared specifically to the buyer and the quality characteristics are customer-specific. Government services are also problematic. What is the quantity/quality of "public administration" or "defence" and how do you split it into a price, quantity and quality component?

Some even argue the increase in the *variety* of products also should be a part of economic growth. Gordon (2016) makes the point that the many choices which people nowadays have compared to people a century ago is a major improvement in welfare. Some authors have even tried to value this increase in variety. Brynjolfsson et al. (2003) found that, at that time, the number of book titles available at Amazon.com was over twenty-three times more than the books at a typical Barnes & Noble superstore. They calculated that the increased product variety of online bookstores enhanced consumer welfare by $731 million in the year 2000.[10]

The problems related to measuring price changes and growth have been extensively discussed in academic journals as well as statistical fora. Important commissions such as the Boskin Commission in the US and the Bean Commission in the UK have looked at these issues.[11] These difficulties mean that the actual economic growth could be significantly over- or underestimated. In addition, the divergence in methods across countries may have impacts on the comparison of growth rates between countries.

Uncertainty and Data Quality

One of the striking aspects of national accounts compared to survey-based statistics is that it is hard to calculate the uncertainty ranges of the estimate. You will not hear a statistical office reporting that "economic growth was 1.2 per cent this year, plus or minus 0.4 percentage points". Yet everyone who is involved in producing national accounts knows that there are error margins, and there have long been calls to collect and publish them.[12]

Very few statistical offices have attempted this although there is one common practice which does give a hint about the degree of error: the various vintages of national accounts figures. Typically a statistical office will publish three growth figures for a given quarter: one after 30–45 days, one after six months and one after a year.[13] The first is meant to satisfy the people who want a quick estimate, but accept that it is "quick and dirty" in the sense that much of the necessary data is not available within forty-five days. The six-month estimate makes use of more data sources and the one-year estimate has all data available. So there is a trade-off between speed and quality. In terms of attention, the "quick and dirty" estimate usually gets the most media attention while the "best estimate" will often hardly get mentioned at all, yet the differences in the estimates can be quite significant.

Another way of assessing the errors ex post is the so-called benchmark revisions. Once every couple of years a statistical office will define a benchmark year. This is a year in which new data sources and estimation methods are introduced. But once these have been set, the data source and methods are kept constant for a while because the temporal comparability is best served by this continuity. After a couple of years a new benchmark is set and the size of the economy changes (usually upward) once the new data and methods are introduced. The most shocking benchmark revisions have emerged in Africa over the last few years. In 2010 Ghana published a new figure for 2006 which raised GDP from 21.7 billion cedi to 36.9 billion cedi, a 70 per cent increase![14]

These benchmark revisions can have important implications. Coyle (2014) recounts a fascinating story about Britain's in 1976: the GDP figures showed a recession which forced the UK to apply for IMF money and introduce draconian budget cuts. The Labour government was swept out of power by Margaret Thatcher three years later, but when the benchmark revision was later produced, it turned out that there never had actually been a recession.

A final piece of uncertainty might come through the pressure from politicians. Governments are anxious to show good growth figures and might pressure their statistical offices to deliver these positive numbers. Famous is the trial of the head of the Greek Statistical Office, Andreas Georgiou. He was recruited in 2010 in the aftermath of the financial crisis in Greece. The manipulation of the statistics in the previous years had hidden the true nature of Greece's economic problems. Yet when new figures were published Georgiou was accused of manipulating them and siding with foreign creditors. In 2017 he was convicted and in 2018 this was upheld under appeal, despite significant criticism from abroad.

IT IS EVEN MORE DIFFICULT BECAUSE OF ICT AND GLOBALISATION

The growth of computing power started in the 1950s and expanded rapidly for the following decades. These developments are often discussed in the context of Moore's law, which refers to the prediction by Gordon Moore in 1956 that computing power per dollar would double every year for the next ten years after that. In fact, Moore's law has held for several decades, although the doubling time is assumed to be around eighteen months now. There is also dispute about how long the "law" will continue.[15]

Starting from the 1990s the proliferation of electronic computers and devices and later their connection to the internet have brought ICT to the masses. Our smartphones of today have more computing power than the supercomputer which covered a whole floor of a building in the 1960s. Raw computing power allows people to shop in webshops rather than on high streets. It allows people to contact people just about anywhere in the world. Nowadays, desk jobs are done almost exclusively on computers using specialised software packages. ICT has led to productivity gains, although there is debate about whether the gains are already behind us. ICT developments have also led to sophisticated robots which are increasingly threatening jobs, or at least certain jobs.[16]

In terms of measurement ICT leads to various challenges. The first is the issue of consumption. The products and services that are consumed have changed significantly and the channels through which they are purchased have also shifted. A sizeable quantity of goods and services are now bought over the internet and not in a local store. In some cases, people will not even realise which country the vendor is from. In the past, an airline ticket would be bought at a local travel agent; now it is bought on a website which could be from any country.

Another issue is that many services are provided free to the general public. Social networks such as Facebook or Twitter are provided free of charge. In the national accounts this means that there is actually no payment for these services. In fact, in the national accounting sense the only output of social networks is that they sell advertising. Similarly, there is a large variety of open-source software which is produced by programmers from around the world and provided free. These developments are not reflected by the SNA in production or consumption

On the other hand, the internet provides opportunities for households to earn more money in the "sharing economy". A person can now use their car as a taxi or rent their house like a hotel. It is also possible to open a website for a small amount of money and be visible to everyone on the planet. People can earn money for clicks on YouTube videos. Through the internet small businesses can serve niche global markets. In the future it is thought that people will start to manufacture some of the products for themselves using 3D printers. Instead of buying certain products, they will simply buy the material input for the printers and manufacture those products themselves. In a way, economic production is being democratised beyond the traditional company. Everyone can be a home producer in one way or another.

The internet has also affected the financial world through the introduction of crypto currencies such as Bitcoin and Ethereum, whose use is expanding. Given the volatility of these currencies and the fact that their use may be hidden from regular measurement, this also presents a major challenge to quantify.

ICT and the internet also make the concept of "a price" more difficult to observe. In the past an airplane fare would be a fixed price in a catalogue. There was an economy and business class fare, but generally there was little price differentiation. Nowadays, the price of an airplane ticket will vary from day to day, or even hour to hour. Airline companies have complicated computer optimisation systems that try to get the most income from filling the seats in the airplane.

They also offer additional options including baggage, various seat classes, insurance and food and beverage options. In a single airplane comparable seats can fetch very different prices depending on the date they were booked and the tailor-made options which the consumer selected.

ICT has also had a tremendous impact on global production patterns. Since the early 1990s, international trade has been expanding at a faster rate than GDP. It is definitely not the first time that globalisation has increased. Richard Baldwin, in *The Great Convergence*, argues that there are two periods of "unbundling" of global trade; the first was the result of lowering the costs of transporting goods across the world. Not only did transportation costs reduce significantly but tariffs were also lowered between 1820 and 1990.[17] The "second unbundling" started around 1990 and was caused by the lowering of communication costs, which makes it easier for ideas (technology) to cross borders. It therefore makes it easier to manage subsidiary companies in a foreign country. Developed countries were able to open factories in low-wage countries while adopting modern technologies – a highly profitable business model.

Production processes have started to fragment towards many different countries. These complex supply-chain dynamics are sometimes referred to as global value chains.[18] There are however signs that the nature of globalisation has changed since the 2008–2009 financial crisis. Growth in trade slowed and in 2015 even shrank. Some refer to this phenomenon as "peak trade" but it is unclear whether globalisation has reached some kind of limit. Given the trade disputes which started during the Trump presidency, it is uncertain how globalisation might develop further.

The age of globalisation also has led to the growth of multinational enterprises (MNEs). Although these types of corporation have existed for centuries, they have expanded significantly since the early 1990s. *The Economist* reported that the number of multinationals doubled in the period 1990–2015.[19] MNEs provide particular challenges to statisticians because of the intra-firm flows that cross borders. These flows have no market price because they are the delivery of one part of a firm to another. When reporting these flows multinational corporations have to estimate the market prices of these deliveries, but this mechanism is also used to lower the tax burden through "transfer pricing".

ICT and globalisation have a profound impact on economic issues such as production arrangements and can ultimately have an impact on inequality in society.[20] Frey and Osborne (2017), for example, pinpoint certain jobs that are most susceptible to automation. Brynjolfsson and Mcafee (2014) discuss ICT and robotisation and the impact that might have on inequality. Globalisation has resulted in industrial jobs shifting away from developed countries to low-wage countries such as China.[21] This also leads to a shifting of environmental pressures. As manufacturing has shifted towards China and other countries in "factory Asia" so have the environmental pressures moved.[22]

From a measurement perspective both ICT and globalisation present many challenges. Given these huge changes in society one might expect that the revision of the SNA 1993 would have led to many changes in the SNA 2008. On the issue of globalisation this is indeed the case. The revision process has spent quite a while looking at the various ways in which globalisation has influenced production, remittances and financial flows. A number of follow-up task forces and reports have been commissioned by major international institutes.[23] As a result statistics is also starting to focus on the global economic system rather than viewing 200 individual economies in isolation.

In the area of ICT and technological change the SNA 2008 has not really introduced any major changes. The word "e-commerce" appears once; "digital camera" is named once as an example. The words "internet", "website" and "social network" do not appear at all. The implication is that SNA accounting rules do not need to be changed because they apply to the old and the new economy alike.[24] However, it is doubtful whether the SNA rules are fully satisfactory in order to measure the complex technological economy that has rapidly changed our society.

GDP DOESN'T MEASURE WELL-BEING

From the very start, Kuznets was a proponent of a system that was geared towards measuring social welfare. He criticised the direction taken in the SNA discussion after the war. He also said that consumers incur intermediate costs, much like producers. For example, the costs of driving to a job are not final consumption, but rather intermediate, because it is a cost that is necessary to maintain the current living standard. It is not a net addition to welfare.[25]

In line with this thinking, economists have introduced the concept of "green accounting" in which they "correct" national accounting indicators by subtracting costs and adding benefits that are not included in the regular national accounts.

One of the most visible debates about the difference between GDP and well-being is the famous Easterlin paradox. In 1974, Richard Easterlin published "Does Economic Growth Improve the Human Lot?", in which he showed that in some countries subjective well-being, measured by surveying people's opinions about their well-being, had not grown while GDP had increased significantly.[26]

Since this finding, hundreds of scientific papers have tried to unravel the question "does money buy happiness?" One of the arguments is that for poor countries there is a clear relationship between increasing well-being and GDP. Poorer countries report low well-being compared to rich countries. The relationship does however display diminishing returns: for every $10,000 extra the amount of additional well-being diminishes. The Easterlin paradox is still debated in the literature, with 10–30 articles a year published in scientific journals.[27]

The literature has not just focused on the overall scores but also on the "drivers" of well-being. Dolan et al. (2008) provide a comprehensive overview of 153 papers which were published starting from 1990.[28] They categorise the evidence on many different influences.[29]

They conclude: "The evidence suggests that poor health, separation, unemployment and lack of social contact are all strongly negatively associated with SWB." In the regressions, the impact of income is already corrected for, so these results show that these non-monetary impacts are important explanations of people's happiness.

This type of research is now part of the blossoming field of "happiness economics" and has yielded many insights into how well-being can be measured and also what drives life satisfaction and happiness. These topics will be discussed further in Chapters 4 and 10.

GDP DOESN'T MEASURE INEQUALITY

GDP is a measure of the total economic activity but it says nothing about how income is distributed. Just looking at economic growth doesn't tell you about changes in the income distribution between subgroups in society.

Inequality has long been a popular topic for many economists but recently has experienced a resurgence, in large part because of the work of French economist Thomas Piketty, whose *Capital in the Twenty-First Century* was a global bestseller.[30] Piketty starts off his book with some praise and criticism of Simon Kuznets's work (him again!) on inequality. Kuznets had moved on to inequality data after his initial work on the national accounts in the 1930s–1940s. In the early 1950s Kuznets showed that income inequality had dropped for the period 1913 and 1948 in the United States. This gave rise to the so-called "Kuznets curve" which implied that the relationship between inequality and GDP was a bell curve: inequality rises at first as income grows but beyond a certain threshold inequality starts to drop. This was quite a revelation at the time, based on unique data that Kuznets and his colleagues had collected.

Piketty does not challenge the validity of Kuznets's statistics; in fact he is complimentary on this point. What Piketty criticises is the automatic mechanism that Kuznets curve suggests and which Kuznets failed to refute sufficiently. The Kuznets curve suggests that in the early stages of economic development the benefits of growth are beneficial to just a minority while during the more advanced phases of growth inequality falls because a larger portion of the population profits.[31] The findings were very welcome in the context of the Cold War. It directly contradicted the Marxist ideology which predicted that capitalist growth would lead to untenable social inequality.

Using long-term datasets, Piketty shows that no such automatic relationships exist between growth and inequality. The episode of diminishing inequality which Kuznets observes (1913/1948) did in fact exist, but Piketty shows that it was caused by the world wars and the Great Depression, which had a tremendous impact on the wealthy members of society. Piketty argues that Kuznets was aware of this but that the positive narrative of the Kuznets curve, within the context of the Cold War, was too attractive to resist for the economics profession in the United States.

Piketty shows that starting around 1980 income and wealth inequality has grown in many developed nations. Other books, such as Milanovic (2016) and Stiglitz (2013), have also added to the debate. All these books show that real wages have remained fairly constant in developed countries for a couple of decades, despite the fact that GDP has grown significantly over that period. Overall, the labour share in GDP has been shrinking.[32] This shows that economic growth does not automatically benefit the working population.

Starting from the 1980s, inequality has risen quite rapidly to levels reminiscent of a century before. GDP does not measure these developments and economists have therefore always stressed that far more should be done to measure the distribution of income and wealth. The dominance of GDP is therefore overshadowing a really important development in society.

GDP DOESN'T ACCOUNT FOR THE ENVIRONMENT/FUTURE

GDP does not account for the environment impacts which have been generated by society. These damages are not accounted for in the national accounting and if they are included it leads to rather perverse outcomes: environmental damage can actually be good for the economy. For example, during an oil spill, companies will have to spend money cleaning beaches and coastal areas, thereby raising GDP. Cutting down rainforests leads to timber sales, which raise GDP. Air pollution has a positive impact on the economy if it leads to additional trips to the doctor or sales of medicines.

Overall, the impact of humans on the natural environment has increased significantly since the start of the industrial revolution. The rate of change has however skyrocketed since the 1950s, which is why it is sometimes called the "1950s syndrome".[33] Population in combination with growing affluence has caused tremendous pressures on the natural systems. The pressures caused by the human system on the natural system are sometimes represented by the famous IPAT equation:[34]

$$\text{Impact} = \text{Population} * \text{Affluence} * \text{Technology}$$

where "affluence" is equivalent to the economic prosperity per capita and "technology" is the amount of environmental pressure per unit of economic output. In this relationship one of the most important debates for environmental economists has been the "growth debate", which asks whether the economy can continue to grow, while at the same time reducing environmental pressures.[35]

In the growth debate there are various viewpoints. In the 1990s there was an active debate about the so-called Environmental Kuznets Curve (EKC), which was inspired by the original Kuznets curve for inequality. Just like the inequality Kuznets curve there is an inverted U-shaped hypothesis: initially as the economy grows environmental pressures increase but beyond a certain threshold the environmental pressures start to diminish while GDP continues to grow. There are various time periods for certain environmental pressures where the empirical data bears this out. Just like the original Kuznets curve, the EKC also has a simple (rather optimistic) narrative. The underlying hypothesis is that the environment is a luxury good which can only be afforded beyond a certain threshold of wealth. This perspective has rather far-reaching implications: to protect the environment *more* economic growth is needed.

The EKC has been criticised using many of the same type of arguments which Piketty uses against the original Kuznets curve: where it is found it is either typical of that period or of a specific environmental pollutant only. Most importantly, it is criticised for implying an automatic (and optimistic) relationship between the environment and the economy.[36]

The total opposite of the EKC hypothesis is the notion of "de-growth".[37] This stream of literature says that the economy has to stop growing altogether or perhaps even shrink in order to remain within the limits of the earthly environment. From this perspective, the only solution to the environmental issues is to stop growing the economy and reduce consumption.

There is also a new third perspective called "a-growth", which makes the argument that if GDP doesn't measure social welfare then society should be ambivalent about its growth. The object of society should be to increase social welfare while staying within environmental limits. Whether this is with or without increases in economic output is not really relevant and should be ignored.[38]

These are academic debates but the opinion of the general public is rarely surveyed. Box 3.1 discusses a novel study that surveyed the general public about what they thought about the relationship.

Some environmental issues have profound current effects. Air pollution and emissions to water can lead to immediate health effects or damage to ecosystems. On the other hand, some impacts might take place far in the future. Depletion of natural resources, climate change or species extinction might not have large impacts on society today but will affect the lives of our children and grandchildren significantly.

The future sustainability of society is something which is also not measured by GDP. Yet the ability of future generations to meet their own needs is an important dimension of societal progress.

> **BOX 3.1 Public attitudes in the growth debate**
>
> Drews and van den Bergh (2016) surveyed a representative sample
> of Spaniards to assess their opinion of economic growth and the
> environment. They conclude:
>
> > We find that most respondents favor GDP growth rates of more than 3%.
> > A majority views growth and environmental sustainability as compatible
> > (green growth), while about one-third prefers either ignoring growth as
> > a policy aim (agrowth), or stopping it altogether (degrowth). Only very few
> > people want growth unconditionally (growth-at-all-costs). About one-third
> > of the respondents believe that growth may be never-ending.

Note that the future is a broader issue than just the environment. Apart from stocks of "natural capital" which are left to the next generation, the people that live now are also investing in roads, buildings and machines that will be available in the future. They are also investing in education in order to maintain or expand the stock of human capital.

The SNA does actually cater to some of these future aspects through so-called asset accounts, designed to measure the stocks of capital. These asset accounts include produced assets (such as machines and buildings), financial assets and also some natural capital. There are calls by many others to expand the number of assets to include full accounting for natural capital as well as human and social capital. However, despite many economists arguing for more wealth measurement few countries produce these figures.

Finally, there is a rhetorical trick that is often used in the Beyond-GDP literature. The trick is to malign the accounting rules of the SNA by pointing to some counterintuitive development. Some have been used in the sections above. What is perhaps not realised is that all these statements have a particular pattern. Many of them fall under the rhetorical rules shown in Box 3.2.

BOX 3.2   **Have a look at these crazy accounting rules!**

1. *Increase in economy = Decrease in well-being*

    Example: When you have a non-fatal heart attack it is good for the economy because it raises the output of the health sector. If your house burns down it is good for the economy because you will have to replace your house, furniture and belongings.

    Example (vice versa): When a person decides to work fewer hours to have more leisure time, the economy shrinks because their income lowers.

2. *Increase in environmental pressure = Increase in economy*

    Example: An oil spill is good for the economy because the services of cleaning up raise GDP.

3. *Administrative change = Change in economy*

    Example: If a housecleaner marries their boss, GDP drops. Before the marriage the housekeeper was a paid employee (and therefore part of GDP) and after the marriage the cleaning is done within the household, and so is not included in GDP.

What these examples highlight is that GDP is meant to measure the size of the economic activities and not the well-being effects or environmental consequences. In addition, examples such as the housekeeper show that the border of the production boundary may sometimes seem arbitrary. The question is whether pointing out strange aspects of the accounting rules, or any of the other topics above, really resonate with the general public. How many housekeepers marry their bosses anyway?

Yet these accounting rules do sometimes lead to strange outcomes. In May 2014 Statistics Netherlands reported the latest quarterly GDP figures using the following headline: "Lower gas consumption has negative effect on Dutch economy". The main reason for lower GDP growth was that the Netherlands had experienced a mild winter. Since the Netherlands extracts natural gas and this is part of GDP, when the demand for gas reduces the economy "suffers". This makes perfect sense from a standpoint of economic output, but the consumers will not have felt that their well-being suffered when their gas bill declined (unless they were a big fan of the Elfstedentocht[39]).

GDP IS NOT A GOOD PROXY FOR WELFARE

So given these criticisms of GDP, why is it still in use? One reason might be a lack of knowledge about how GDP is measured. It is certain that many people in society are oblivious. Even amongst economists one might wonder how many know exactly what it takes to measure this metric. Economic courses are also teaching less and less national accounting, or only giving a broad-brush overview. Detailed knowledge is therefore rare. How many people have read all 700+ pages of the SNA?

Most macroeconomists will know the arguments made in this chapter. Yet, in practice, many will still use this data in empirical macroeconomic applications anyway. An important reason is the overwhelming availability of GDP data. From the perspective of the range of countries, historical time series and quarterly figures, vast datasets can be downloaded in a couple of minutes. The availability of better measures for the economy or for Beyond-GDP is far from perfect and presents a significant hurdle.

Yet there is another reason which is used to justify the use of GDP figures. While GDP might not be a direct measure of social welfare, some argue that it is a pretty good proxy.[40] It is the long-term perspective that makes for the most compelling argument. Figure 3.1 shows data for the world population and GDP per capita from 1750 to the present. Thanks to the work of the economic historian Angus Madisson there exist estimates for these two factors going back two millennia. The graph could have started from year 1, but nothing much happens in the first 1,750 years. Population is estimated to have been 226 million in year 1 with around 467 Geary-Khamis dollars per capita.[41] In 1750 population had increased by a factor of nearly three while GDP per capita had not even doubled (615 Geary-Khamis dollars).[42] From the perspective of population and economy, the period from 1750 to the present is truly a unique period in history.

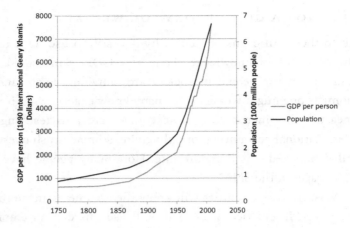

FIGURE 3.1 World GDP and population (1750–2008 AD)

The mid-eighteenth century is the start of the "industrial revolution" which began in Great Britain. Production of goods started to move to large-scale factories which were adopting the latest steam-powered machines (first industrial revolution) to increase production. The end of the nineteenth and beginning of the twentieth century was the period of the second industrial revolution, which was based on electricity and the internal combustion engine. This changed people's lives even further by bringing mobility and electrification to all domains of life. The latest stage is the ICT revolution, which is sometimes referred to as the third industrial revolution which has radically changed digital applications and connectivity.

In the period from 1750 to now the standard of living has risen significantly in nearly all aspects of life. On average, people live far more comfortable and healthy lives than 270 years ago. Take, for example, the United Kingdom, the country in which the industrial revolution started and for which there exist long statistical time series. For the period 1820–2010, GDP per capita increased twelvefold. Simultaneously, impressive progress has been made in health and education. Life expectancy at birth has doubled from around forty years in 1820 to over eighty years in 2010. In 1820, the average length of schooling for a UK resident was 1.8 years. By 2010 this had increased to 13.3 years.[43] Looking just at these statistics, it seems that GDP and the standard of living pretty much grow hand in hand.[44]

It seems self-evident that the quality of life of the average person nowadays is much better than in 1750. It is also obvious that technological advances led to productivity growth which fuelled a much higher standard of living. Taken in that light, it seems quite reasonable to view economic growth as a proxy for long-term social welfare improvements.

Literature from various quarters suggests that sometime after the war the relationship between social welfare and GDP changed in developed countries. The Easterlin paradox suggests that after a certain threshold, increases in income since the war have not raised well-being scores. Gordon (2016) also argues that the greatest welfare improvements lay in the period up to 1970. Other literature has shown that around the 1970s, GDP continued to grow while green accounting aggregates start to stabilise or fall. For example, Victor (2010) shows that the Index of Economic Well-being decreased after 1970 while the Genuine Progress Indicator peaked in 1978.[45] The reason is that many of the negative components of green accounts started to increase rapidly (e.g. higher inequality and environmental damage).

For developing countries it might still be argued that GDP and quality of life correlate quite strongly because economic prosperity is needed to provide for food, shelter, health and education. However, the idea that economic growth would *automatically* lead to higher wages, lower inequality (Kuznets curve) or lower environmental damage (environmental Kuznets curve) have unravelled. Green accounting literature and happiness literature suggest that the relationship has in fact stagnated or become negative for developed countries. In the future, issues such as climate change, population growth, digitisation and ageing populations will make the relationship even more complex. There is no basis to assume that GDP will be a good proxy in future either.

One of the primary reasons why GDP has remained so dominant, despite all the criticisms raised in this chapter, is that there is no clear alternative. If there had been a powerful Beyond-GDP metric, which had had worldwide support, this might have threatened the dominance of GDP. The next chapter will discuss the history of Beyond-GDP and why it has, thus far, failed to deliver a powerful alternative.

4 Why Is Beyond-GDP Not Successful?

FROM A COTTAGE INDUSTRY TO A LARGER COTTAGE INDUSTRY

The realisation that GDP does not measure crucial aspects of society has inspired many researchers and institutions to create alternative metrics. Their aim is to create a better "compass" for society than GDP which signals whether society is travelling in a right or wrong direction.

The term "Beyond-GDP" immediately reveals a problem: it is a negatively defined term which only makes clear what should *not* be measured. This term captures a plethora of underlying approaches, debates and methodologies with varying ideas about the measurement object. In fact some of these would not even consider themselves part of "Beyond-GDP" because their aim is not to replace GDP but to measure an entirely different concept.[1]

It is difficult to pin a precise number on the quantity of measurement systems that have been suggested. The biggest database, the Compendium of Sustainable Development Indicator Initiatives, listed around 900 initiatives all around the world but not all of these are at the national level.[2] Some are corporate social responsibility initiatives or sustainable city indexes. Note that the Compendium was updated up to 2011 and has since been taken offline. If it had continued after 2011, it is clear that there would be significantly more entries. The largest active repository of Beyond-GDP initiatives is wikiprogress. org, which is an OECD initiative that provides information about well-being and sustainability projects from around the world. This currently lists around 500 initiatives.[3]

These databases have a specific reach and do not provide comprehensive overviews of Beyond-GDP initiatives.[4] They do not cover

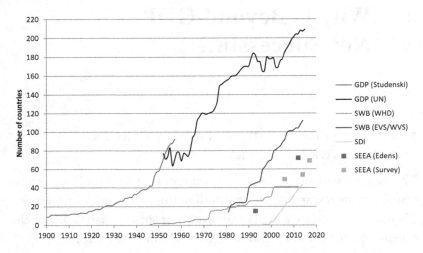

FIGURE 4.1 Number of countries with experience in GDP, SWB, SEEA and SDI
Sources: See Annex

all the initiatives which have emerged over the many decades that Beyond-GDP has existed. Nearly all countries have multiple initiatives spread over many institutes and researchers. For the purposes of this book it can safely be assumed that there are hundreds of measurement systems, especially if we take on board city, provincial and measurement systems for companies. If anyone ever tried to do a complete overview it should not come as a surprise to find that the total exceeded a thousand.

Compared to GDP, it is hard to provide a neat and tidy overview of the chronological development of Beyond-GDP. For example, in Chapter 2 the history of GDP was split into four periods. This is not as easy in the case of Beyond-GDP because the various approaches have their own development paths. Figure 4.1 provides a partial view of the development of three areas of Beyond-GDP: namely Subjective Well-being (SWB), the System of Environmental and Economics Accounts (SEEA) and Sustainable Development Indicators (SDI). For SWB two sources have been used (World Happiness Database and the European/World Values Survey). For the SEEA, estimates by

Edens (2013) are used as well as responses to the Global Assessment of Environmental-Economic Accounting which is carried out by the United Nations Statistics Division.[5] See the Annex for details.

The y-axis of the figure shows the number of countries which have applied these methodologies. By setting it against the development of GDP it is possible to make an assessment of the Schumpeterian Dream. How close are these efforts in terms of global coverage compared to GDP?

The measurement of SWB started just after the war and the number of countries has shown steady growth ever since. The proliferation of the EVS/WVS shows a rapid expansion of the number of countries that have taken part in at least one wave of this research. The expansion of SEEA and SDI in terms of countries is quite rapid. Overall one might say that the Beyond-GDP initiatives are currently breaking through the "rich-countries barrier". Just like GDP, the early adopters are developed countries with the most advanced statistical systems. Slowly but surely, less developed countries are also starting to measure Beyond-GDP. So in terms of the number of countries, progress is being made. However, there are some caveats. One is that the initiative is not always annual (let alone on a quarterly basis). For the EVS/WVS waves take place once every 4–5 years and there are only a few countries which take part every time. The second issue is harmonisation and institutionalisation, where there is still a long way to go.

Note that there are Beyond-GDP indicators with global coverage which are not shown in Figure 4.1. For example, the Human Development Index (HDI) is available for 188 countries at data.un. org, the ecological footprint is calculated for 186 countries by the Global Footprint Network and the Sustainable Society Index has data for 154 countries. Also, the most recent Gallup polls on SWB cover around 140 countries. However, it is important to note that these datasets are done by a single institute. This has the advantage that it is fairly easy to harmonise methodologies.[6]

In the case of GDP, the statistical infrastructure is more complex because the production of the statistics is decentralised to

Table 4.1 *Historical overview of Beyond-GDP initiatives*

		1945–1969	1970–1974	1975–1979	1980–1984	1985–1989
	Conferences/ Initiatives (International organisations)	Problems of Modern Society	Stockholm Conference		World Commission of Environment and Development	
	Publications (International organisations and other)	SNA53 SNA69 Affluent Society Population Bomb Silent Spring Tragedy of the Commons	Limits to Growth Easterlin Paradox			Our Common Future
TYPE 1	Subjective Well-being	US, MX, JP, IN, UK, FI	NO, BE, DK, FR, DE, IE, IT, LX, NL EuroBarometer	AT, KR	GR, AR EVS1 WVS1	ES, PT, RU
TYPE 1	Green Accounting		Measure of Economic Welfare (MEW) Sustainable National Income (SNI) Total Income System of Accounts (TISA)	Adjusted GNP	Economic Aspects of Welfare (EAW) Integrated Economic Accounts	Index of Sustainable Economic Welfare (ISEW) Gross Private Domestic Product
TYPE 1	Other					
TYPE 2	Composite Indicators		Life Situation Index (LSI)			
TYPE 3	Non-conceptual indicator sets		Gross National Happiness			
TYPE 4	Conceptual indicator sets					

209 countries, while at the same time working with a harmonised methodology. This is also the case for the SDI, SEEA and SWB initiatives shown in Figure 4.1. These are examples where the calculations are done in each country individually. From a coordination perspective this is a far more daunting challenge than a single institute calculating an index for all countries.

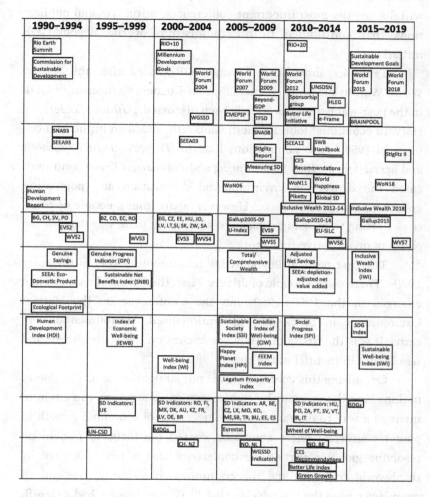

Sources: See Annex

HISTORICAL OVERVIEW OF INFLUENTIAL CONFERENCES, INITIATIVES AND PUBLICATIONS

Figure 4.1 shows the development of SDI, SEEA and SWB by analysing the country proliferation. There are however many more Beyond-GDP methodologies. Before these other Beyond-GDP measurement systems are discussed, this section first provides historical context. It will discuss the most important conferences, initiatives and publications that contributed to the momentum of the Beyond-GDP initiatives.[7]

Table 4.1 shows that Beyond-GDP started after the Second World War. In previous chapters, Simon Kuznets's criticism of GDP in the post-war period has already been discussed. *Affluent Society*, by Harvard economist John Kenneth Galbraith, added an influential critique in 1958.[8] Also publications like the *Tragedy of the Commons* and bestsellers such as *Silent Spring* and *Population Bomb* communicated the dangers of environmental degradation and population growth to a wider audience.[9] However, apart from a couple of countries starting to measure subjective well-being, little was done in the realm of quantitative indicators.

The first peak in Beyond-GDP measurement was in the early 1970s. There were a couple of drivers. First, the Green Movement had emerged in the 1950s/1960s but the Conference on the Human Environment in Stockholm institutionalised environmental concerns. It was the first global UN conference on the environment and was highly influential at the time.

Organising this conference was not straightforward. The poorer nations saw the attempt by rich countries to focus on the environment as a way to distract from the necessity of economic growth in poorer countries. These countries wanted the focus to remain on resolving global poverty. The conference was nearly boycotted by third-world countries and the communist bloc but in the end all countries signed the joint declaration.[10] The conference had a significant effect on the institutionalisation of environmental issues. It created the United Nations Environmental Programme, which stimulated governments all over the world to set up environmental ministries. Up to that point governments rarely had a separate minister for the environment.

1972 was also the year that the seminal *Limits to Growth* report of the Club of Rome was published. This report played a major role in raising environmental awareness. The report provided scenario projections of the population and economy which showed that resources would run out within several decades. The main message was that exponential growth could not continue indefinitely. The study made use of the most advanced computer simulation techniques at the time, which had been developed by a Massachusetts Institute of Technology (MIT) professor, Forrester. The models represented a huge step in environmental modelling and did a lot to raise public awareness of environmental problems. The report also stimulated attention to the relationship between growth, resources and environment in the young field of environmental economics.[11]

Social concerns also provided momentum for Beyond-GDP initiatives in the 1970s. The student protests of 1968, youth culture, the Vietnam War, the civil rights movement and other issues were causing friction in society. It is no wonder that the OECD, the bastion of economic growth after the Second World War, set up a programme to solve "The problems of modern society", which ran from 1968 to 1974. At that time it was becoming abundantly clear that the spectacular economic growth of the 1950s–1960s did not automatically create a better society.

The social indicator movement was an eclectic movement that aimed to overcome the dominance of economic indicators. The main result was a major boost in the measurement of subjective well-being. The importance of subjective well-being measures was further bolstered by the academic discussion about the Easterlin paradox in the early 1970s.

Yet the early 1970s would turn out to be a false start for Beyond-GDP. The economic turmoil of the 1970s meant that governments were frantically looking for ways in which to rekindle economic growth. This actually reduced attention to environmental and social issues. For example, the OECD sidelined the programme on the "problems of modern society" after member countries urged the organisation to get back to its original mandate of GDP growth policies.[12] The social indicators movement lost momentum and the green accounting initiatives remained mostly academic.

The real game-changer in Beyond-GDP measurement was the seminal publication by the United Nations World Commission on Environment and Development (WCED) in 1987. The commission's report, *Our Common Future*, is often referred to as the "Brundtland Report", after Gro Harlem Brundtland, the chairperson of the commission.[13]

This report led to the popularisation of the term "sustainable development". Ever since then, sustainable development has been a catch-all term which defines societal progress as the balanced development of the economic, environmental and social dimensions of society. It provided a narrative to speak about global environmental issues and other social issues such as third-world poverty under a common heading.

The term "sustainable development" was further institutionalised due to the "Earth Summit" in Rio de Janeiro in 1992. Just as the Stockholm Summit in 1972 started the institutionalisation of environmental problems, the Rio Earth Summit in 1992 institutionalised the term "Sustainable Development". At this conference, Agenda 21 was adopted which included a recommendation for countries to monitor their progress towards sustainable development.[14]

Ten years later, the "Rio+10" conference led to renewed momentum of Agenda 21. In the period after the Rio+20 Conference, the other international institutes started to take up this topic. The OECD started convening the World Forum's "measuring well-being and societal progress" once every 2–4 years from 2004. The OECD also launched the Better Life Initiative/Index at the fifty-year anniversary of the institute in 2011.

Eurostat (the statistical office of the European Union) started work on Sustainable Development Indicators in 2005. The European Commission held a large-scale conference on "Beyond-GDP: Measuring progress, true wealth, and the well-being of nations" in 2007 and funded projects such as e-Frame and BRAINPOoL (Bringing Alternative Indicators into Policy), which dealt specifically with Beyond-GDP indicators. The World Bank published the "Wealth of Nations" reports in 2006, 2011 and 2018.[15]

World leaders also started to join in. In 2009, Nicolas Sarkozy, President of France, set up the Commission on the Measurement of Economic Performance and Social Progress. This report, which was produced by the CMEPSP, is commonly referred to as the Stiglitz Report. David Cameron, Prime Minister of the UK, started a process to measure subjective well-being, including a programme to measure SWB on a quarterly basis and to create a Wheel of Well-being. There are also other initiatives such as the *Human Development Report*, *The World Happiness Report*, *The Global Sustainable Development Report* and the *Inclusive Wealth Report* as well as Thomas Piketty's book on inequality (*Capital in the Twenty-First Century*), which has had a significant impact on the Beyond-GDP debate.

The period 2002–2015 also saw a number of harmonisation efforts such as the Working Group for Statistics of Sustainable Development (WGSSD) (2004–2009) and the Task Force for Sustainable Development (TFSD) (2009–2014), which were led by the UN-ECE, OECD and Eurostat. The OECD's *Guidelines on Measuring Subjective Well-being* was published in 2013. The biggest impulse to conceptual harmonisation was probably provided by the Stiglitz Report, which was published in 2009.

The Rio+20 Conference in 2012 led to renewed momentum. The main legacy of that conference is that the Sustainable Development Goals were conceived at that conference. However, 2012–2015 was a fruitful period for many other Beyond-GDP initiatives. Apart from the SDG process, the financial crisis of 2008 also bolstered support for Beyond-GDP. The crisis has strengthened the narrative that a world which is too much led by economic figures and short-term profits is susceptible to this type of implosion.

TYPOLOGY OF BEYOND-GDP METHODOLOGIES

The next couple of sections will provide a more detailed overview of the various Beyond-GDP initiatives. To bring some order to the

Table 4.2 *Beyond-GDP methodologies*

	Index	Set of indicators
Conceptual	TYPE 1 (e.g. Subjective Well-being, Genuine Progress Indicator, Ecological Footprint)	TYPE 4 (e.g. Stiglitz Report, CES recommendations, Better Life Index)
Non-conceptual	TYPE 2 (e.g. Human Development Index)	TYPE 3 (e.g. Sustainable Development Goals)

Beyond-GDP alternatives, this section uses a methodological typology of four conceptual categories, which are summarised in Table 4.2. The methodologies have two dimensions. First, some measurement systems strive to capture societal progress in one index while others try and capture the society's developments using a set/dashboard of indicators. The second dimension describes the conceptual foundation of the measurement system. In some cases, a conceptual framework is used, while in other cases no conceptual basis is used at all. For example, a political process or stakeholder consultations might be used to choose the various indicators.

Table 4.2 shows the types which exist for these four permutations and some examples. The next few sections will discuss these in more detail. The discussion are based on Table 4.1 (for a full overview of sources see the Annex).

TYPE I: CONCEPTUAL INDEX (SUBJECTIVE WELL-BEING)

The OECD defines Subjective well-being as: "Good mental states, including all of the various evaluations, positive and negative, that people make of their lives, and the affective reactions of people to their experiences."[16] The most common way of measuring this is by asking respondents to evaluate their lives, e.g. on a scale from one to ten. A typical question might be: "Overall, how satisfied are you with life as a whole these days?" This type of questionnaire emerged after the Second World War, starting with the first survey in the United States in 1946.[17] This was the period in which survey sampling came of age and it therefore became possible to obtain various social indicators through questionnaires.

In the "golden age" of economic measurement after the war, SWB measures expanded gradually to a couple of countries.[18] SWB survey life evaluations got a boost from the "social indicators movement" in the early 1970s. Overall, this movement was unsuccessful in creating a similar framework to the SNA but did raise the profile of social measures, notably SWB.[19]

From 1973, SWB questions started to be asked in the European Union's Eurobarometer survey. From 1981, academic groups started to work on the European Value Survey and World Value Survey in order to compare various SWB and other attitudes over multiple countries. Even commercial parties have started to implement surveys on SWB. The Gallup World Poll started in 2005 with 26 countries and had expanded to around 140 countries by 2018.[20]

The SWB literature is dominated by analysis of life evaluations where people are asked to evaluate their "happiness" or "life satisfaction". However, the OECD guidelines speak of three concepts of well-being: Life evaluation, Affect and Eudaimonia (psychological "flourishing"). Life evaluation is only one of the approaches. The main difference is that affect measurement captures the feelings experienced by the respondent at a particular point in time. This type of well-being research is advocated by a field called hedonic psychology, the proponents of which include Daniel Kahneman, a psychologist, one of the founders of behavioural economics and winner of the Nobel Prize in economics in 2002.

This type of approach measures the emotions of people at specific moments in time. This is an expensive survey and quite intrusive for respondents, which is why cheaper and easier survey methods have been devised.[21] Survey questions on affect might ask respondents to score emotions such as Positive, Negative, Good, Bad, Pleasant, Unpleasant, Happy, Sad, Afraid, Joyful, Angry or Contented. Kahneman and Krueger (2006) suggest that any episode can be quantified as positive or negative. Based on this, they propose the "U-index", which records the percentage of time spent on unpleasant activities.

The third SWB approach, Eudaimonia, refers to deeper psychological motivations such as Competence, Engagement, Meaning, Optimism, Positive relationships, Resilience, Self-esteem, Emotional stability and Vitality. The OECD guidelines argue that each of these perspectives on SWB provide important and complementary dimensions to well-being.

Most data that is collected is about life evaluation but the availability of other SWB measures has increased through programmes such as EVS/WVS, which has grown from around 20 countries in 1981 and is expected to have around 70–80 countries by 2019.

TYPE I: CONCEPTUAL INDEX (GREEN ACCOUNTING)

Although SWB surveys started earlier, many economists take the year 1972 as the starting point for Beyond-GDP. That was the year the Measure of Economic Welfare was created by Yale economists Nordhaus and Tobin.[22] This was the first prominent example of a "green accounting" aggregate.

This type of index takes a macroeconomic aggregate as the foundation but a number of additions and subtractions are made. For example, for the MEW, the value of leisure time and home production were added because these provide a positive contribution to welfare.[23] Environmental damage, expressed in monetary terms, was subtracted because it is detrimental to welfare. This is referred to as "green" accounting, although usually it does more than correct for environmental damage.[24]

The MEW can be seen in the tradition of Simon Kuznets's critique of national accounts. Kuznets argued that some of the components of GDP did not contribute to welfare and should therefore not be included in national income. Also, some externalities are detrimental to welfare and these should be subtracted. Using methods that are based on welfare economics, a monetary value can be estimated for these impacts. The idea is that the aggregate index provides a better estimate of economic welfare.[25]

The MEW methodology inspired the Index for Sustainable Economic Welfare (ISEW), which was proposed in 1989 by Daly and Cobb.[26] The ISEW later evolved into the Genuine Progress Indicator (GPI).[27] The ISEW/GPI is used regularly in the economics literature and there have also been successes at the policy level. Two US states, Maryland and Vermont, have introduced official GPI measures and there are more that are exploring them.[28] In practice the ISEW/GPI applications differ methodologically because there is discussion about what exactly it is supposed to measure as well as practical differences and data availability. There is therefore a call to strive towards a harmonised "GPI 2.0" methodology.[29]

The MEW/ISEW/GPI approach is from the same family of green accounting aggregates. A different, rather unique, approach was proposed in 1974 by Roefie Hueting: Sustainable National Income.[30] Instead of adding benefits and subtracting damages from existing macroeconomics indicators, the SNI approach took environmental limits as the foundation of the methodology. The indicator quantifies the question "how high would national income be if the current technology were used to stay within sustainability limits?"[31]

A third variety of green accounts emerged in the 1990s and is based on a different economic method, the capital approach. This method starts from the premise that society has certain assets (produced, financial, human, natural and social capital). John Hicks, back in 1939, defined real income as the maximum amount that could be spent on consumption without reducing the capacity to maintain the same consumption stream over time.[32] For non-declining "Hicksian income" it is necessary to maintain a non-declining stock of capital. This is sometimes seen by economists as the conceptual equivalent of the term "sustainable development".

Based on this capital theory, the genuine savings indicator was suggested in 1993.[33] This indicator shows the additions to the various stocks of capital. For example, an investment in education is recorded as an increase in human capital while depletion of natural resources is a reduction in a capital stock.

One can also measure the total value of each stock, which is known as wealth accounting. This variety of green accounting is influential because the World Bank has adopted this approach and publishes "adjusted net savings" and "total (or comprehensive) wealth" indicators. The United Nations University, under the leadership of Partha Dasgupta, proposed the Inclusive Wealth Index (IWI). The System of Environmental and Economic Accounts, which will be discussed later on, also includes a couple of indexes which follow this theoretical approach.

Table 4.1 shows that there are many other green accounting aggregates which have not been discussed in the text. Ever since the early 1970s, new proposals have been published in the economic literature on a regular basis.[34]

TYPE I: CONCEPTUAL INDEX (ECOLOGICAL FOOTPRINT)

The ecological footprint also starts off with macroeconomic data, namely the consumption of a country. It then converts all the goods and services into the land area that is required to produce them. The unit of measurement is therefore not money but land area. For example, the consumption of food is translated into the area that is necessary for agriculture. The ecological footprint is therefore equal to the biologically productive area needed to provide all the products that people use: fruits and vegetables, fish, wood, textiles, and space for buildings and roads. It also includes the absorption of carbon dioxide from fossil fuel use by estimating the area of forest that will need to be planted to compensate for these emissions.

Communicatively, the ecological footprint works very well because it can be contrasted to the biologically productive area available within a region or the world (biocapacity). This can then be used to show that human consumption is greater than the area on earth. In fact the World Wildlife Fund, which promotes the use of the ecological footprint, states that humanity needs 1.6 Earths to maintain its current consumption patterns. The message which is communicated is clear: society is living beyond its means.

Many scientific articles have been published on the ecological footprint, both pro and con. It has also led to the development of other related indicators, such as the carbon footprint, water footprint and material footprint. The harmonisation of ecological footprint data is done by the Global Footprint Network, which currently has a database of more than 200 countries.

TYPE 2: NON-CONCEPTUAL INDEX (COMPOSITE INDICATORS, E.G. HUMAN DEVELOPMENT INDEX)

A non-conceptual index aggregates multiple sub-components using a mathematical procedure. It is not based on a conceptual framework but provides a simple basis upon which to combine indicators into a single index. This type of aggregation has existed for a long time in the Beyond-GDP discussion. For example, in the early 1970s the Life Situation Index (LSI) was produced in the Netherlands.[35]

By far the most famous composite indicator is the Human Development Index. In 1990, the United Nations' Human Development Report used HDI for the first time. The HDI aggregates numerically the economy, health and education into a single index. It is loosely based on Sen's capability approach.[36] This framework argues that welfare should not only be measured according to realisations of people's lives (functionings) but also the potential people have to live the life that they want (capabilities).

The capability approach is philosophically challenging and critiques welfare economics in particular. Sen was not in fact in favour of capturing the many dimensions of society in one index. He thought such indexes were "vulgar".[37] Nevertheless, he was convinced by the UN representatives to go ahead with a highly simplified version of his theory.

The HDI is probably one the most successful Beyond-GDP initiatives but many others have been proposed as well. Table 4.1 shows that many composite indicators have been proposed, especially in the 2000s. Composite indicators are generally good for ranking of countries.[38] This is also why they have become popular in fields that are not related to Beyond-GDP. Examples include the Competitiveness Index published by the World Economic Forum and the Global Innovation Index. The country rankings of composite indicators are easily communicated to the general public and therefore capture media attention.

TYPE 3: NON-CONCEPTUAL INDICATOR SETS (E.G. SUSTAINABLE DEVELOPMENT GOALS)

Type 3 are indicator sets that do not have a conceptual basis. One of the earliest and most cited Beyond-GDP initiatives is the programme on Gross National Happiness which was initiated by the King of Bhutan in the early 1970s. In practice, a number of dimensions are distinguished and a survey is taken of the population to measure each of these dimensions.

The Brundtland Report in 1987 and the Rio Earth Summit in 1992 were instrumental in promoting Type 3 Sustainable Development Indicators (SDI). In 1995 the Commission for Sustainable Development (CSD) proposed such an indicator set. The CSD indicators were based on stakeholder deliberations between the various countries of the UN. They were a major boost to the measurement of Beyond-GDP and were supposed to be the benchmark indicator set for sustainable development. Countries could adapt the CSD set according to their preferences, but the adoption of the CSD set was not compulsory.

As Table 4.1 shows, these types of non-conceptual indicator sets subsequently became very influential. The use of sustainable development indicator (SDI) sets increased amongst official government institutes and statistical offices. The Rio+10 Conference in 2002 stimulated many countries that had not yet done so to create an SDI set. However, there was significant divergence in which indicators were used. The CSD set was generally not followed, with each country creating its own SDI dashboard. All EU28 countries created their own indicator set, and there was also a European SDI which was produced by Eurostat. Indicator sets also became popular for other topics outside of sustainable development. For example, Eurostat's Well-being Report has a range of indicators and the UK's Wheel of Well-being is another example of a Type 3 indicator set.

By far the most influential initiative is the Sustainable Development Goals, introduced in 2015. This was a worldwide process where the governments of the world agreed to define 17 goals and 169 targets for sustainable development. The process started at the Rio+20 Conference in 2012. At that conference, it was decided that the Millennium Development Goals (MDGs), which ran from 2000 to 2015, would be replaced by the SDGs. These targets would be set for the 2015–2030 period. In just three years of negotiations, this process has managed to achieve a level of harmonisation that is unprecedented in Beyond-GDP. Many countries that had their own Type 3 SDI sets have since shifted to SDGs or are considering it.

TYPE 4: CONCEPTUAL INDICATOR SETS (E.G. STIGLITZ REPORT)

In the 1990s/2000s the vast majority of indicator sets were non-conceptual. However, in the mid-2000s a couple of countries started to create indicator sets based on conceptual frameworks: Switzerland, Norway and New Zealand. Later the Netherlands and Belgium also introduced Type 4 indicator sets.

Although the number of countries which have adopted these indicator sets is limited, Type 4 has been influential in the various harmonisation efforts. In 2004, the UNECE, OECD and Eurostat (European Commission) created the Working Group for Statistics on Sustainable Development (WGSSD). The group built on the idea of wealth accounting, which had gained prominence in the 1990s and is also popular at the World Bank. However there was much resistance to the idea that sustainability was simply a summation of monetised capital stocks.[39] The final report discusses monetary indicators for capital but also the advantages of providing a set of non-monetary indicators for these assets.

The WGSSD Report was published in 2009 and had a significant influence on the Stiglitz Report, which was also published in that same year. The Stiglitz chapter on "sustainability" leans heavily on the WGSSD report. At the same time the Stiglitz Report is highly critical of creating monetary indexes (i.e. Type 1). Methodologically speaking, the Stiglitz Report can be seen as a compromise between Type 1 and Type 3: the green accounting demand for a single indicator is dropped but at the same time the proponents of indicator sets accept a conceptual (economic) foundation rather than a stakeholder process.

In 2009, just after the publication of the Stiglitz Report, the joint UNECE/OECD/Eurostat Task Force on Measuring Sustainable Development (TFSD) was created. This was the institutional successor to the WGSSD. The TFSD built on the conceptual framework of the Stiglitz Report and also created a set of (Type 4) indicators. The report was endorsed by the Conference of European Statisticians and the CES Recommendations on Measuring Sustainable Development have been adopted by a couple of countries so far. However, the SDG process seems to have shifted the momentum back towards non-conceptual indicator sets (Type 3).

An influential indicator set is the Better Life Index (BLI), which was launched by the OECD at its fiftieth anniversary.[40] It is actually an indicator set but it can also be aggregated into a single index using a web-based application. Initially, equal weights are set for the indicators to calculate the index. However, the website also allows users to define their own weights to calculate the BLI.

SYSTEM OF ENVIRONMENTAL AND ECONOMIC ACCOUNTING (SEEA)

The final Beyond-GDP initiative that will be discussed in this chapter is the SEEA. This is a successful initiative which is hard to classify because it is an accounting framework that produces both Type 1 and

Type 4 indicators. The idea of environmental accounts had already started in the 1970s in Norway and France and in the 1990s in the Netherlands.[41] During the process that led to the SNA 1993, the topic of environmental pressures and sustainable development were high on the agenda because of the Brundtland Report/Earth Summit.[42] It was an opportunity for green accounting to be included in the SNA. However, it was decided that rather than put environmental aspects and social issues into the "core" SNA framework, it was better to allow for a "satellite" account for the environment.[43]

The harmonisation process for environmental accounts of the early 1990s led to the first handbook in 1993.[44] The SEEA 1993 includes a green accounting indicator called the eco-domestic product (EDP) which is obtained by subtracting environmental costs from the Net Domestic Product.[45]

Although the SEEA 1993 is related to the green accounting movement, there is a marked difference. The largest part of the SEEA handbook deals with the physical accounts which record the flows and stocks of an economy. This includes physical flows in terms of mass and energy units as well as resource use or emissions by industry. These physical accounts can be used 1) separately for policy purposes or 2) to create green accounting indexes.[46] The SEEA is therefore a modular accounting framework with both a physical and monetary dimension. The monetary green accounting aggregates are far less prominent than one might expect of an initiative that grew out of this discussion.

The SEEA 1993 was an important first step towards harmonisation of environmental accounting. By the time the second edition (SEEA 2003) was published the other international institutes had joined the UN as co-authors.[47] The SEEA 2003 had also grown to a 598-page document. Yet on many crucial issues it was not prescriptive. In terms of green accounting aggregates, various alternatives were described, but no definitive choices were made. Ten years later there was a new attempt. After a lengthy deliberation process the *System of Environmental Economic Accounting 2012 – Central Framework* was adopted by the Statistical Commission of the United

Nations.[48] The SEEA was prepared under the auspices of the six major international institutes. The SEEA has the same standing as the SNA since they are both "statistical standards". In fact, the SEEA has also dropped the term "satellite account" and is seen as on an equal footing with the SNA.

The SEEA has a lot of information about physical flows such as natural resource use and emissions in production and consumption. The SEEA also proposed green accounting aggregates called "depletion-adjusted net value added" and "depletion adjusted net domestic product", which are obtained by deducting consumption of fixed capital and depletion from gross value added and GDP.

Viewed from a historical point of view, the green accounting movement has managed to get an index elevated to a statistical standard – the highest rung in the statistical pantheon. Yet the correction to GDP is only for depletion of natural resources. No reductions in quality of the environment (degradation), health issues or other externalities are included although these are common in the green accounting community.[49]

The success of the SEEA process is reminiscent of the success of the macroeconomic community. Table 4.3 compares the two. The SEEA is in a good position to become the "common language" for environmental macroeconomics. The goal of this community is to manage the economy within environmental limits. Table 4.3 shows that there is a clear structure to the community in terms of policy science, accounting framework and key indicators. The common language (the SEEA framework) took two decades to complete. The SEEA has had significant institutional success. Getting this handbook agreed by six international institutes and all the statistical offices of the UN member states is a major achievement. The European Commission made it legally binding for all European countries to produce six of the SEEA accounts. The UN Statistical Division has made it its explicit aim to have a hundred countries start producing SEEA account by 2020.[50] Yet, despite these successes, the SEEA is still far from the dominance of the SNA.

Table 4.3 *Comparing the macroeconomic and environmental-macroeconomic communities*

Community features		Macroeconomics (GDP multinational)	Environmental (macro)economics
Goal		Economic growth	Managing the economy within environmental limits
Community structure	Policy Science	Macroeconomics	Environmental Macroeconomics
	Accounting Framework	System of National Accounts	System of Environmental and Economic Accounts
	Key Indicator	Gross Domestic Product	Various Physical and Monetary Indicators
Common language		System of National Accounts	System of Environmental and Economic Accounts
		First edition: 1953	Start: 1993
		Completion: 1993	Completion: 2012
Institutionalisation		Around 200 countries	Around 70 countries 100 countries by 2020

THE NEED FOR A COMMUNITY

Why have none of these Beyond-GDP initiatives managed to overcome the dominance of GDP? Other literature has previously tried to provide an explanation. Some have argued that vested interests are actively working against the adoption of alternative indicators. There is also evidence to support this view. The environmental accounts of the United States were discontinued in the 1990s by the US Congress.

A decade later a green accounting initiative in China was put on hold when the results were published and led to controversy.

The second perspective is that Beyond-GDP should do a better job. Bleys and Whitby (2015) probably provide the most comprehensive assessment in this direction. It names timeliness, robustness and communication as well as a standardised methodology as important requirements for success.[51] Hayden and Wilson (2016) investigate the "disappointing" uptake of Beyond-GDP indicators in Canada. They conclude euphemistically that the idea that simply producing an indicator will suddenly change society "is certainly not borne out by the Canadian experience to date".

In a novel paper, Costanza et al. (2017) liken society's focus on economic growth to a real addiction. They explore how methods that are used for addicts might be adopted at the societal level. For example, Motivational Interviewing (MI) is based on engaging addicts in a positive discussion of their goals, motives and futures. Costanza and colleagues explore what the MI therapy might look like if applied to society's addiction to GDP.

This book argues that the crux of the matter is that the macro-economic community is more powerful than the well-being and sustainability community. Our historical overview has shown that it was not just the indicator GDP which transformed society; something far more fundamental happened. A scientific community was formed with a clear goal, structure and common language which institutionalised in the 1950s and 1960s. The Beyond-GDP cottage industry cannot compete with this GDP multinational. The well-being and sustainability community is a loosely connected group of initiatives. Some are aimed at well-being, some at environmental issues, some at broader measures of sustainable development. In terms of the structure there is a variety of scientific disciplines (e.g. happiness, behavioural, environmental and ecological economics), some accounting frameworks (e.g. SEEA) and a multitude of indicator systems (hundreds).

In terms of the common language the situation is dire. The various communities involved all speak different languages, dialects and accents.[52] This makes mutual communication difficult and the message to the general public ineffective. Finally, the issue of institutionalisation has only seen partial success. Many of the initiatives can claim some degree of institutional progress in convincing international institutes and national governments to adopt their methodologies. Yet these efforts are done in isolation and in some cases are contradictory. There is no coherent and authoritative initiative that provides an overall community for well-being and sustainability science.

However, there are hopeful signs. The SEEA is probably the most successful example in the Beyond-GDP scene. It has a clear goal, structure and common language (SEEA), and the harmonisation process took less than twenty years. Institutionalisation is happening fast.

The SDG process also proved that international institutes can be very effective in fostering a global agreement. However, despite these successes, overall progress is insufficient. The Beyond-GDP situation will not improve unless a new strategy is adopted. The strategy is quite simple but also daunting: to build a coherent institutionalised community that can compete with the macroeconomic community.

PART II The New Strategy: A Community for Well-being and Sustainability

5   Outline of the Strategy

Chapter 1 introduced the idea of the Schumpeterian Dream to illustrate the hope that Beyond-GDP might one day replace "one of the greatest innovations of the twentieth century", Gross Domestic Product. Based on the analysis of Chapter 2 and Chapter 4 it is possible to assess the advancement of the Schumpeterian Dream in Figure 5.1.

The GDP story is a true rags-to-riches success story but it was only in the period 1929–1944 that the measurement of GDP really took off. Economists started using national accounts to provide insights and create policies to alleviate the effects of the Great Depression and the Second World War. Yet the period after that (1944–1973) was the crucial "golden age" which laid the foundations of the GDP multinational. Economists became more prevalent in academia, the private sector and an essential part of the government. The emergence of "big government" and international institutes enhanced the demand for economists.

Soon after the war, GDP growth became the primary goal of society – a perfect symbol of the importance of economics in the post-war world. Governments in the 1950s and 1960s started to set growth targets. Cold War rivalry helped to instil a further urgency to this development. In the West, economic growth was seen not just as a luxury but rather as a means of surviving ("expand or die"). In fact, economic thinking started to be applied to other "non-economic" domains. For example, at the OECD, education and science were reframed in the 1960s as engines of growth rather than independent policy areas.[1] This dominance of economics over other sciences is sometimes referred to as "economic imperialism".[2] Thurow (1977)

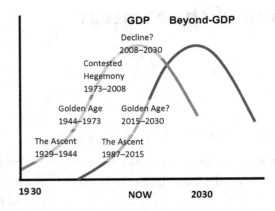

FIGURE 5.1 The innovation cycle of GDP and Beyond-GDP

observed: "If the early 1960s were the golden age of economics when economists were perceived as knowing all of the 'right' answers, the late 1970s are the age of economic imperialism. The influence of economists has never been greater."

The GDP multinational has kept growing although criticism has also increased. This is why the period 1973–2008 is referred to as "contested hegemony". The economic crisis of the 1970s as well as social and environmental problems led to a variety of alternative indicators and scientific fields such as environmental economics. This type of criticism might eventually weaken GDP. In fact, in Chapter 2 the question was asked whether the period after the 2008 financial crisis will lead to the demise of the GDP multinational. Big data, movement away from statistics or lack of interest in low-growth GDP development might all contribute.

Will Beyond-GDP lead to the creative destruction of GDP? It is difficult to put Beyond-GDP in the same Schumpeterian framework; nevertheless the period 1987–2015 has been dubbed "The Ascent" in Figure 5.1. Some might argue that this should start around 1972 (the first green accounting index) or even back in 1946 (the first SWB survey). But the 1970s were a bit of false start for Beyond-GDP. Although green accounting, the social indicators movement and

SWB gained in momentum, they remained mostly academic or later faltered. As such, the period 1946–1987 in Beyond-GDP is comparable to the period 1665–1929 for national income.

The introduction of the term "sustainable development" by the Brundtland Report, and its further institutionalisation through the Rio conferences (1992, 2002, 2012) were major factors in promoting Beyond-GDP. The term "sustainable development" reached its institutional pinnacle in 2015 because of the adoption of the SDGs. Yet the SDGs are only one of hundreds of initiatives that have emerged with many different methodological approaches. Overall, institutionalisation and harmonisation are fragmented.

What is next for Beyond-GDP? Will the period 2015–2030 be a "Golden Age" in the Beyond-GDP innovation cycle? Will it grow from a Beyond-GDP cottage industry to a multinational, which replaces GDP? Is there something that can be done to achieve this? This is the topic of Part II of this book.

ALTERNATIVE STRATEGIES

The crux of the golden age of GDP is that an effective macroeconomic community was formed. The crux of the failure of Beyond-GDP is that it is not a coherent community. The strategy proposed in this book is therefore straightforward: create a community for Beyond-GDP which is equally or even more powerful than for macroeconomics.

What should be the basis of the community? This section will explore some strategies which might be adopted. One approach would be to simply choose one of the existing dominant Beyond-GDP initiatives and institutionalise it. A number of options which would be able to garner significant support will be discussed below.

Green Accounting

There are quite a few prominent environmental economists that favour a green accounting aggregate. But which green accounting aggregate would one choose? There are three alternatives that might be considered.[3]

The first option is the Genuine Progress Indicator which is based on the MEW and ISEW and which has a lot of support in the environmental-economic community. These indicators are based on economic welfare theory, which is used to quantify the negative and positive externalities. The GPI has recently enjoyed some institutional success when several US states adopted it.[4]

A second option is green accounting indicators that are based on the capital approach. For example, the World Bank uses wealth accounting to count the total monetary value of produced, natural and human capital. It also calculates the "adjusted net savings", which indicates the increase in capital (savings) between two periods. The World Bank, in its latest Changing Wealth of Nations report, calculated data for 141 countries. The United Nations University has collected similar data on the Inclusive Wealth Index for 120 countries.[5]

The third option is a green accounting aggregate from the SEEA. The SEEA Central Framework has proposed depletion-adjusted aggregates. A major selling point is that the SEEA has been adopted as a statistical standard by the major international institutes and has been adopted in dozens of countries.

However, keep in mind that green accounting has existed for nearly fifty years. It may be popular with academics but the end results are a little disheartening: the GPI (twenty-five years old) is used by two US states, wealth accounting (also twenty-five years old) is used on a fairly regular basis by the World Bank but has no official status. The SEEA is far more institutionalised but it is mostly the physical accounts – not the green accounting aggregates – which are produced by statistical offices.

These are definitely some hopeful signs but hardly resounding successes. The UN process to measure sustainable development has hardly been influenced by green accounting. The CSD of the 1990s and the SDGs of 2015 were both indicator sets without a conceptual basis – the polar opposite of a green accounting approach. Given the narrative of "economic imperialism" this is definitely a field which economists have failed to "colonise".

Why would this change in the future? Some might say that the vested interests might be working against green accounting and this power dynamic needs a resolution. An alternative explanation is that economists have failed to convince society that creating monetary indexes on the basis of welfare theory or the capital approach is the solution.

Stiglitz Report/CES Recommendations

The Stiglitz Report is broader than green accounting, in terms of its conceptual foundation. Although it includes welfare theory and the capital approach, it also includes insights from a broader range of economic thinking, such as Sen's capability approach, happiness economics and behavioural economics. The Stiglitz Report is also different in a second way: it argues for a set of indicators rather than just one index.[6] It recommends one set of indicators for current well-being and one set of indicators for future well-being (sustainability).

The Stiglitz Report has enjoyed a certain amount of institutionalisation. It was the basis for the CES recommendations (UNECE/OECD/Eurostat) and an EU sponsorship group was set up to implement many of the recommendations. The Better Life Index (which measures current well-being) of the OECD is also based on the conceptual foundation provided in the Stiglitz Report.

However, the Stiglitz Report has been around for over a decade without it having a truly transformative effect. This is perhaps because it did not provide precise guidance on which indicators to use. The CES recommendations did provide indicators based on the Stiglitz Report but this has also failed to be adopted in many countries.[7]

Sustainable Development Goals (SDG)

The SDGs have proven to be a "game changer" in the field of Beyond-GDP. Within the space of a couple of years, this process has led to a globally agreed list of 17 goals and 169 targets. It has the backing of the UN, which has thereby propelled the term sustainable development to the next institutional level. A great advantage of the SDGs is that they have a global reach.

The SDG process builds on the institutionalisation of the term sustainable development, which has gone from strength to strength. This development has been stimulated by the three UN-led Rio conferences in 1992, 2002 and 2012. There is already a powerful and growing community around the SDGs. The fact that the targets are set for the year 2030 means that this momentum is likely to continue and even expand.

The SDGs are based on a political process of the governments of the world. Such a political process usually stirs up enthusiasm and support because stakeholders are given a role. Note however that the political process does not automatically translate into a measurable target.[8] Politicians negotiate about words, but do not necessarily take on board the *measurability* of what they are saying. Even when the SDGs are measurable, the appropriate data may not exist. The UN Statistical Division has had a hard time suggesting indicators and collecting data to measure the SDG targets.[9] This is not just the case for the developing countries but also for developed countries.[10]

SHOULD POLITICIANS BE IN THE LEAD?

Of the three options discussed in the previous section, two are based on economic theory (green accounting, Stiglitz Report) and one is based on a political process (Sustainable Development Goals). This, and the next section, therefore asks the crucial questions: Should politicians/economists be in the lead?

The SDGs is the most successful political process in the Beyond-GDP realm. This does not mean that scientific input was not sought. Just like many government processes, scientists have been consulted at various steps to identify the most urgent goals and targets for sustainable development. However, the definitive list of SDGs was decided through negotiations between member states of the UN. This process has already had a significant effect on the Beyond-GDP discussion and countries are already abandoning their

Sustainable Development Indicator systems and replacing them by SDG monitoring systems.

The outcomes of a political process are however lacking in certain respects. Political compromises might mean that some topics (governance, equality) might not make it onto the list although they are relevant from a scientific perspective. More fundamentally, the SDGs do not define what the ultimate goal of sustainable development is. There is no model that relates the 169 indicators to an end goal. This also means that it is unclear how the goals are linked to each other. There is no underlying framework that links education to health to environment to gender issues to employment. Yet in real life these are interconnected phenomena.

If the SDGs were defined in the context of a coherent scientific measurement system, the connections become clearer and a more effective policy mix can be established. The OECD refers to this type of integrated perspective as policy coherence in sustainable development.[11]

SHOULD ECONOMISTS BE IN THE LEAD?

Should the new community be based on economic concepts and ideas (such as green accounting or the Stiglitz Report)? Economists created the successful community based on macroeconomics/SNA/GDP. Should economists also be in the lead for Beyond-macroeconomics/Beyond-SNA/Beyond-GDP?

To many people the answer is "yes". When President Sarkozy of France was forming the Stiglitz Commission in 2008 he filled the group with mostly economists.[12] It is true that the members were broadminded economists with expertise and interests outside of mainstream approaches. They included experts in behavioural economics, the capability approach and inequality, but the vast majority were none the less economists. Other social sciences fields (sociologists, political scientists, psychologists[13]) were underrepresented in the commission. There were no natural scientists, climatologists or ecologists, although there was a prominent environmental economist.

Was this choice by Sarkozy a reflection of the scientific knowledge that was needed to answer the question? Or is it a reflection of "economic imperialism" where economists are given the lead over "non-economic" policy domains?[14]

The primacy of economics is also evident in statistics. The previous section has already discussed the concept of "satellite accounts".[15] Phenomena outside of the "core" economic accounts can be recorded in satellite accounts such as the System of Environmental and Economic Accounts (SEEA).[16] This means that a lot of economic terminology has been transferred to the statistics for "non-economic" phenomena. For example, the term "capital" is used for various social domains (social capital, human capital) or the environment (natural capital).

Terminology and language have profound impacts on discussions. They betray a way of thinking and as a result can alienate non-economists. The terms human, social and natural capital imply that these assets are production factors for the economy. It imposes an anthropocentric view of the world in which the only value is the "services" which these factors provide. Nature is important only if it provides "ecosystem services" to humans. The term "externality", which refers to the side effects of economic growth, clearly demarcates that there are things which happen inside the economic system (the core) and things which happen outside (satellites).

This way of thinking implies that the economy is the centre of attention and other aspects are peripheral. The terminology also links to certain quantification methods and policies. For example, capital needs to be valued using asset valuation techniques. Externalities are valued using welfare theory. It also leads to certain policy options dominating. For example, the standard economic policy to resolve externalities is to "internalise" them by creating a market and an appropriate price.[17]

However, mainstream economic methods, such as welfare theory, can only provide a partial view of well-being or sustainability. There are also areas where welfare theory falls short, especially in the social dimensions of life. What is the monetary value of family and friends? How do you put a monetary value on inequality? Even when methods are available, economic theory can lead to widely divergent results. For example, the social cost of carbon (SCC) can range from a couple of dollars to hundreds of dollars per ton of carbon.[18]

Capital theory also has limitations. While the measurement of ecosystem services (a flow) is prevalent, the valuation of a "stock of ecosystems" is fraught with methodological difficulties. Human capital valuation only includes the income-generating capacity of persons while the monetisation of social capital is rarely attempted.

But what about economic methods beyond welfare theory and the capital approach? Fields such as happiness economics and behavioural economics definitely further the understanding of subjective well-being and the underlying psychological foundations. Especially in the field of current well-being, these methods of "heterodox economics" are valuable (although less so for analysis of long-term environmental sustainability). These economic schools are inspired mostly by psychology and sociology so in essence these are already multidisciplinary sciences.

Mainstream (or heterodox economics) methods in economics do not have all the answers that are needed to tackle the topics of well-being and sustainability. As Kenneth Boulding put it: "Economic problems have no sharp edges. They shade off imperceptibly into politics, sociology, and ethics. Indeed, it is hardly an exaggeration to say that the ultimate answer to every economic problem lies in some other field."[19]

Economic methods are not applicable to all situations. What is needed is a science which is truly multidisciplinary in nature. Economics, both mainstream and heterodox, should be included in the science but economists should not be in the lead. Terminology aligned to welfare theory and the capital approach should be replaced by more neutral terms. The aim is to create a community for well-being and sustainability *science* rather than well-being and sustainability *economics*.

CREATING A COMMUNITY FOR WELL-BEING AND SUSTAINABILITY SCIENCE (WSS)

The previous chapters have argued that neither politicians nor economists should be in the lead of the new community. The new strategy is centred around the creation of a multidisciplinary community for well-being and sustainability science. The strategy should include insights from green accounting, the Stiglitz framework and the SDGs as well as the decades of research on Beyond-GDP science and indicators. It is hardly necessary to start from scratch!

When it comes to the architecture of the community it seems that the GDP multinational provides a pretty good template: it has a clear goal, a coherent structure, a common language and is heavily institutionalised. These four aspects of the community will be discussed below.

Goal: Well-being and Sustainability

In the case of macroeconomics there is a clear goal, which is to understand the sources of economic growth and to devise policies that stimulate its development. It also studies how to prevent recessions and how to recover from them when they occur.

So what should be the aim of the new community? Out of all the terms in the Beyond-GDP field the term "sustainable development" is a prime candidate. Many terms have come and gone, but the ever-increasing institutionalisation of this term means that it has been around for over thirty years. Due to the SDG process it is bound to last until at least 2030.

The Brundtland definition is: "Sustainable development is the kind of development that meets the needs of the present without compromising the ability of future generations to meet their own needs." This has intuitive appeal. It resonates well with underlying ethical philosophies and feelings of intergenerational fairness. However, it is also rather open to interpretation. Already in 1991, Lélé (1991) argued that "if SD is to have a fundamental impact, politically expedient fuzziness will have to be given up in favour of intellectual clarity and rigor". In fact the interpretation of the term sustainable development has varied over time.[20] One of the perpetual criticisms has been whether sustainable development was actually an oxymoron because perpetual economic growth is not possible on a finite Earth. This is especially true when sustainability is reduced to only environmental matters and development is equated to GDP growth.

The "intellectual clarity" of the term sustainable development has not truly been realised. It is common to split sustainable development into three pillars: social, economic and environmental, which should be "balanced".[21] But the adoption of the SDGs confirms that a conceptual basis to the term has not been found, despite thirty years of history. It seems fair to say that sustainable development is a successful term which has struck a chord with society. At the same time the term has failed to converge towards a clear conceptual definition.

The conceptual approach which comes closest is the capital approach because it stresses the importance of intertemporal trade-offs. It allows one to distinguish current and future well-being. The Stiglitz Report (p. 17) clearly articulates this using the following metaphor:

> The assessment of sustainability is complementary to the question
> of current well-being or economic performance, and must be
> examined separately. This may sound trivial and yet it deserves
> emphasis, because some existing approaches fail to adopt this
> principle, leading to potentially confusing messages. For instance,
> confusion may arise when one tries to combine current well-being
> and sustainability into a single indicator. To take an analogy, when
> driving a car, a meter that added up in one single number the
> current speed of the vehicle and the remaining level of gasoline
> would not be of any help to the driver. Both pieces of information
> are critical and need to be displayed in distinct, clearly visible areas
> of the dashboard.

To summarise, it is the current human well-being (well-being) and the future (sustainability) which are at stake. The time dimension, "here and now" vs. "later",[22] helps to structure the debate. Rather than defining the goal of the science as the rather ambiguous "sustainable development", it is better to break down this term into two component parts: "well-being" and "sustainability".

The communal goal of WSS is therefore to understand the determinants of well-being and sustainability and devise policies to enhance these phenomena. Implicit is also the fundamental trade-off between the present and future.

Coherent Structure: Science–Accounts–Indicators

In the case of the GDP multinational there is clear policy science (macroeconomics), an accounting framework (SNA) and a key indicator (GDP), which provide a coherent framework for scientific inquiry and empirical application. Well-being and sustainability science should also adopt such a coherent structure.

An important feature of the structure is that it is multidisciplinary. It should include insights from psychology, demography, sociology and other sciences that shed light on societal developments. Furthermore, natural scientists such as hydrologists, climatologists, geologists, ecologists and biologists are needed to understand the functioning of our planet and its environmental limits. Nevertheless, economics is an important part of the WSS. Traditional economics methods such as welfare economics provide valuable insights about efficient policies due to market-based theories. Heterodox economic methods will also be part of the new science because they are able to provide additional insights beyond welfare economics.

Common Language: System of Global and National Accounts (SGNA)

The foundation for a successful community is that the members speak the same language. Not only does it lead to internal coordination of thought but it also helps to send a coherent message to society. Kate Raworth, in her best-selling book *Doughnut Economics*, makes a similar point when she argues that economists have been so successful because they have managed to create iconic pictures which have affected and influenced society.[23] She therefore praises the power of communication that economists have created and suggests that Beyond-GDP requires new pictures and narratives. In this book, a similar argument is made about the importance of communication but the importance of language is stressed.

The WSS community also needs an accounting framework to act as a common language. In this book, it will be referred to as the System of Global and National Accounts. This accounting framework will formalise the vocabulary and "grammatical conventions" of the community. The decades of work on Beyond-GDP have produced more than enough scientific and practical guidance for such an endeavour. However, it is important to keep the language as neutral as possible to reflect the multidisciplinary nature of the science. Given the importance of this common language, it is expanded upon later in this chapter.

Institutionalisation

The final factor for a successful community is institutionalisation. In the case of macroeconomics, the community has been entrenched in society and government, both formally and informally. In the case of well-being and sustainability science, it will also be necessary to do so by 2030. This is a realistic time frame given previous harmonisation efforts. This deadline also coincides with future revisions of the SNA and the SDGs which provide opportunities to align with these initiatives.

It is important to note that institutionalising such processes is part and parcel of what governments and international institutes do. What has been achieved in the field of macroeconomics by the SNA and GDP has been done in other fields too.

The Intergovernmental Panel on Climate Change (IPCC) is an example where climate scientists worked together to harmonise their accounting framework for the carbon cycle, created headline indicators (temperature change and CO_2 concentration) and created policy options. Climate scientists have created a common language and the IPCC has achieved a great deal of institutionalisation. As a result, climate scientists are providing a coherent narrative to society.

Similarly, Chapter 4 has described the success of the SEEA, which is an accounting structure with headline indicators (both physical and monetary) and which is used by many environmental economics and ecological economics researchers. This successful community is undergoing rapid institutionalisation and will most likely become more important in the future.

START WITH A COMMON LANGUAGE: SYSTEM OF GLOBAL AND NATIONAL ACCOUNTS (SGNA)

The many scientific disciplines that are involved in well-being and sustainability science will have to agree on an accounting framework which will be the common language. This is an important but difficult task, which is why Part II of this book will spend most time on this topic.

The first question that is important is to provide clear demarcations of the systems which are being described. Figure 5.2 provides an overview of the five sub-accounts underlying the System of Global and National Accounts.

System Accounts

The first three accounts deal with the three core systems: the environment, society and the economy. This is not a novel concept; it is a demarcation that has been adopted in many publications about sustainable development. Note that the environment is named first and the economy last. This is a subtle but symbolically important aspect of the System of Global and National Accounts. In the age of "economic imperialism" the economy is the central framework and impacts on society and the environment are "externalities". In this framework, nothing is external and the economy is not the core system.

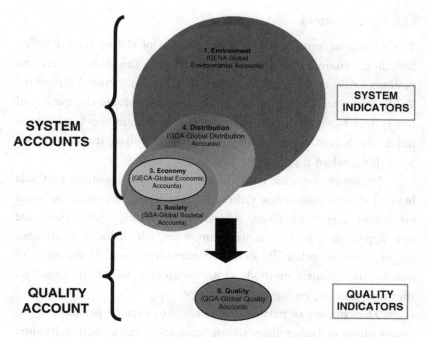

FIGURE 5.2 The System of Global and National Accounts (SGNA)

The fourth account (Global Distributional Accounts) describes the distributional aspects of society and the economy. It accounts for inequality in society in the broadest sense of the word. It is not just about the distribution of income and wealth between households but also about the inequality of other factors such as education, health and social networks. It also looks at the distribution between countries, and difference between small and medium sized enterprises (SMEs) versus multinationals or the disparities between various levels of government (city-level, regional and national).

Together these four accounts are called system accounts. The SGNA is "global" in the sense that its measurement scope is aimed at the worldwide environment, society and economy. The SGNA is also global in the sense that the implementation should be done by all countries and international organisations rather than just by a small group of developed countries.

Quality Accounts

The system accounts provide a description of the systems (stocks) and their dynamics (flows) but do not answer the question: are the systems working well? Is it going in the "right" or "wrong" direction? To do this assessment you need a method to evaluate the quality of the system's dynamics. For example, welfare economics is a basis to judge which developments are good or bad. If welfare increases it is a good thing; when it goes down it is bad.

However, there are many kinds of quality assessment methods beyond welfare economics. Other anthropocentric methods are based on survey responses about subjective well-being. Also, there are new approaches, such as neuro-economics, which looks at changes in the brain or other physiological measurements. There are also non-anthropocentric methods to assess quality, which are based on thermodynamics, biology or technology.

The concept of networks also leads to various perspectives to assess quality. Rather than adding up quality from each individual actor, it assesses the functioning of the total network. For example, how *resilient* is society to sudden changes? These are concepts that are used often in disciplines such as ecology or computer science to assess the quality of complex systems.

In terms of the units of measurement there is a vast range of possibilities. They will depend on the quality assessment method adopted. Mainstream economic approaches generally have monetary units but if a wide range of methods are used, other units are possible.

This issue of quality assessment is the area which scientific disciplines will disagree about most vigorously. This is one of the prime advantages of the modular nature of the SGNA framework (which is inspired by the SEEA framework). The system accounts of the SGNA are fairly uncontroversial because they provide a neutral accounting framework which simply describes the functioning of the various systems. On the other hand, opinions and approaches about the quality assessment will be a source of contention. By separating the two it is possible to create an area in which various disciplines can converge and cooperate while also having a domain in which discip-lines can disagree.[24] We will expand on this "structured multidisci-plinarity" in Chapter 11.

The overall effect of the modular SGNA will be to broaden the range of quality assessment methods. This will also help to wean society away from the dominant economic methods such as welfare economics and the capital approach. This does not mean that these approaches should be rejected. These economic perspectives defin-itely have value, but they are currently too dominant in society's perception of when things are getting better or worse. A second advan-tage is that the quality accounts might lead to multidisciplinary cooperation which provides even more valuable perspectives beyond what a single scientific discipline can provide.

System and Quality Indicators

The system and quality accounts provide various indicators. The system indicators are summary measures which are related to the functioning of the respective system. They might include the CO_2 concentration in the air, land areas of ecosystems, pollution, popula-tion levels, education levels, social networks and institutions, GDP, household income, etc.

On the other hand, the quality accounts provide key indicators on whether the systems are getting better or worse. It is these quality indicators which ultimately should replace GDP. They will be dis-cussed further at the end of Chapter 10.

BUILDING BLOCKS OF THE SGNA: STOCKS/FLOWS, NETWORKS AND LIMITS

How can the system accounts be set up in such a way that a wide variety of scientific disciplines relate to it? How do you create a language that economists, climatologists, psychologists, demographers, etc. under-stand? What are the commonalities between these disciplines?

There are scholars of linguistics who study these commonalities between real languages. For example, all languages, whether they are spoken in downtown Mexico City or on a Pacific Island, have nouns and verbs. It is like a universal grammar which transcends language barriers. Something similar needs to happen for well-being and sustainability science. The universal grammar underlying the many scientific disciplines needs to be found. What are the underlying concepts that connect these scientific fields?

In this book three core concepts are proposed as building blocks for the SGNA: stock/flows, networks and limits. Whether you are looking at nature, society or the economy, these three concepts play some role in the theoretical apparatus. Although the various scientific disciplines might have different terminology, these are foundational concepts.

Are these the only concepts which underlie the various disciplines? Probably not. Yet in the description of the subsequent chapters, they seem to be able to cope with a wide variety of literature and topics. Perhaps in future other commonalities will be uncovered but for the moment they provide a solid basis for the SGNA.

Stocks/Flows

The notion of accounting for stock and flows is universal to many scientific fields. A stock is a level of some variable at a discrete point in time. Changes in these stocks are referred to as flows. Stock accounts for the economy, demography and environment might be measured in different units (money, number of people and mass/ number of a given species respectively) but they all adhere to the same stock-flow accounting principles.

In his Nobel Prize lecture, Richard Stone said: "By organising our data in the form of accounts we can obtain a coherent picture of the stocks and flows, incomings and outgoings of whatever variables we are interested in, whether these be goods and services, human beings or natural resources, and thence proceed to analyse the system of which they form part."[25]

Some stock/flow accounts are ruled by the laws of physics and are therefore particularly robust. Examples include accounts in mass/

energy/time units. But there are many other accounting units that are equally robust. The number of species, the size of the human population, the number of cars are all accounted in discrete numbers. Although measuring these variables might present practical problems, from a theoretical point of view the stock-flow accounts are straightforward.

Stock/flow accounting has been the basis of financial accounting since double-entry bookkeeping was formalised by Luca Pacioli for the merchants of Venice.[26] Some parts work just like a physical stock-flow account. For example, a product sold by one party is bought by another. This means that the balance of goods and services (that are bought/sold) automatically balance because they are recorded on the selling and receiving end. However, in other cases various "balancing items" are used to accommodate losses and gains in value.

Networks

The environment, society and the economy are made up of many actors that are linked and interdependent. Therefore, the concept of networks plays a role in each domain and should be part of a common language.

All living beings, whether human or not, are connected through many types of relationships. For example, networks exist *within* species because they mate and nurture their young but also *between* species because they are prey or hunter or have some other relationship. The intra- and interspecies networks together form the ecosystems around us. The feeding relationships are captured by food webs and food chains.

In society, networks between people have similar properties to the intra-species networks discussed above. People do not operate as individuals; they form all types of connections to others. They find spouses, operate within families, live in neighbourhoods, work with colleagues and "friend" people on Facebook. They also form larger groups of villages, cities and countries which have governments and other organisations that govern the communities. The norms, rules and laws that are adopted are referred to as the "institutions" of society.[27]

An economy can also be seen as the activities between actors within a network. There are relationships between companies, banks, households and governments in terms of products, income and financial flows.[28]

Limits

All systems, whether they are environmental, societal or economic, have limits. The stocks, flows and networks underlying the environmental–societal–economic domains are restricted by thermodynamic, physical, practical, temporal, spatial, biological or other boundaries. The systems change over time but will sometimes be confronted by these limits.

Over the years, some economists have drawn attention to the limits of the economy. Amongst others, the work of Malthus, Georgescu-Roegen and the *Limits to Growth* publication were influential in pointing out that growth can lead to overshooting of environmental limits. More recently, the idea of planetary boundaries has become popular.

Limits are phenomena that can be generalised. For example, an important limit is time. A day has twenty-four hours. However hard a person tries, they cannot make a good day last one second longer or a bad day an hour shorter. From a human perspective all people have 8,760 hours to spend per year. This is both the upper and lower limit. The stock of time decreases hour after hour, minute after minute. There is no way to tweak the system.

In some cases, the limits are not strict boundaries. A biological example is the number of pregnancies per woman or the minimum number of hours of sleep. Another example is the number of durable goods a person owns, which is often limited because of practical restrictions. A household might, for example, own a washing machine but it is rare that a household would own two or three washing machines. It is not physically impossible to own two washing machines, and it happens, but in practical terms one is the limit. Similarly, the maximum number of cars for most households is one per adult in the family. There are of course households with more cars but these are exceptions to the general rule.

In some cases, the limits indicate a hard boundary, especially when considering thermodynamic and time limits. In other cases the limit indicates a point whereby the system shifts from one condition to another. In ecological research this is known as a critical limit beyond which an ecosystem shifts from one state to another.[29]

Data about limits is not collected systematically. Yet it might have important implications when analysing system dynamics. If this type of data becomes more readily available, the opportunity to include these limits in models will also increase.

READING GUIDE TO PART B

This chapter has outlined the strategy of creating a community for well-being and sustainability science. It has argued that the creation of a common language is the most crucial aspect of the strategy. That is why the largest part of the book will deal with the accounting framework: the SGNA.

The five accounts of the SGNA are discussed in next chapters: Global Environmental Accounts (Chapter 6), Global Societal Accounts (Chapter 7), Global Economic Accounts (Chapter 8). Chapter 9 provides insights into the distributional aspects of society (Global Distribution Accounts). All chapters on system accounts will discuss stock/flows, networks and limits but they will not discuss any quality assessment techniques. They will simply focus on the "uncontroversial" description of the three systems and distribution.

Quality assessment is left to Chapter 10, which looks at the many ways in which one may assess whether systems are doing well or not. This chapter also discusses the system and quality indicators of the SGNA which will eventually replace GDP.

After having covered the SGNA, Chapter 11 looks specifically at the practical aspects of the strategy. It addresses the feasibility and the practical steps necessary to implement the strategy.

6 Global Environmental Accounts (GENA)

There is perhaps no greater complexity than the environmental system of the planet. The interplay of geology, climate, materials, nutrients and water with living creatures have made for a planet that is habitable for many species. It is not quite known how many species exist on Earth but one estimate is around 8.7 million, while others believe this is a lower bound.[1] Societies have been trying to understand the processes that govern the functioning of the earth for many millennia, sometimes through religious philosophies or sometimes through scientific inquiry.

Homo sapiens is just one species in the larger complex system. But humans are not insignificant. Quite the contrary, the human population has had profound impacts on natural resources, climate and biodiversity. It is not without reason that Paul Crutzen coined the phrase *Anthropocene* to reflect the significance of humans in this era.[2] Yet humans are dependent on the natural system for their existence. Nature provides the air we breathe, the food we eat and the climate we live in. It also provides the materials and energy that are needed in factories and homes. Humans cannot live without nature, but nature would still exist, albeit in an altered state, if there were only 8,699,999 species left.

The aim of the Global Environmental Accounts (GENA) is to provide a framework for all the abiotic and biotic parts of the planet and the interrelationship with human society. The abiotic part, the non-living components of Earth, include the geosphere, atmosphere and hydrosphere. The biotic part, all living beings on the planet, live in one or more of these "spheres".

The geosphere includes all the stocks of minerals and the fossil fuels in the Earth's mantle. It includes the land and soil which are used for agricultural activities, human settlement and nature. The atmosphere and the hydrosphere are amongst the most active parts of the natural system because there is a constant flow of gases and water. The various natural cycles, such as the nitrogen and carbon cycles, take place in all three "spheres".

The vast majority of environmental problems that exist today can be defined from the perspective of mass and/or energy. Acid rain, smog, climate change, resource depletion, plastic soup, etc. are all related to mass and energy flows. In many cases energy and mass are both part of the story. For example, climate change is caused primarily by humans extracting fossil fuels (a flow in mass terms) from a fossil-fuel reserve (a stock which can be accounted for in both mass and energy terms). The fossil fuels are used as an energy source (energy flow). The mass of carbon that is emitted (a flow) in these processes leads to higher CO_2 concentration (a stock of CO_2 gas) in the atmosphere and oceans. The CO_2 in the atmosphere leads to higher temperatures (energy), which in turn melts the polar ice and increases the mass of water in the oceans, leading to higher sea levels. Fundamentally, these processes can be understood by looking at the stocks and flows of mass and energy in the various spheres.

Other natural cycles, such as the hydrological cycle or nitrogen cycle, can also be accounted for in mass units. Mass and energy are essential accounting units because under the first law of thermodynamics they are never lost (at least under most conditions on Earth). If all the inputs of mass into a system are added up, it must exactly equal the mass of the outputs. The same holds for energy. From an accounting perspective, this is a prerequisite for an appropriate unit: input must equal outputs.

The living part of Earth, the biotic system, adds even more complexity. It includes plants and animals that exhibit autonomous behaviour which requires more than thermodynamic laws to explain.

The existence of varying degrees of intelligence makes each of these species a complex study object in its own right. What is more, the living beings also interact both within their species and between species, in ecosystems.

From an accounting perspective, there are a couple of units that are appropriate. For example, the number of species per region might be counted. However, the knowledge of the number of species is limited. When they estimated that Earth had 8.7 million species, Mora et al. (2011) noted that a sizeable part of them have not been scientifically classified: "In spite of 250 years of taxonomic classification and over 1.2 million species already catalogued in a central database, our results suggest that some 86% of existing species on Earth and 91% of species in the ocean still await description." So in theory one could make a stock/flow account for the number of species and the number of individuals in each species. But from a measurement perspective it is practically impossible.[3]

The stocks/flows perspective is just one way of looking at species. In a network point of view the interrelationships between species in ecosystems are stressed. Ecosystems are complex networks of species that live in, sometimes, delicate ecological balance. Some of the relationships are predatory while in other cases they are symbiotic. If the population of a certain species grows too fast, it can pass a critical limit when the ecosystems shift to another state.

To complicate matters even further, the biotic and abiotic systems are interconnected. Species, humans in particular, play particular roles in the various natural cycles. The interrelationships between and within the biotic and abiotic system are subject to complex dynamics.

MINOR ADJUSTMENTS TO THE SEEA (WITH BIG IMPLICATIONS)

The modular nature of the System of Global and National Accounts, i.e. splitting the systems accounts from the quality account, is inspired by the SEEA. The SEEA has promoted this modular structure since the early 1990s and the SEEA Central Framework (SEEA)

became an international statistical standard in 2012. The basis of the
SEEA accounts are descriptions of the stocks and flows of mass and
energy. These system accounts also yield many country-level environmental indicators such as greenhouse gases emitted, material
extraction or water use.

However, when creating indicators to assess whether things are
going well or not, a quality assessment approach is needed. The SEEA
uses capital theory to produce "depletion-adjusted aggregates". In the
Experimental Ecosystem Accounts of the SEEA (SEEA-EEA), a separate handbook, approaches from welfare economics are used to estimate the value of "ecosystem services". The modular structure of the
SEEA is therefore a perfect model for the SGNA. Its foundation is
physical flow accounting, but at the same time it allows quality
assessment methods to be linked to these accounts. Nevertheless,
the GENA is different to the SEEA. While these changes are relatively
minor in conceptual terms, they do have significant symbolic and
practical implications.

The first change to the SEEA structure is to expand the range
of quality assessment methods. The current SEEA is strongly linked
to traditional economic theories such as the capital approach and
welfare economics. In the multidisciplinary SGNA approach, these
methods are not rejected, but are seen as two options within a broad
range of quality assessment methods (see Chapter 10). The SEEA itself
is quite candid about the limits of welfare economics and the capital
approach. For example, the reduction in the quality of the environment, known as degradation, is not included. The SEEA simply says:
"the measurement of degradation in physical and monetary terms is
not pursued in the Central Framework".[4]

Similarly, in the SEEA-EEA, the estimation of ecosystem services (flows) is given extensive treatment using welfare theoretical
approaches. However, on the estimation of ecosystem assets (stocks)
the SEEA-EEA is circumspect: "5.121 The measurement of NPV
based estimates of ecosystem assets raises a number of challenges."
In UN-speak this means this is a big red flag. To calculate the ecosystem assets one would need to estimate future ecosystem services.

Underlying this calculation would be assumptions about the "asset life" (the expected period of time over which the regenerating eco-system services are to be delivered), understanding dependencies between ecosystem services and assets and selection of an appropriate discount rate. These are not minor issues and the SNA-EEA con-cludes: "5.122 Given all of these considerations, careful thought should be applied before applying standard NPV approaches to the valuation of ecosystem assets."

The fact that the SEEA Central Framework and SEEA-EEA use the capital approach and welfare economics has also affected the terminology. A case in point is the definition of the environmental assets (a synonym for "natural capital"): "Environmental *assets* are the naturally occurring living and non-living components of the Earth, together comprising the bio-physical environment *that may provide benefits to humanity*" (SEEA 2012, paragraph 2.17; italics added). The word "assets" is a clear reference to the capital approach while the concept of "benefits to humanity" is related to welfare theory.

Originally, the SEEA was conceived as a "satellite account" of the SNA and the definition of assets in the two systems are similar, although not identical. The original SNA-definition is: "An asset is a store of value representing a benefit or series of benefits accruing to the economic owner by holding or using the entity over a period of time. It is a means of carrying forward value from one accounting period to another."[5] The SNA includes produced capital (machines and buildings), non-produced capital (goodwill and marketing assets) and financial capital (savings, stocks and bonds, etc.) and some forms of natural capital (such as natural resources and land). By "owning" these "assets" an economic owner is able to obtain "benefits" over time. The SEEA has maintained the concept of "benefits" and has also adopted the term "assets". However, the SEEA has dropped the own-ership criterion because many parts of the environment are not held by an "economic owner".[6]

The primary problem is that the SEEA definition is still guided by these economic methodologies. It stresses that the natural system is an "asset" to be used for the benefit of humans. The value of "ecosystem services" is linked to the ability to provide these "bene-fits". By implication, nature or environmental stocks/flows which do not provide any "services" to humans have no value.

This type of terminology is not consistent with the SGNA–GENA philosophy. The language used should be as neutral as pos-sible. Some natural scientists find terms such as ecosystem services too economic. For example, the Intergovernmental Science-Policy Platform on Biodiversity and Ecosystem Services (IPBES) recently experienced a significant setback in its deliberations. Opponents of the term ecosystem services proposed to speak of Nature's Contribu-tion to People, because it was less economic and more reflective of how indigenous people see the role of nature.[7]

In the SGNA, the terminology should not be based on one of the quality assessment approaches, whether economic or otherwise. This is surprisingly easy. It can be achieved by dropping the last six words (*"that may provide benefits to humanity"*[8]) of the SEEA definition and changing "assets" to "stocks": "Natural stocks are the total of all naturally occurring living and non-living components of the Earth, together comprising the bio-physical environment."

The definition also leads to the second difference between the SEEA and the GENA. The SEEA only includes environmental assets *inside* economic boundaries (i.e. the area under the jurisdiction of nation states). Yet around a half of the world's surface is not legally owned by any country. From the SEEA perspective, all the coral, species and minerals that are beyond territorial boundaries are not considered "environmental assets". The atmosphere is also not included within the SEEA boundary. And fauna are included only if "effective ownerships rights are exercised". This implies that two of the most important environmental problems of this era, climate change and biodiversity loss, do not get a full global accounting treatment in the SEEA.[9]

The SEEA boundary might make sense to an economist because it is the same boundary as the national economy, but from a natural scientist perspective it is inconceivable to exclude large portions of the planet's surface and the entire atmosphere. The GENA is therefore an accounting framework with a global scope. It aims to capture the entire environmental system of Earth. Of course, the national boundaries are important demarcations within the GENA but only in the context of the worldwide description of the natural system.

While these changes are conceptually fairly minor, they have important symbolic significance. Firstly, the importance of economic methodologies is diminished (but not rejected outright). Secondly, environmental accounting shifts the focus from the economy–environmental interactions (SEEA) to a global description of environmental cycles and human impacts (GENA). The GENA does include the SEEA accounts, but starts from a global rather than a national perspective.

These changes have practical consequences. National statistical agencies can measure the things that are occurring within their borders but the statistical responsibility for the open seas and the atmosphere has not been defined. The GENA as it is currently envisaged may seem ambitious but the next section will make clear that GENA-style accounts already exist.

STOCKS/FLOWS: THE CASE OF THE CARBON CYCLE

The GENA can best be illustrated by discussing one of the most important environmental problems of today: climate change. The SEEA would tackle this problem by looking at the emissions per country. In the case of the GENA the global situation is the starting point.

Figure 6.1 shows a simplified version of the carbon cycle as reported by the IPCC in 2013. The report says of the figure:

> Numbers represent reservoir mass, also called "carbon stocks"
> in PgC (1 PgC = 1015 gC) and annual carbon exchange fluxes
> (in PgC yr–1). Black numbers and arrows indicate reservoir mass
> and exchange fluxes estimated for the time prior to the Industrial
> Era, about 1750. [Grey] arrows and numbers indicate annual
> "anthropogenic" fluxes averaged over the 2000–2009 time period.

The carbon cycle, thus illustrated, is a stock/flow system that is measured in mass units. The associated numbers underlying Figure 6.1

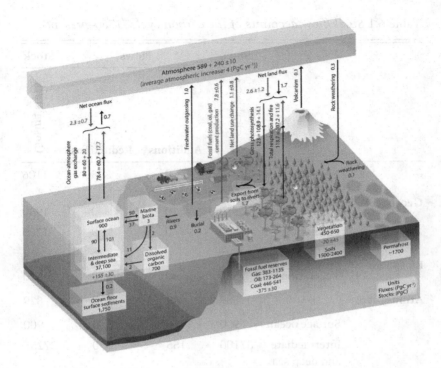

FIGURE 6.1 The IPCC simplified schematic of the global carbon cycle
Source: Ciais et al (2013). Reproduced with permission of the IPCC.

are shown in Table 6.1. The stocks are the "boxes" that are shown in the figure. For the sake of the exercise the average has been taken wherever a range is provided. For example, the figure shows the following range for gas (383–1,135), oil (173–264) and coal (446–541). By taking the average of all three, the final figure of 1,471 PgC is obtained. For the sake of the exercise, the uncertainty ranges are not taken into account. For example, the reduction in fossil fuels is estimated to be 365 ± 30. I have ignored the 30 and simply used the 365.

Given these assumptions, Table 6.1 shows that the total stock of carbon on Earth has not changed: 46,713 PgC.[10] However there has been a shift in where the carbon is located. There is a lower amount in the geosphere due to fossil fuel reductions (365 PgC) and lower levels in the biosphere due to land use changes (30 PgC). This additional carbon

Table 6.1 *Stock/flow accounts of the carbon cycle (1750–present)*

		Stock — Opening stock	Flows — Additions	Flows — Reductions	Stock — Closing stock
Geosphere	Fossil fuels reserves	1471	0	365	1106
	Soils	1950	0	0	1950
	Permafrost	1700	0	0	1700
Biosphere	Marine biota	3	0	0	3
	Vegetation	550	0	30	520
Atmosphere		589	240	0	829
Hydrosphere	Surface ocean	900	0	0	900
	Intermediate and deep sea	37100	155	0	37255
	Dissolved organic carbon	700	0	0	700
	Ocean floor	1750	0	0	1750
Total		46713	395	395	46713

Source: Authors own calculation based on Ciais et al. (2013)

has ended up in the atmosphere (240 PgC) and the seas (155 PgC).[11] Table 6.1 might not be as visually appealing as the graphical representation, but it is clear that the system is essentially a simple stock/flow accounting system in which for each component (Geosphere, Biosphere, Atmosphere and Hydrosphere) the following equation holds:

$$Opening\ stock + Additions - Reductions = Closing\ stock$$

Given the conservation of mass, the sum of additions and subtractions must equal each other. The carbon never "disappears".

Total additions (Geosphere, Biosphere, Atmosphere
and Hydrosphere)
= Total reductions (Geosphere, Biosphere, Atmosphere
and Hydrosphere)

To explain the dynamics of the various components of Table 6.1 requires different scientific expertise. If you would like to explain why 365 PgC of fossil fuels have been extracted then it is probably best to ask an environmental economist with knowledge of the long-term economic, demographic and technological developments which have influenced fossil fuel use. Yet you will need a climatologist to explain how CO_2 disperses into the atmosphere and the seas. At the same time an ecologist is needed to estimate the carbon content of vegetation and land use cover changes over time.

The beauty of this stock/flow system is that it simplifies the work of all these disciplines into an easy-to-interpret summary. The economist, climatologist and ecologist all understand the stock/flow account. In fact, anyone with simple arithmetic skills is capable of grasping these concepts. It is not burdened by unnecessary economic (or other) terminology such as "natural capital".

Table 6.1 provides an overview of the total flows since 1750 and the resulting changes in stocks. From this overview it is possible to "zoom in" on the human contribution to this problem. Table 6.1 shows that fossil fuel depletion contributed to a 365 PgC reduction in carbon over a 260-year period. The vast majority of these fossil fuels will have been combusted. Table 6.2 shows where these emissions of CO_2 have taken place since the start of the industrial revolution.[12] The sheer orders of magnitude are quite staggering. The quantity which was emitted in the first 150 years (12.2 PgC) is not very much higher than what is emitted annually nowadays (9.2 PgC).[13]

Table 6.2 clearly shows the shifts in countries that dominate the global economy. The United Kingdom is prominent in the first period

Table 6.2 *Historical emissions of carbon (1751–2013)*

	Emissions (PgC)				
	UK	USA	CHINA	Rest of world	TOTAL
1751–1900	4.6	2.9	0.0	4.8	12.2
1901–1950	6.1	22.1	0.5	22.2	51.0
1951–1970	3.2	17.0	2.3	28.9	51.3
1971–1990	3.2	25.2	8.7	64.5	101.7
1991–2010	2.9	29.6	24.8	80.5	137.9
Total 1751–2010	**20.0**	**96.9**	**36.3**	**200.8**	**354.0**
2011	0.1	1.4	2.7	4.8	9.0
2012	0.1	1.4	2.7	5.0	9.2
2013	0.1	1.4	2.8	4.9	9.2

Source: Carbon Dioxide Information Analysis Center (CDIAC)

because this is where the industrial revolution started. The United States dominates the rest of this historical overview, with more than a quarter of all historical emissions between 1751 and 2010. However, China has recently overtaken the United States (in 2006, according to Carbon Dioxide Information Analysis Center) as the largest annual emitter. Of course, in terms of per capita emissions, China is still behind the developed countries.

From Table 6.2 it is possible to zoom in even further. Take for example the 0.1 PgC emitted by the UK in 2013. Table 6.3 shows the breakdown of these emissions into nineteen economic sectors. These come from the air emission accounts of the SEEA and it is possible to compare these emissions to economic variables such as value added.

In just three simple accounting steps, the global carbon cycle has been linked to economic activities in one specific country for one specific year. Each of these steps is comprehensible to a wide variety of scientific disciplines. Nevertheless, the underlying system dynamics of each of the elements requires expert knowledge.

Does this type of accounting sound ambitious? Well actually this type of stock-flow accounting is already being done. The Global Carbon Project has already published carbon "budgets" data for the

Table 6.3 *Emissions of the UK in 2013 (10^6 tonnes of carbon)*

	CO_2 emissions
Electricity, gas, steam and air conditioning supply	40.8
Manufacturing	23.4
Transportation and storage	20.8
Mining and quarrying	4.6
Wholesale and retail trade; repair of motor vehicles and motorcycles	3.5
Agriculture, forestry and fishing	1.8
Public administration and defence; compulsory social security	1.5
Human health and social work activities	1.3
Education	1.0
Accommodation and food service activities	0.9
Administrative and support service activities	0.7
Water supply; sewerage, waste management and remediation activities	0.7
Professional, scientific and technical activities	0.6
Arts, entertainment and recreation	0.4
Information and communication	0.4
Other service activities	0.4
Real estate activities	0.2
Activities of households as employers	0.1
Financial and insurance activities	0.0
Total	**102.9**

Source: Eurostat Environmental Accounts (CO_2 emissions converted to carbon content by author)

period 1959–2016, which provides a consistent overview of annual emissions and global stocks. All of the above accounts could be produced for that period.[14] This type of accounting could act as a model for all natural cycles (nitrogen, water, oxygen, etc., or use of natural resources), although in each case pragmatic choices need to be made about which elements are relevant. The GENA should also include energy fluxes on the planet which could be linked to the energy accounts of the SEEA.

In fact the current SEEA includes an account which describes *all* the physical flows of the economy. It includes the physical interactions with the natural cycles (such as CO_2 emissions) and as such is a perfect accounting system to link to. The physical input–output table (PIOT) will be discussed in the Chapter 8 because in the SGNA this account is actually part of the economic accounts.[15]

INTERMEZZO: GLOBALISATION AND CARBON RESPONSIBILITY

In the previous discussion, carbon emissions were assigned to the economies that generated them. Most of these fossil fuels are used by companies in the production of goods and services, which is why this is often known as "production responsibility" or "production accounting". However, these goods may be exported to another country and used by a consumer there. The responsibility could therefore also be assigned to this final consumer ("consumption accounting"). This is sometimes also called the "carbon footprint" and it assumes that the consumer who actually buys the end product is responsible.[16]

Since the early 1990s, globalisation has increased rapidly. This has caused an increasing difference between production and consumption accounting totals, as shown in Table 6.4. At the beginning of the period (1991–1995), the production and consumption perspectives were just about equal for the United States, around 7,200 10^6 tonnes of carbon. By the end of the period the consumption-based emissions far exceeded production-based totals, because the United States started importing more and more goods and services from abroad, especially China. And this shift was happening throughout the developed world: manufactured goods were being

Table 6.4 *Production and consumption-based accounting* (*10^6 tonnes of Carbon*)

	Production-based accounts		Consumption-based accounts		Difference consumption–production accounts	
	US	CHINA	US	CHINA	US	CHINA
1991–1995	7,200	3,958	7,185	3,510	15	448
1996–2000	7,898	4,631	8,070	3,993	–171	637
2001–2005	8,208	6,275	8,782	5,580	–573	695
2006–2010	8,000	10,333	8,675	8,600	–675	1733
2011–2015	7,484	13,764	8,132	11,186	–648	2578

Source: Global Carbon Budget 2017

imported in ever greater quantities from "factory Asia".[17] This is why the trend is the opposite for China.

The overall trend is therefore that CO_2 emissions are shifting from developed to developing countries. The difference between the two perspectives on responsibilities is therefore growing. It must be noted that the shift in production is detrimental to global emissions because production usually shifts from countries with superior technologies to countries with more inefficient, and CO_2-intensive, production. Hoekstra et al. (2016) show that 18 per cent of the increase in global emissions between 1995 and 2007 was caused by this technology difference.

Other ways of assigning responsibility have also been proposed.[18] An intriguing example is what happens if the responsibility is assigned to the country or company which mines the oil and gas. In one rare example of this type of analysis, Heede (2014) traces historical extraction of fossil fuels and finds that 63 per cent of the total extraction can be linked to a small group of just ninety "carbon major" entities, the big oil and gas companies, for the period 1751–2010.

STOCKS/FLOWS: SPECIES AND ECOSYSTEMS

Stock/flow accounts can also be used to measure the concepts of ecosystems and species.[19] If there are n species living in m ecosystems then their development can be described in stock–flow terms.[20] In the short term, the number of species is fixed or reduces as a result of extinctions. If the account is viewed on a (very) long time scale, new species might emerge because of evolution. Conceptually, the total number of species and the species per ecosystem can be measured at the beginning and the end of the accounting period. The difference between these two periods is the net additions and subtractions which can be caused by deaths, births and migration flows.

Although this is conceptually simple it is practically impossible. It is already hard to produce demographic accounts which record the number of humans, let alone for the millions of other species. It is also questionable whether it is really necessary to know exactly how many species there are in each ecosystem. Nevertheless, there are many instances where a stock-flow account actually makes a lot of sense. For example, it might be useful for some large mammals, especially endangered species, to have a demographic account for the last couple of hundreds of individuals. For example, the World Wildlife Fund reports the numbers of rhino for five different species on its website; it has estimated that only 58–68 individuals of the Javan rhino are left. Since they live only in the Ujung Kulon National Park, it is possible to make pretty accurate demographic accounts (including sex and age characteristics) for this endangered population.[21]

The SEEA-EEA does not show a stock/flow account of species. Instead it uses the area covered by the ecosystem as its accounting foundation, shown in Table 6.5.[22] Land area is of course a useful accounting unit because the quantity of land area is easily identifiable and fairly constant over time.

Human activities obviously affect ecosystems in many direct and indirect ways.[23] In some cases, such as change in land use, the impact is quite direct. Also when national parks are defined, the

Table 6.5 *Ecosystems asset – extent*

| Ecosystems | Stock | Flows | | | | | | | Stock |
| | | Additions | | | Subtractions | | | |
	Opening stock	Managed expansion	Natural expansion	Upwards reappraisals	Managed regressions	Natural regressions	Downwards reappraisals	Closing Stock
Artificial surfaces								
Crops								
Grassland								
Tree-covered area								
Mangroves								
Shrub-covered area								
Regularly flooded areas								
Sparse natural vegetation areas								
Terrestrial barren land								
Permanent snow, glaciers and bodies of inland water								
Coastal water and inter-tidal areas								

impact of humans is obvious. Humans can be the direct cause of plants or animals being killed, through poaching, hunting, road kill, etc. However, far more often humans have an indirect effect on the health of ecosystems and the population of a given species though air pollution, climate change and land use fragmentation.

Taking the ecosystem as the unit of measurement has conceptual advantages. In the SEEA-EEA these areas provide "ecosystem services" which are then quantified using welfare economics. These services are assigned to ecosystems rather than individual species. When one walks through a forest, the recreational service which the forest is providing is the result of the entire ecosystem, not individual species. This is no different to normal market commodities. When assessing the benefits of a car, it is the entire machine which provides the service. It is not possible to attribute the benefits to the engine, wheels or windscreen wipers separately.

NETWORKS: ECOSYSTEMS

Having only information about the ecosystem area is not sufficient.[24] A network perspective of these complex systems is also required. E.O. Wilson, a highly respected scholar of biodiversity, said: "The greatest challenge today, not just in cell biology and ecology but in all of science, is the accurate and complete description of complex systems."[25]

Ecosystems are networks of interdependent species which are also interacting with their abiotic surroundings. Work on food webs describes which species are feeding on which other species.[26] In some cases the work on food webs creates matrices of prey–predator relationships. For example, Cohen et al. (1990) have 130 of these matrices. Williams and Martinez (2000) show the food web of Little Rock Lake, Wisconsin, which currently is the largest food web in the primary literature.[27]

Mass and energy play an important role in the functioning of these networks. Food webs and chains are driven by the energy and nutrient requirements of the various species. Brown et al. (2004) has suggested that theories of ecology, species and ecosystems should be based on mass/energy because they are governed by the laws of physics.[28]

The SEEA-EEA does not provide a network perspective on ecosystems. This is partly due to the fact that the concept of ecosystem services is sufficient in order to create valuation approaches based on welfare economics. However, a more important problem is data availability. Although a couple of hundred peer-reviewed articles are published each year about food webs/chains, they are mostly case studies for small ecosystems or of individual species. E.O. Wilson (1998) puts the challenge thus:

> The paramount challenge to ecology in the foreseeable future is the cracking apart and resynthesis of the assemblages of organisms that occupy ecosystems, particularly the most complex ecosystems such as estuaries and rainforests. Most studies in ecology focus on only one or two species of organisms at a time, out of the thousands occupying a typical habitat. The researchers, forced into reductionism by practical necessity, start with small fragments of the whole ecosystem. Yet they are aware that the fate of each species is determined by the diverse actions of scores or hundreds of other species that variously photosynthesize, browse, graze, decompose, hunt, fall prey, and turn soil around the target species.

Ecosystems are finely balanced systems. Once an ecosystem crosses a certain threshold, for example if the population of one species becomes too dominant within the network of species, the state of the ecosystem may change. The ability to resist these changes is called resilience.[29] Some ecosystems will be more sensitive than others. To assess the quality and resilience of an ecosystem it is imperative that a network-oriented approach to ecosystem accounting is included in the SGNA.

Yet getting data is difficult. Given the advances in ICT and satellite imaging and the growing number of ecological case studies (of foods webs and chains) it is conceivable that by 2030 there will be new ways of obtaining data that help in the study of ecosystems networks. The GENA should therefore keep open the possibility of creating an account from this perspective.

LIMITS: PLANETARY BOUNDARIES

The idea that the environmental system has certain limits has a long history. Scientists have warned that human populations will lead to environmental collapse for many centuries. Amongst the first economists was Thomas Malthus, who in 1798 warned that agricultural production could not keep up with the growing population.[30] In the 1960s/1970s books like *Population Bomb* and the *Limits to Growth* report brought Malthusian-type fears to a wider audience.[31]

The idea of limits is rare in standard theories of economic growth. Economic growth theories rarely take on board the physical boundaries of our planet. This was most eloquently articulated by Kenneth Boulding, who lamented that "Anyone who believes exponential growth can go on forever in a finite world is either a madman or an economist".[32]

Yet there are certainly (economic) research groups that have propagated the importance of environmental and thermodynamic limits. As far back as 1969, Ayres and Kneese (1969) stressed that physical limits are insufficiently heeded in economic theory. Georgescu-Roegen (1971) pointed out that economic theory violates the laws of thermodynamics. Ken Arrow, a Nobel Prize winner, and colleagues argue for the importance of looking at the carrying capacity in *Science*.[33] Many other Nobel Prize winners and prominent economists have warned of this blind spot in the mainstream models.

There have also been many suggestions about how to create economies that operated within these limits Boulding (1966), Daly (1992), Lovelock (1979), Jackson (2017) and Raworth (2017) suggested "spaceship earth", "steady state economics", "Gaia", "Prosperity without growth" and "Doughnut Economics" respectively. These are all influential books that make clear that the Earth is a closed system which is limited by certain boundaries.

Two environmental problems have boosted this type of thinking: biodiversity loss and climate change.[34] With respect to species
loss, some authors have argued that the planet is currently experi-
encing the "sixth mass extinction".[35] In terms of climate change the
debate is whether human-induced warming can be kept below catastrophic levels.

A recent influential publication in the field of environmental
limits is the work of Rockstrom et al. (2009), who listed seven "planetary boundaries". According to this publication, these are the boundaries "within which we expect that humanity can operate safely.
Transgressing one or more planetary boundaries may be deleterious
or even catastrophic due to the risk of crossing thresholds that will
trigger non-linear, abrupt environmental change within continental-
to planetary-scale systems". The authors concede that it is hard to
measure but argue it is an important field which requires more
research. The authors quantify seven of the nine planetary boundaries
and even provide specific measures for each:

1. Climate change
2. Ocean acidification
3. Stratospheric ozone
4. Biogeochemical cycles for nitrogen (N) and phosphorus (P)
5. Global freshwater use
6. Land system change
7. Rate at which biological diversity is lost

They estimate that three planetary boundaries have already
been transgressed, namely climate change, rate of biodiversity loss
and changes to the global nitrogen cycle. Note that five of the planetary boundaries are measured in mass units, one in terms of area and
one in terms of number of species. The two categories for which
Rockstrom was unable to set a planetary boundary (atmospheric
aerosol loading and chemical pollution) will almost certainly have
a mass unit. The boundaries can therefore easily be linked to the
SGNA system.

It is a matter of discussion whether the planetary boundaries are really "limits", in the sense that is being proposed in this book. The concept of natural limits in the SGNA should show the limits of complex systems. These may be biological, thermodynamic, practical or otherwise. For example, the gestation period of the Javan rhino is a limit. The availability of fossil fuels and minerals is limited. The amount of sunlight reaching the earth's surface is a limit. The extinction of a species is an example where a lower limit has been reached. In that sense, the 2-degree target for climate change is not a limit. It is not the case that at 1.9 degrees society is fine while at 2.1 the global natural system transitions into another state. The impacts of climate change are gradual, and even if there is tipping point it is hard to pinpoint. This does not mean that the 2-degree target is not an important policy target, but it is not a limit in the strict sense proposed in this book.

FINAL THOUGHTS

The GENA will provide the accounting structure of the biotic and abiotic systems using the concepts stocks/flows, networks and limits. The GENA is based on the SEEA Central Framework, which is already a global statistical standard that is rapidly being deployed in the world. The United Nations Statistical Division (UNSD) wants to have 100 countries produce SEEA accounts by 2020 (see Chapter 4).

The GENA is, however, different to the SEEA. It strips away unnecessary economic terminology and expands into a truly global accounting system. This means that it not only looks at countries but also at the global commons. It includes stock/flow accounts for mass and energy for all the natural cycles that can be linked to human societies. A great example of a GENA account is the Global Carbon Budget project, which is historical, annual, national, global, stock and flow data on carbon emissions and concentrations. It also includes responsibility indicators from the consumption perspective, which are important to understand the significance of globalisation.

Measurement of the biotic system is the greatest challenge. Nevertheless, the availability and quality of satellite data has increased significantly in the last couple of years and will be of great use in this field. Perhaps the greatest obstacle is to introduce the ideas of networks in the measurements of ecosystems. Given that the SGNA-GENA has a timeline of 2030, there is still time to take advantage of new statistical sources and burgeoning knowledge of ecosystem functioning.

7 Global Societal Accounts (GSA)

After discussing the environmental accounts it is time to zoom in on our own species. This will be done in two steps. This chapter will discuss the societal accounts. The economic system, which is a sub-system of the societal accounts, is discussed in Chapter 8.

The foundation of Global Societal Accounts (GSA) is the number of people (stock) as well as demographic changes (flows) such as births, deaths and migration (How many are we?). The GSA, however, also includes the characteristics of the individuals of the populations such as age, skills, health and where they live (Who are we?).

Furthermore, the GSA are also designed to record how society is organised. People organise themselves into all types of formal and informal groups and institutions, such as households, sports clubs, companies and governments, which enable society to function. All these institutional units are linked to each other in a complex network system which is governed by various norms, customs or laws (How are we organised?).

The final part of the account is to understand what people do in society. By tracking their activities in terms of their time use, it is possible to get a good grip on what our daily lives look like. It makes clear where we are, what we are doing and with whom (What do we do?).

Taken together, the data provides an important picture of society. Comparing these statistics across nations tells you a lot about the features of a nation including its culture and its institutions. The accounts provide a solid foundation to understand the well-being of the citizens and what factors play an important role in determining that. The GSA also provide context for an economic analysis of society, although this is developed further in Chapter 8.

STOCKS/FLOWS: DEMOGRAPHIC ACCOUNTS

Throughout history, it has always been an important exercise to count the number of citizens of a country. Remember that in the Bible, Mary and Joseph are travelling to Bethlehem because of a census of the population by the Romans. Having this type of information about the population is important for many reasons, especially for tax purposes. Furthermore, knowing the size and whereabouts of your population is crucial for democratic societies. This is why population statistics are the only data that is obligatory under the US constitution. In that document the US Congress is tasked to generate a census once every ten years and has done so ever since the first one in 1790.

Demographic statistics have gone through a similar international harmonisation process as the SNA. The first handbook was issued in 1958. Around that time the World Programme on Population and Housing Censuses led to worldwide implementation of censuses. Since the 1950s many countries have conducted censuses: more than 1,600 censuses have since been conducted worldwide. The 1958 handbook was updated in 1998 (*Principles and Recommendations for Population and Housing Censuses, Revision 1*). Revision 2 followed in 2008.[1]

The accounting unit of population is the individual person. The stock-flow system is rather simple (see Table 7.1). At the beginning of a year there are a certain number of people. If all births and deaths in the world are accounted for in a year, then the closing balance of the stock of the global population can be derived. However, from a country perspective, there is a third flow factor: migration. People move from one country to another. Net migration is zero at the global level, but for a single country there can be a significant net influx or outflow of people.[2]

Table 7.1 *Demographic accounts – population*

	Opening stock	Additions		Reductions		Closing stock
		Births	Immigration	Deaths	Emigration	
Country 1						
Country 2						
Global total						

Demographic statistics are compatible to national boundaries but this does not mean that it is always easy to measure the population. There are difficult groups of people such as those who move between countries a lot. They might do so for work, study or for a long trip. This is why demographic accounts define the principle of "usual residence" to assign a person to a given country.[3] In practice it might happen that this person is being counted twice in two different countries or not at all. Given the importance of globalisation and the influence this has had on the movement of people around the globe, this issue will probably become more significant in future.

The UN Principles and Recommendations for Population and Housing Censuses, Revision 2, states:

> Aside from the answer to the question "How many are we?" there is also a need to provide an answer to "Who are we?" in terms of age, sex, education, occupation, economic activity and other crucial characteristics, as well as to "Where do we live?" in terms of housing, access to water, availability of essential facilities, and access to the Internet.

These are all important characteristics which affect the well-being as well as the economic performance of a person. The most often cited are age, health, level of educational, skills and housing situation. After his work on the SNA, Richard Stone worked in the 1970s on

Table 7.2 *Demographic accounts – age*

Opening stock	Additions			Reductions		Closing stock
	Births	Ageing	Migration	Deaths	Emigration	
0–1						
1–5						
5–18						
18–65						
65+						
Total						

producing demographic and social accounts which measured these types of characteristics of the population.[4]

Age is the easiest to account for since its development is predictable over time. The only unpredictable aspect is whether someone dies or leaves the country, which is only a fraction of the total population. The stock/flow accounting system shown in Table 7.2 is similar to the core demographic account shown in Table 7.1.

Education is the next characteristic that is accounted for in the demographic accounts. The economic literature tends to look at humans in their role as production factors in the economic process. This interpretation, the "human capital revolution", started in the 1960s and viewed the education levels of the population as a capital stock. The seminal work by Theodore Shultz and Gary Becker on education began at that time.[5] But apart from additional income, education has "non-economic" benefits too.[6] This is reflected in the OECD definition, which states that human capital is "the knowledge, skills, competencies and attributes embodied in individuals that facilitate the creation of personal, social and economic well-being".[7]

Table 7.3 shows the opening and closing stocks of skills and educational levels. This account records the number of people in each category. In principle, the skill levels are of interest because these are

Table 7.3 *Demographic accounts – education*

	Opening stock	Additions		Reductions		Closing stock
		Addition	Graduation	Reduction	Deaths	
Skill 1						
Skill ...						
Skill n						
Education level 1						
Education level ...						
Education level n						

more relevant in economic performance, but the education level is easier to measure because it is a discrete variable.[8] You either have a diploma or you don't. It is also easier to set up a stock-flow account because things like graduations and deaths can be linked directly to a closing stock. In the case of skill (e.g. ICT or language skills), it is harder to define what a skill is, how you acquire them and how quickly you "forget", except by observing this at the beginning and end of the period.

Finally, the health of a person is an important driver of economic performance and well-being. Poor health can easily ruin a life in both these dimensions. The most common way to judge the health of a population is usually to look at the life expectancy. This can be augmented by information about the causes of death in Table 7.1. However, this is quite a crude estimate of what the health of population really is. But what is good heath? The World Health Organization, in its Preamble to the WHO Constitution, stated that "Health is a state of complete physical, mental and social well-being and not merely the absence of disease or infirmity".[9]

One of the issues of measuring health as defined by the WHO is that it is a far more volatile human situation than education level or age. It may change from day to day in abrupt and unpredictable ways. Just measuring health on 31 December in one year and comparing it with health a year later does not tell you everything about the health of the population. You might be perfectly healthy at those two times, while the rest of the year you had a serious ailment. It is useful to measure the incidence of certain chronic diseases in this fashion, but for other minor ailments (e.g. the flu) it is better to record these aspects in the time-use accounts.

STOCKS/FLOWS: INSTITUTIONAL UNITS

The demographic accounts of the GSA only provide information about the number and characteristics of the population. However, persons organise themselves into all types of groups in society, either informal or formal. Probably one of the most important groups is the household. Despite the fact that societies all over the world have many different household living arrangements, the vast majority will have a family or extended family living with each other in the same dwelling.

Households provide a really important foundation for the well-being of an individual. Firstly, this has to do with the characteristics of the dwelling. That is why the *UN Principles and Recommendations for Population and Housing Censuses* also include many questions related to the quality of the houses. Second, the relationship between the inhabitants of the dwelling is probably one of the most important sources of happiness (in the case of a harmonious family) or unhappiness (in the case of abuse or impending divorce).

An additional demographic account would therefore indicate the number of different households in society. These would need to include the many different living arrangements which exist throughout the world. These accounts would provide a snapshot of the differences between the various nations. The household account should also include variables related to the quality of the housing so that it is clear how many people are living in comfortable dwellings, slums or perhaps even on the street.

The household is probably one of the most important ways in which societies organise themselves. But there are countless other groups in society. Social life can be structured around families, friends, religious groups and other social clubs. People also organise into companies which produce products and services and generate income, or people work in the government to create and uphold the laws of society or to provide government services. Schools and hospitals are groups of individuals that work together to provide education and medical services.

In fact, the SNA provides a start to identifying the groups in society. It specifies the following five "institutional sectors": Non-financial corporations; Financial corporations; Government units; Non-profit institutions serving households (NPISHs);[10] and Households. In layman's terms, these are the companies (regular and financial), government, non-profit organisations and households. The institutional sectors are made up of individual institutional units, e.g. there are literally millions of non-financial corporations ranging from multinationals to one-man shops. In the SNA these units are described as follows: "The defining characteristic of an institutional unit is that it is capable of owning goods and assets, incurring liabilities and engaging in economic activities and transactions with other units in its own right."[11]

For the definition of the SGNA-GSA, this economic definition of the groups in society is too restrictive. It is important to strip away any unnecessary economic bias from this definition, just as was proposed for the SEEA. The SGNA needs to define all institutional units that are important for *society*, not just economic transactions. Clearly, people organise themselves in many different types of formal and informal networks. Individuals are parts of families, groups of friends, or neighbourhoods which have important impacts on well-being. In the case of the SGNA, the institutional units are defined as *all* groups in which people congregate to achieve a common goal. Note that this does not always mean that the group is "good" for society; criminal organisations or hacker networks are groups which are beneficial to themselves but not to society in general.

It is not true to say that the economic units (SNA) are important only for the economy and that the other groups are only important for well-being. Companies provide a working environment which can contribute significantly to well-being though the working conditions and the friendships between colleagues (and bosses). On the other hand, family, friends and neighbours can affect economic outcomes as well. Alumni organisations or "old boy networks" are informal but can still provide important momentum during a career.

One could approach the accounting for institutional units in one of two ways. Firstly, one could create demographic stock/flow accounts for all these institutional units in a similar way to the population accounts. In the case of the institutional units as defined by the SNA, they are often legal entities. Nevertheless, it can be surprisingly hard to estimate "the number of companies in a country". Despite the fact the demography of the companies in a society is important for economic statistics, mergers, fusions and shell companies make it hard to produce reliable figures. Many countries lack a good business register, which basically is a stock account for the number of companies in a country.[12]

In the case of the non-SNA institutional units it is even harder because there is rarely a legal foundation (marriages and parent–child relationships being an exception). Groups of friends don't go to a lawyer to have their friendship formalised. Some of these groups therefore do not have clear boundaries. For example, who is included in a "group of friends" and who isn't? One may also question whether it is necessary to know how many "groups of friends" there are in a country. On the other hand, the number of neighbourhoods or places of worship might provide important information about a society, while still being statistically feasible.

There is another way to look at the issue, by taking the perspective of the individual. "Membership accounts" register whether a

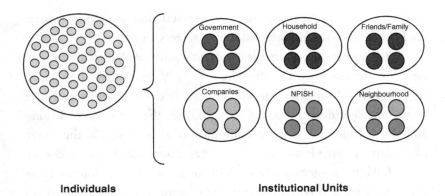

Individuals   **Institutional Units**

FIGURE 7.1 A network perspective on the structure of society

person is part of group. For example, it records how many people are members of churches, sports clubs or whether they have close friends. Such surveys are already done in many countries. This may split into age, education levels, ethnicity, etc. These types of accounts could also record how many people are employed by corporations or other SNA institutional units. This could include information about the employment relationship (active/not active, employee/self-employed, part-time, full-time, industry, etc.). The account could also take the form of a stock/flow account to show how the membership of these groups fluctuates over time.

NETWORKS: THE STRUCTURE OF SOCIETY

Figure 7.1 shows the individuals and groups in society, both economic and otherwise. On the left are all the individuals, depicted by smaller circles. To the right are institutional sectors, which are made up of institutional units. In fact each institutional unit is itself a network. A company can be viewed as a single unit but at the same time it is also a collection of persons cooperating using customs and norms in a hierarchical and complex organisation.

An individual person can be a part of multiple institutional units. For example, they might be a family member in a household, a government employee and an owner of stock of a listed company. In fact, some relationships might endure in different settings. For example, a good bond with a colleague at work might also turn into a friend who you see outside of the office.

Apart from the network between individuals, there are also network relationships between institutional sectors and units. For example, companies buy goods and services from other companies. In addition, governments and corporations have many types of relationships including regulation, taxation, or as a customer. Corporations also spend money on political campaigns or assist governments in implementing policies in society.

There are countless network relationships between individuals and institutional units. Basically, one can connect each circle in Figure 7.1 to another circle. Each of these network relationships is bound by contracts, social norms, laws or trust relationships. The networks may result in flows of goods, services and information or it may be a source of love or laughter.

Understanding the networks and groups is vital to understanding the functioning of society. Creating such a network account would start by 1) defining a set of institutional units that go beyond the SNA; 2) network relationships have to be classified; 3) the various flows between the institutional units need to be defined. This might also be a fruitful way of operationalising concepts such as social capital and institutions, which are not clearly defined in the literature.

The term social capital has existed for quite a while but has eluded a precise unambigious definition.[13] The term is known in the sociological and economic literature and its importance has been argued in many ways. Social capital is usually associated with the interpersonal relationships between individuals. A significant component of the networks is the trust and the shared norms involved. Despite the differences in definition, the literature does show that social capital can be seen as an important contributor of economic growth as well as of well-being[14] or inequality in mortality[15] or as a means to solve environmental issues.[16]

The quantification of social capital has suffered because of the lack of an agreed conceptual foundation. Membership of societal groups or the numbers of people volunteering are sometimes taken as proxies. One of the key indicators that is sometimes adopted is "generalised trust". It is measured by asking people: "Generally speaking, would you say that most people can be trusted or that you can't be too careful in dealing with people?"[17] When the data is compared between countries a robust pattern of high-trust versus low-trust societies emerges. Places such as Scandinavia and northern Europe generally score well in these data.

The literature on institutions is also a field that might benefit from further development of the concepts. In fact, the relationships of society proposed in this chapter are reminiscent of Douglass North's definition: "Institutions are the humanly devised constraints that structure political, economic and social interaction. They consist of both informal constraints (sanctions, taboos, customs, traditions, and codes of conduct), and formal rules (constitutions, laws, property rights)."[18] North goes on to say that "Institutions provide the incentive structure of an economy; as that structure evolves, it shapes the direction of economic change towards growth, stagnation, or decline." In our case, the institutions are also affecting well-being.

The power differences between institutional units are also the rationale behind the "extractive institutions" narrative which is proposed by Acemoglu and Robinson (2012). In their book they argue that in unsuccessful countries it is possible for a small elite to change the institutions of a country to their advantage. The relationships of this small elite (their connections to government, the army or companies) are so powerful that it tilts the system in their favour. The power of the other groups is not sufficient to stop it. Other developments, such as rising inequality, are also sometimes explained in these terms. We will return to this point in Chapter 9 on distribution accounts.

These institutional settings vary per country and the reliance on formal and informal institutions differs as well.[19] The network perspective proposed in the GSA could provide a framework for social capital and institutions which would enable further formalisation, harmonisation and quantification.

FLOWS/LIMITS: TIME USE

What are all the individuals in society actually doing? And what role do the other institutional units and networks play in daily life? Time use is the area of the last account of the SGNA-GSA. Time is an excellent accounting unit. Whether it is a human, a machine or a network, each of these have exactly the same amount of time in a given year. For example, the US has around 320 million people. Assuming that the population stays the same, that amount of human time for each year is 1.2E+11 days, 2.8E+12 hours, 1.7E+14 minutes and 1.0E+16 seconds.

Time is the ultimate democratic resource. Each human, assuming they are alive the entire year, has exactly the same amount of time available. There might be great inequality between Warren Buffet and his cleaning staff, but in terms of time they have exactly the same twenty-four hours. The inequality lies in the discretion that people have to choose what to do with their time, which also affects the quality of a life. Another source of inequality is the time use over an entire lifetime. Some humans pass on at a young age while some survive to the ripe old age of 100 (around 876,000 hours).

A twenty-four-hour day can be split into various activities. The data in Table 7.4 is taken from the Harmonised European Time-Use Surveys (HETUS), which makes European surveys comparable. The table shows the time use of various European countries according to five main categories for both males and females.

The table is also a perfect illustration that the economy is only a relatively small part of daily life. Of the five countries shown, the males work around 3.27–4.21 hours per day. For females it is 1.52–2.2.4 hours per day. Participation in economic production is therefore only a small portion of total time spent. Another dimension

Table 7.4 *Time use of persons (mean hours per day – activity)*

	France	Germany	Italy	Spain	United Kingdom
MALE					
Personal care	11:44	10:40	11:16	11:11	10:22
Employment	3:48	3:27	4:15	4:21	4:10
Study	0:15	0:15	0:11	0:18	0:08
Domestic	2:24	2:22	1:35	1:37	2:18
Leisure	4:44	5:42	5:05	5:16	5:22
Travel	1:03	1:29	1:35	1:16	1:30
Unspecified	0:02	0:05	0:03	0:02	0:08
FEMALE					
Personal care	11:53	10:58	11:12	11:05	10:43
Employment	2:17	1:56	1:52	2:06	2:24
Study	0:14	0:13	0:14	0:20	0:09
Domestic	4:34	4:14	5:20	4:55	4:15
Leisure	4:05	5:15	4:06	4:26	4:55
Travel	0:54	1:19	1:14	1:05	1:25
Unspecified	0:03	0:05	0:03	0:02	0:10

of the economy is consumption of goods and services. These commodities are consumed during the other activities which are shown in the table. Cars or public transport tickets are needed to travel, gym subscriptions and television are used during leisure time and pyjamas and a bed are needed for sleep (part of personal care in the table), etc.

Social networks[20] are also crucial to time use and well-being. Many of the activities in Table 7.4 are with friends, family members or colleagues. The American Heritage Time Use Survey therefore also includes questions about who people spent time with. The location of the activity (home or otherwise) is another important characteristic which affects the contribution of an activity to well-being. Together, the interaction between time, networks, goods and services and location provide a fairly complete overview of the characteristics which govern instantaneous well-being (see the section on affect measurement in Chapter 10).

Time-use categories can be subject to biological, technological, practical or other limits. For example, each human needs to spend at least some time sleeping and eating. Some might only need a couple of hours of sleep, while others need ten hours, but no one can go without for an entire year. Similarly, given the distance between a person's home and their work, there is a technological limit to how fast a person can commute to the office.

Over the last couple of decades there have been dramatic shifts in time-use patterns which clearly show how society had changed. Aguiar and Hurst (2007) provide long-term trends in time-use data for the United States. The data shows that woman have shifted from staying at home to engaging in formal employment. At the same time there has also been a dramatic increase in amount of leisure time for both men and women. They showed that because men started working less, their leisure increased by about six to nine hours per week. For women, leisure time increased by roughly four to eight hours per week because of less home production.

There are therefore differences in leisure time between genders, but also between other groups in society. Some people might have more "free" time than others. This has also led to research in "time poverty" which looks into the phenomenon that people have too little leisure time.[21] However, others have pointed to the fact that people have a lot of discretion in how they spend their time and that the feelings are therefore partially subjective.[22]

INTERMEZZO: EFFECTS OF ICT/GLOBALISATION ON THE STRUCTURE OF SOCIETY AND TIME USE

Our daily lives are different in many ways when compared to thirty or fifty years ago. This is partially because of the enormous impact which ICT has had on society. The economy has also undergone profound changes due to globalisation. As a result, the GSA need to be able to cope with these developments. I will focus here on the role which these developments have played in the creation and use of networks and time use.

As a consequence of ICT, institutional units are increasingly global in scope. These units are no longer bound by national borders. This is the case for multinationals which have affiliates in many countries. However, other groups are forming at the global level because of the internet. For example, scientists can be part of both formal and informal global networks which enhance their scientific endeavours. Some co-authors on scientific papers will have never met face-to-face. Virtual networks are forming in all areas of life. In the past, location was an important criterion to connect to people. People can now have friends online, form an online knitting community or a hacker collective. In the past, forming friendship or other groups required some kind of physical proximity; this limit has been removed.

The internet and online devices (phones and tablets) have transformed the way people work, communicate and amuse themselves. This has a profound impact on the way time is spent: In the past there was only the option of a telephone, but through emails, social network programmes and chatting applications people are able to communicate with many other people simultaneously. This can have positive effects but also negative ones (e.g. cyber bullying or social media addiction). What is certain is that ICT has a profound impact on the way social interactions occur.

Multinationals are also a reflection of our globalised era, and pose a huge challenge from a statistical perspective. The number of multinationals has doubled in the period from 1990 to now. Although this type of company has existed for a while,[23] it has really started to take off during the last couple of decades. Statistical issues arise when production is divided over many countries. Some of the trade flows are difficult to measure or value. For example, international trade between company subsidiaries do not have a market price. In this case the multinational is asked to record the transaction at "arm's length value", which is the market value that would have existed if they had had to buy it on the market. This is obviously difficult and in reality many multinational companies use "transfer pricing" in order to minimise the taxes they have to pay.

Another problem is the use of R&D. In many cases, R&D takes place in one country and is used in a factory in another nation. Measuring these flows of knowledge is a major challenge. There is an increasing tendency to shift the measurement of multinationals from national statistical offices to international agencies which are better equipped to analyse the full scope of the multinational and its subsidiaries (e.g. the Eurogroups project).

FINAL THOUGHTS

The GSA describe the people, structure and functioning of society. The GSA comprise four elements. The first counts the number of people while the second records the characteristics of the population including their age, skills and location. The third element provides a way to account for the structure of society by viewing it as a large network of individuals, institutional sectors and institutional units. The institutional units of the SGNA are groups in which humans cooperate or congregate towards common goals. These may be formal institutional units such as those in the SNA or informal groups such as friendship groups. All of these institutional units are important for economic and well-being outcomes. Finally, this chapter looked at time-use accounts to measure the daily lives of the individuals in a society.

Some parts of the GSA are already in use and methodologies are well developed. For example, population has been measured for centuries. The demographic accounts are based on the *Principles and Recommendations for Population and Housing Censuses Revision 2*, which is used in censuses.[24] However, the accounting structure is also inspired by Richard Stone's work on social and demographic accounts. Population stocks and flows are provided by the UN Population Division for long time series and even include projections up to 2100.[25] This information might be augmented by data from the UN Refugee

Agency (UNHCR) on migration/refugees and from the World Health Organization (WHO) on causes of death.

The other characteristics, education and health, are more difficult. Incidence of diseases might be obtained from the WHO (health). The UN has recently also estimated "years of schooling". The OECD has statistics on skills and competencies of children and adults.[26]

The way in which the networks of society are organised is probably the biggest challenge in terms of measurement. It includes all the networks between people amongst each other and with institutional units. In future, new big data sources are likely to make it easier to collect data about these networks.

The availability of data is also a problem when it comes to time use, because of expensive surveys. In an overview, Charmes (2015) describes only around a hundred surveys for sixty-five countries for the previous decades. If there are no great leaps forward in terms of new statistical techniques then this account will be hard, if not impossible, to finance globally on an annual basis. Again, new big data techniques will be needed in order to make this type of statistic less expensive (see Chapter 11).

8   Global Economic
    Accounts (GECA)

A VERY IMPORTANT SUBSYSTEM

Chapter 3 makes clear that the economy is not an objective phenomenon but rather a measurement convention. For example, the production boundary, which defines what is included in economic production, has been the focus of debate for many centuries. The SNA convention doesn't just dictate what is internal to the economy, but also defines what is *external*: the societal and environmental stocks, flows and networks which are considered to be "non-economic".

The asset boundary, which defines which stocks have economic value stored in them, has also been debated for several decades. The SNA includes financial assets, produced tangible assets such as machines and buildings and intangible assets such as intellectual property products. It also considers natural resources such as oil and mineral reserves to be part of the economy. However, many have argued that additional natural capital categories, human capital and social capital should also be included as production factors because they contribute to economic development. The debate over what is inside and outside the economic accounts should therefore be seen in the long-term discussion about the appropriate measurement convention.

However one defines the economic accounts, it is clear that it is a subsystem of the societal accounts. That does not mean that the economic accounts are unimportant. Quite the contrary. Economic activities contribute significantly to societal and environmental change. The economic accounts are therefore an important component of the SGNA. But how is the SGNA-GECA different to the SNA?

Just like all the other accounts, the GECA are truly global in scope. While the SNA is solidly based on the idea of a national economy, the GECA starts from the premise of a global economy. Of course, this economic data is split into 200 countries, but all within the context of a worldwide account. Given the current globalised situation, it is important to look at the economy as a global system which covers all the country data and intercountry relationships.

The second important difference between the GECA and the SNA is the role of non-monetary data. The SNA restricts itself almost exclusively to monetary transactions. The only exceptions are that in the back of the SNA there are chapters on population, labour and "capital services". However, in this chapter it is argued that when analysing technology, consumption and the limits of an economy, non-monetary information is essential.

To illustrate the importance of non-monetary data take the example of a recent influential book in economics. *The Rise and Fall of American Growth* by Robert Gordon is about the long-term economic growth of the United States.[1] Although its topic is economic growth, the book leans heavily on non-monetary data such as labour force participation, time use and ownership of durables. These are important variables that help explain how American society has changed in the last centuries. If the book had been written purely based on monetary data it would have been less compelling (and it would definitely have been a lot shorter!). All the monetary data in the book is derived from the national accounts, while all the non-monetary data on the economy is not. Why should money be the only measurement unit of the economy? Why should the non-monetary dimension not be treated with the same accounting rigour as the rest of the economy?

Perhaps surprisingly, the GECA does *not* contain proposals to change the production or asset boundary. Despite the fact that many authors have advocated them, this is not done within the context of the GECA. The reason is the idea by Ingvar Ohlsson which is discussed in Chapter 3. He proposed in the 1950s that it did not make sense to define one boundary for an economy but rather that the boundary should be dependent on the research question you are trying to answer. If people want to expand the economic boundary, the various SGNA accounts provide ample data (time use, networks, inequality) to do this.[2]

When stretching the boundary of production and assets, one needs to use a quality perspective. For example, a lot of non-market externalities (leisure time, environmental pressures) can be assessed using techniques from welfare economics. The value of a capital stock will be based on capital theory. These expansions to the economic boundary should therefore be done in the context of the global quality accounts. Why? The reason is that the GECA restricts itself to a factual observation of the economic stocks and flows, both in monetary and non-monetary terms. They are accounts which simply provide a description of how the economic system functions, but not the underlying "value".

This assessment of quality is left to the GQA. In the quality accounts, it is possible to create a production boundary using a broader notion of welfare. This would be done using data from the environmental, social and economic accounts. For example, if one wants to create a green accounting indicator one would take a macro-economic total from the GECA (e.g. consumption), CO_2 emissions from the GENA, leisure time from the GSA and income inequality from the GDA and then value the latter three phenomena using techniques from welfare economics. The GECA should therefore concentrate on recording economic stocks and flows while the questions of quality should be left to the GCA (see more on this in Chapter 10).

STOCKS/FLOWS: CAPITAL, INVESTMENT AND DEPRECIATION

At the basis of an economy are its "assets". They are the resources that are available for production or to provide other benefits in the future. These assets are owned by institutional units such as companies or households. Table 8.1 shows an asset account as defined by the SNA. The "Produced capital" refers to items such as buildings, infrastructure and machines which economists traditionally refer to

Table 8.1 SNA assets accounts

| | | Opening balance sheet | Capital and financial accounts | Other changes in the volume | Nominal holding gains and losses | Neutral holding gains and losses | Real holding gains and losses | Closing balance sheet |
					Revaluation account			
Non-financial assets	Produced assets	Dwellings						
		Other buildings and structures						
		Machinery and equipment						
		Weapons systems						
		Cultivated biological resources						
		Costs of ownership transfer on non-produced assets						

Intellectual property products
Inventories
Valuables

Natural resources
Contracts, leases and licences
Goodwill and marketing assets

Monetary gold and SDRs
Currency and deposits
Debt securities
Loans
Equity and investment fund shares/units
Insurance
Pension and standardised guarantee schemes
Financial derivatives and employee stock options
Other accounts receivable/payable.

Non-produced assets

Private assets/liabilities

Financial assets/liabilities

Net worth

Source: Adaptation of SNA 2008 (EC et al, 2009)

as "capital". These are assets that are the result of "production" by other institutional units or by itself. The list also includes several "non-produced assets", including a number of resources which occur naturally. Somewhat surprisingly, goodwill and marketing assets are considered non-produced, despite companies spending money on advertising to build up their brand. Chapter 10 will reflect further on this point. Finally, the SNA also includes financial assets and liabilities, which are the various ways in which institutional units can own debt or credit.

The asset boundary of the SNA is not static and was debated during the last SNA revision process. The SNA 2008 now defines R&D efforts and creative originals as produced assets. When this was introduced in the US national accounts a *New York Times* op-ed piece asked: "What Is 'Seinfeld' Worth?" to indicate that TV formats and movie originals were now considered assets.[3] Collecting this type of data on intellectual property products is challenging and the valuation of the assets is difficult.[4]

The SNA asset accounts record the quantity of these assets on 1 January of a year (opening balance sheet). Various flows, both additions and reductions, contribute to the closing stock at the end of the year. The capital and financial accounts show the "regular" items of consumption of fixed capital and gross capital formation, which are technical terms for depreciation and investment respectively. However, there are also unexpected items such as "Other changes in asset accounts" and "Holding gains and losses". The former is used for irregular changes "that result from flows that are not transactions",[5] which may include "catastrophic losses" or "uncompensated seizures". The latter refers to the fact that the value of an asset may change over time and this is called a holding gain or loss. Especially in the realm of financial capital, these types of differences can have a large impact on the value on 1 January and 31 December of a year.

This is the SNA approach, but the GECA is different. The non-monetary balance sheets are the foundation of the account. Only financial capital is measured exclusively in monetary terms. For the other types of capital there are underlying non-monetary dimensions. For example, the number of dwellings, the area of cultivated biological resources, the number of cars, or the kilometres of roads and railroad tracks can all be used to create asset accounts in non-monetary units. In fact, these types of data are often already collected and more prevalent than monetary asset accounts. For example, the World Development Indicators (WDI) database of the World Bank already includes data on rail lines (route-km), the number of tractors, the amount of automated teller machines (ATMs), patent applications as well as the area of many types of land (arable, forest, permanent cropland, terrestrial protected areas). This non-monetary data about capital stocks provides a great deal of information about a country's economic situation. Yet such data is not formally part of the SNA.

In cases that are particularly important for well-being, the characteristics of the capital stocks should be included. For example, simply reporting the total value of all dwellings of a country does not tell you all that much. The *Principles and Recommendations for Population and Housing Censuses, Revision 2* asks as many as thirty-eight different types of questions about the characteristics of the home.[6] These include questions about rooms, bedrooms, useful floor space, water supply system, drinking water, type of toilet, sewage disposal, bathing facilities, kitchen, fuel used for cooking, lighting and/or electricity, solid waste disposal, heating type, piped gas, construction material of outer walls, floors, roof, elevator and more. Although the total value of a house might be a summary statistic of its quality, these characteristics come closer to a connection with well-being.

In the GECA, the monetary assets accounts are no longer part of the economic accounts. They are moved to the GQA because they require a particular quality assessment approach (the capital approach) to assess the value of the capital stocks. These valuations are based on the non-monetary data in the GECA.

The use of non-monetary data has practical advantages and provides possibilities to collaborate at the global level. For example, for some types of large standardised machines it should be relatively easy to create detailed physical stock/flow accounts for the whole world. For example, the number of aircraft, trains, trucks and cars (per type) can be estimated at the global level by looking at the production by large manufactures, vehicle ownership statistics and losses though crashes or redundancy. If the data is split into types of cars/planes/trucks and who owns them, it provides valuable information to compare countries and sectors. The data could be produced most efficiently at the global level and then distributed to individual countries as an input to their non-monetary asset accounts.

FLOWS/NETWORKS: THE GLOBAL ECONOMY

The SNA includes an account which shows the flows of transactions within the production and consumption network. Such a matrix is called an input–output table.[7] It shows many elements of the "economic cycle" such as production, consumption, investments, imports, exports, taxes, subsidies and wages, mixed income, etc. However, the SNA only covers the national economy. The basis of the SGNA-GECA is a global input–output table.

Table 8.2 shows a rudimentary global input–output table in monetary units. The basis of an input–output table is that in the columns it shows the inputs (uses) of industries while in the rows it shows their output (supply).[8] For example, the column for agriculture in country A shows the use of commodities from other industries (both domestic from country A or imports from country B). The column also shows the other gross value added categories, such as the salaries or profits. The row shows the deliveries to other industries (intermediate demand in country A and B) as well as final demand (households, government and investment in both country A and B). The columns and rows balance because inputs must equal output.

The taxes and subsidies on production and consumption are an important part of the monetary table. They represent a significant share of government revenue and outlays. But taxes and subsidies are not just revenue components, they are also important tools that a

Table 8.2 Global input-output table in monetary units

		Intermediate demand						Final demand						Total
		Country A Industries			Country B Industries			Country A			Country B			
		Agriculture	Industry	Services	Agriculture	Industry	Services	Households	Investment	Government	Households	Investment	Government	
Industries	Country A													
		Agriculture													
		Industry													
		Services													
	Country B													
		Agriculture													
		Industry													
		Services													
Taxes and subsidies														
Labour wages														
Mixed income														
Gross value added														
Total														

government has to change the behaviour of producers and consumers in society. Subsidies might help to trigger innovation, organise social gatherings or stimulate green investment. Taxes can be used to make unhealthy products such as alcohol and tobacco more expensive, or raise the price of environmentally unfriendly products.

The input–output tables provide a comprehensive overview of the monetary flows in society. Many types of economic models use these input–output tables. What makes an input–output table particularly useful is that it is also a representation of economic networks.[9] It shows the many links in an economy through the transactions between industries, and between industries and households and governments. It also shows the networks' relationships with foreign countries through imports and exports.

The network perspective has become important in the context of globalisation research. Since around 1990, developed countries are increasingly importing manufactured goods from other foreign countries. Production processes have been "fragmenting" into the underlying processes in the sense that the various stages of production are increasingly being performed in multiple countries.[10] For example, the production of the iPod was investigated by Dedrick et al. (2010), who found that an Apple iPod had 451 different parts produced by many different companies which combine the technologies of Japan, China and the United States.

The importance of globalisation has stimulated the creation of many global input–output databases which are used frequently to analyse "global value chains". In the last decade or so the proliferation of academic databases such as Global Trade Analysis Project (GTAP), EORA, the World Input–Output Database (WIOD) and EXIOBASE has increased significantly. In addition, international institutes such as the OECD and Eurostat have created the Intercountry Input–Output Table (ICIO) and Full International and Global Accounts for Research in Input–Output Analysis (FIGARO) databases, respectively.[11] The EU and the United Nations have also commissioned reports on how to classify and conceptualise globalisation in the statistical system.[12]

Creating these databases is not easy. One of the biggest problems is the issue of trade asymmetries. This is the phenomenon that if you add up all the imports and exports of countries, they don't add up. In fact, the data for exports is larger than those for imports. This led *The Economist* to the only logical conclusion that statisticians are measuring the "Exports to Mars".[13] It is important to resolve these statistical difficulties underlying these global input–output tables so that the GECA provides an adequate representation of the worldwide economy.

FLOWS: PRODUCTION, TECHNOLOGY AND INNOVATION

The founding father of modern economics, Adam Smith, starts his most famous book, *The Wealth of Nations*, looking at the production line of a pin factory and describing the various steps of the pin-producing process.[14] Economists of that era were also interested in technology and the organisation of production. They would analyse the inner workings of factories. However, as economists started to adopt the "production function", the focus moved away from the engineering aspects of production but turned to mathematical representation of the various inputs. In these types of models it is implicitly assumed that the production process is a black box with regular mathematical features.[15]

At the same time, the macroeconomic growth models which started to emerge in the 1950s confirmed the importance of technology as one of the primary determinants of growth. Yet in the application of the growth models the technology of a country is simplified to a significant extent. One way of relating historical trends in technological change to economic growth is the method of "growth accounting". In this approach the column of a monetary input–output table is considered to be a "production function". Often the intermediate inputs are split into energy, materials and services (E, M and S) while the primary inputs are capital (K) and labour (L) – a so-called KLEMS productivity analysis. This type of analysis is discussed in chapter 20 of the SNA. A growth account analyses the efficiency changes in five types of inputs (KLEMS). For example, when the amount of labour required per unit of output decreases, this is an improvement in labour productivity.

There is also a residual productivity term which is called total factor productivity (TFP) or multi-factor productivity (MFP). This is sometimes interpreted as reflecting overall technological progress but it is also referred to as the "measure of our ignorance". Economists have been trying to reduce this residual by improving their growth accounting specifications. For example, the EU-KLEMS and WORLD-KLEMS databases have data on the number of hours worked at various education levels in order to estimate the quantity and quality of labour input.

KLEMS productivity analysis does not look at absolute technology but rather at *technological change*; it only investigates changes in production functions rather than the absolute technologies. Also, besides the labour component on hours worked, all the rest of the data is monetary, although it is deflated so that the changes represent changes in "volume". However, monetary data is not the natural unit for describing technology. If you go to an engineer at a factory and ask them to describe their technology it is unlikely that they will use monetary units. An engineer will know the amount of steel which is required for a certain model of car or the amount of water and sugar needed in the production of soft drinks but not necessarily the price of these inputs.

The GECA flow account should therefore provide a non-monetary representation of the economy. The monetary account shown in Table 8.2 is therefore a secondary account. Non-monetary accounts are the foundation of the GECA. The SEEA already includes a comprehensive accounting framework: physical input–output tables. This SEEA account is therefore transferred to the economic accounts of the SGNA, rather than being part of the environmental accounts. Table 8.3 shows such a PIOT, which includes the mass of commodities, natural inputs and emissions. Just about all environmental problems

Table 8.3 Global physical input-output table in mass units

		Intermediate demand						Final demand						Emissions	Total
		Country A			Country B			Country A			Country B				
		Agriculture	Industry	Services	Agriculture	Industry	Services	Households	Investment	Government	Households	Investment	Government		
Country A Industries	Agriculture														
	Industry														
	Services														
Country B Industries	Agriculture														
	Industry														
	Services														
Natural inputs															
Total															

can be linked to one or more of these physical flows. The physical input–output table shows these links between an economy and the subtractions from and additions to natural cycles (this is an overlap with the environmental accounts).

Luckily, the collection of physical data has been improving over the last few decades. The Material Flow Analysis (MFA) community has been collecting a lot of data on physical flows. Krausmann et al. (2009) provide long historical time series (1900–2005) for annual global extraction of biomass, fossil energy carriers, metal ores, industrial minerals and construction minerals. At materialsflows.net (of Vienna University), 200 countries are covered for the period 1980 to 2013 for more than 300 different materials (twelve main categories). Physical input–output tables have already been created in a variety of countries and recently for the entire world.[16]

Apart from mass, input–output tables can also be created for other non-monetary accounting units. For example, the SEEA also includes energy accounts which should become part of the GECA.[17] In addition, the input of other production factors should also be accounted in non-monetary units and provide relevant disaggregation.[18] On the labour side, the accounts should include the number of hours worked by skilled labourers as well as the tasks performed in the production process.[19] Time-use accounts may also be created for major machines. For example, a machine or other capital goods might not run twenty-four hours a day. It might be idle because it has broken down, it is being repaired or there is no work to be done. The quality of the various machines involved should also be measured.[20]

The rows of the input–output tables can be depicted in other units because there is a balance in the supply and use of these commodities (only money, mass, energy units balance in both row and column dimensions of an input–output framework). These row-specific balancing units include: number of cattle, m^2, m^3, number of cars, haircuts, number of kilometres of public transport, nights in hotels, etc. These are volume input–output tables which also provide valuable information about the functioning of an economy.

The production descriptions in the PIOT might also be split into sub-processes. The "production function" can conceptually be broken down into smaller steps which show the various stages in production from R&D, to producing the physical product, to marketing, to sale of the product. Many companies outsource one or more of these sub-processes, either nationally or internationally. In these cases, technological change is a matter of shifting processes.[21]

The above description is a rather static representation of a production process. Technologies change over time through "learning by doing", by other forms of autonomous technological change or because of dedicated innovation expenditures.[22] In the SNA, investments in R&D are recorded as investments in intellectual property products. However, there is no link made to the technological changes that actually take place. It would be useful to have more information about which of the industries, inputs or processes the innovations are targeting. Respondents should specify the expenditures in R&D but it might also be good to use different units as well. For example, innovation surveys or patent statistics may be used to try to understand in which areas innovations are taking place.

FLOWS: CONSUMPTION

The input–output tables, both non-monetary and monetary, have a column for the "consumption by households". The information from these input–output tables would provide data on the quantities (number of kWh, loafs of bread and theatre tickets) as well as the prices that were paid.

The first thing to realise about the SNA conventions is that the term "consumption" is somewhat misleading. It records when the goods and services are *purchased*, not *used*. This is a subtle, but important, difference. For example, in the Netherlands about one-sixth of total household consumption is on durable goods.[23] These are goods such as cars, electronics and furniture that are used for a longer period of time. Despite the fact that the commodity is

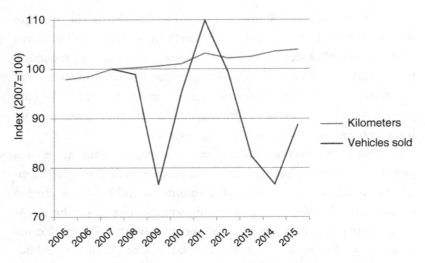

FIGURE 8.1 Sales and use of cars in the Netherlands

used over multiple years, the entire purchase is recorded in the first year.[24]

If the actual use of the commodity is accounted for, this might make a big difference. For example, Figure 8.1 shows that there is a difference in the purchases and use of cars. The number of new cars sold in the Netherlands is volatile and is largely dependent on the state of the economy. On the other hand, the use of the car (in terms of the number of kilometres driven) shows stable growth.[25] Note that in economies that produce many cars (such as Germany, Japan or the United States), the cars sold are an important contributor to GDP. When the sale of cars slumps, this will influence GDP significantly. But this is looking at the economy from a production perspective. If the focus is shifted towards the actual use of products, by spreading the use of durables over multiple years, the macroeconomic data would look far less volatile.

The second point about consumption in the SNA is that the goods and services which are included are highly heterogeneous. To give some insight into this issue, the SNA classifies consumption

---

BOX 8.1　**The COICOP classification of consumption**

COICOP (Classification of Individual Consumption According to Purpose)

- 01 – Food and non-alcoholic beverages
- 02 – Alcoholic beverages, tobacco and narcotics
- 03 – Clothing and footwear
- 04 – Housing, water, electricity, gas and other fuels
- 05 – Furnishings, household equipment and routine household maintenance
- 06 – Health
- 07 – Transport
- 08 – Communication
- 09 – Recreation and culture
- 10 – Education
- 11 – Restaurants and hotels
- 12 – Miscellaneous goods and services (12.1 – Personal care, 12.2 – Prostitution, 12.3 – Personal effects n.e.c., 12.4 – Social protection, 12.5 – Insurance, 12.6 – Financial services n.e.c., 12.7 – Other services n.e.c.)

---

according to the purpose of the commodities (see Box 8.1). There are various "basic needs", such as nutrition (01), clothing (03) and shelter (04, 05), which are necessary for daily survival. However, these categories can also be luxury goods (e.g. caviar and designer clothing). Also, beyond the basic level, excessive consumption can lead to negative side effects such as obesity in the case of food. Similarly, use of alcoholic beverages, tobacco and narcotics (02) can lead to addiction and health damage.[26]

On the opposite side of the spectrum, categories such as recreation and holidays (09, 11) come closest to general ideas of happiness or well-being. However, some consumption categories do not really have a well-being component but are related to maintaining certain standards. For example, many housing costs have to do with the repair, upkeep or cleaning of the house. These services are aimed at keeping living quarters at a certain level of comfort and sanitation.

Similarly, health expenditures (06) might be seen as the "maintenance costs" to combat disease and ailments.

In other cases, the consumption seems more like an investment. For example, education spending (10) can be seen as an investment in "human capital". Communication costs (08) include payments needed to maintain contacts and social networks. They help to maintain a person's social capital. Travel costs (07) may also be needed to visit friends and family but transport may also be used for commuting or leisure.

In some cases, commodities can have multiple functions. For example, water and electricity have many applications. Water may be used for hygiene, drinking or garden upkeep while electricity/energy is used for heating, cooking and a multitude of machines and appliances. Finally, there are also goods and services that help to reduce risks. For example, buying alarms or door locks are ways of enhancing security at home while buying insurance services[27] provides financial security against risks.[28]

Thus, overall the consumption column is a rather eclectic set of different goods and services which play many different roles in our daily lives.[29] As Box 8.2 shows, these goods and services are also changing rapidly because of ICT and globalisation. Economists such as Kuznets have argued that that there are certain consumption categories that might not contribute to well-being or might even be detrimental. For example, Kuznets argued that commuting costs should not be part of consumption. In the "Green accounting" aggregates these types of components are subtracted from the regular macroeconomic indicators. But the green accounting method is discrete in the sense that the contribution to well-being is reduced to a yes/no question. Yet, in reality, the psychological effects of goods and services, networks and dwellings are highly complex. Chapter 10 (affect evaluation) discusses a more continuous approach to assessing well-being.[30]

The data from the GECA will include monetary and non-monetary data, which should also be corrected for actual use of

BOX 8.2 **Effects of ICT/globalisation on the consumption**

The ICT revolution has given society the internet and smart phones and together these have transformed lives in many ways.

Existing products. Current goods and service offerings are changing fast as a result of the ICT revolution. Shops and malls are closing throughout the developed countries because people are shifting to online purchases. From a statistical perspective this is quite hard to measure. In the past one could survey the local retail companies; nowadays, it is also possible to shop online and it is not always clear in what country the websites are located. The internet has also made it possible to create tailor-made prices. For example, airline fares used to be fairly stable. Nowadays, every seat goes for a different price because prices may vary by the hour and there are various types of add-on services which can be ordered when booking online. The emergence of tailor-made prices makes it increasingly difficult to measure inflation of aircraft services.

New services. The internet and smartphones have led to many new services. Social networks, games and many other practical tools are being created at rapid speed. What is more, many of these services are not part of SNA consumption because they are produced free of charge. No monetary transaction is taking place and so nothing is "consumed". Nevertheless, social networking sites, internet search engines and digital encyclopaedias have made lives far easier but come at no cost to the user. In the SNA, these services are not providing a service to consumers but are producing advertising services. This means that these companies do not actually lead to any additional consumption, from a national accounting perspective.

Even if internet services are paid for, there are many services that are a fixed price model. Many communication costs these days (telephone or internet) are fixed rate and are therefore not dependent on use. Streaming services of music or series also charges a fixed price per month. These fixed costs are recorded in the national accounts, but provide no insight into use. One month you might not use the

BOX 8.2   **(cont.)**

streaming service at all while the next month you might binge-watch your favourite series. In other words, the consumption transaction might not really reflect the use of the service. It also raises questions about the appropriate price index.

Redundancy/radical change. As a result of internet services a number of products have become redundant. Who buys encyclopaedias anymore? Other markets, such as music and films, have totally changed their business models from physical CD sales or VHS rentals to digital streaming services. Businesses such as newspapers are still trying to find ways of changing their paper-based products into web-based business models.

Sharing economy. The internet allows consumers to cooperate far more easily. Selling your secondhand stuff or sharing tools has become much easier because of the internet. This means that utility can be created by the sales or free delivery of goods between people. These are flows which are not captured in the current SNA consumption.

Consumers as producers. The internet also makes it far easier for households to become producers. Airbnb means that households can now supply accommodation services and Uber allows individuals to offer taxi services. In future, households might actually start to produce goods which are used at home. It is often speculated that 3D printing will provide opportunities for people to create various products that would otherwise be produced by the market. This would again create a problem for national accountants because they would have to estimate this production process (inputs and outputs).

durable products. Ideally information about the quality characteristics of the commodities are also part of the products. However, all this data does not equate to a measure of the "value" to the consumer. To add all the various components to see whether households are better off from one year to the next requires a quality assessment approach, which is discussed in Chapter 10.

NETWORKS: NEW PERSPECTIVE ON THE ECONOMY

There is increasing interest in looking at economies as networks. The availability of global input–output tables, which has been described in a previous section, has enhanced research into the global network of production. The financial crisis has also shown that the financial interdependencies between sectors can lead to a domino effect with grave consequences.

Is the input–output table the only way in which the SNA deals with networks? The word "network" is actually only used three times in the entire SNA 2008, yet the SNA alludes to network thinking quite a few times. Take for example the definition of non-produced assets such as goodwill and marketing assets respectively:

> Potential purchasers of an enterprise are often prepared to pay a premium above the net value of its individually identified and valued assets and liabilities. This excess is described as "goodwill" and reflects the value of corporate structures and the value to the business of an assembled workforce and management, corporate culture, distribution networks and customer base. It may not have value in isolation from other assets, but it enhances the value of those other assets. Looked at another way, it is the addition to the value of individual assets because they are used in combination with each other.

> Marketing assets include brand names, mastheads, trademarks, logos and domain names.[31]

Many of these terms used are linked to a company's networks: "Customer base", "brand names", "customer loyalty". On the other side there are references to network relationships with other firms. For example, "distribution network" is indicative of the relationships with logistical and retail firms, while assembled workforce and corporate culture refers to the relationships with workers. In fact, CEOs will often stress that the relationships with customers, employees and other companies are the most important assets they have. Metrics are used quite frequently to measure the name recognition and customer loyalty of a brand or company because this is important for current and future sales.

Seen from this perspective it seems a bit odd that these capital stocks are defined as "non-produced assets" in the SNA. "Non-produced" implies that there is no production process which creates these capital stocks, yet advertising is seen as production by the SNA. Clearly, companies spend a lot of money on advertising but this is recorded as intermediate inputs rather than capital formation. It does not take a lot of imagination to think of this as an investment in a company's goodwill or brand. In fact the SNA itself makes this point:

> Marketing is a key driver of brand value and big corporations invest heavily in building and supporting their brands by advertising, sponsorship and other measures to build a positive image with customers. The SNA treats marketing assets as being non-produced and the expenditures incurred in their creation as intermediate consumption. They appear in the balance sheet only when they are sold. The major reason for not treating marketing assets as fixed assets is due to the difficulty of measuring their value.[32]

The reason for this decision is therefore pragmatic rather than conceptual. Economists have been working on developing the methods to estimate "intangibles", which is a related topic. Corrado et al. (2009) created a method to estimate four categories of intangible assets. The first two are computerised information (software) and innovative property (scientific and unscientific R&D). Then there is a category called "economic competencies", which has an internal and external component. The external (brand equity) is similar to the goodwill/marketing assets: "spending on strategic planning, spending on redesigning or reconfiguring existing products in existing markets, investments to retain or gain market share, and investments in brand names". The internal part of the economic competencies is the firm-specific resources which include training and management costs.

The European Commission has even started a project called SPINTAN, which has collected this data for all EU countries.

One other line of thinking is the "network as a business model". In some cases companies actually "own" networks. Social media platforms such as Facebook, Twitter or LinkedIn are owned by these companies. In this case the software that is used is definitely an asset to the company but the value of the companies is primarily dependent on the network of active users. The number of users, the amount of time they spend and the content which they add are the most important fact is in the valuation of these companies.[33]

There are many other ways in which networks are studied in economics.[34] Even in the global financial crisis of 2008/2009 network thinking played an important role. It was the risk of "contagion" or the "domino effect" between financial institutes which was named when justifying the capital injections by governments in banks that were "too big to fail". On the other side of the argument were also people who think that the relationship between Wall Street and politicians is too cosy, thereby leading to soft rules on bonuses and bailouts.[35]

These are just a few of the applications of network thinking in economics.[36] In many cases the SNA cannot provide information which would be useful for this analysis. An important challenge for the SGNA will be to look at the issue of networks and to provide more relevant data. The issue of networks is also related to the issue of inequality, and the power structures within networks. This is discussed further in Chapter 9.

LIMITS: THE CASE FOR NON-MONETARY DATA

The main dimensions of the GECA economic accounting system are consumption, production and investment/capital stocks. These are equivalent accounts to the SNA system, except that it is argued that the basis of these accounts should be the non-monetary units. The GECA, however, adds a new type of data which is not known in the SNA: limits.

It is easier to formulate limits to the economic system using non-monetary units. There does not seem to be a boundary to the amount of money that can be spent on food, haircuts or cars except one: consumption is limited by income, savings and the maximum amount one can borrow. But this is only a temporary budget restriction. Given that most economic theorising is done on monetary data (or only looks at the growth in volumes), it is not surprising that few economists have dwelt on the limits of an economy.

Yet when a non-monetary perspective of the economy is taken there are many limits. Take, for example, technology. A coal-bedded blast furnace uses coal and iron ore or a little bit of scrap metal but it is limited in its capacity. It is technologically impossible to start using electricity instead of coal and 100 per cent recycled scrap metal instead of iron ore.

This is also related to the issue of complementarities of inputs. Berndt and Wood (1979) investigate energy–capital relationships. In the case of labourers' interaction with machines, the co-dependencies are called capital–skill complementarities. Simply put, if a production process has computers you will need computer-literate employees to operate them.[37] Similarly, the relationships between social capital and human capital were investigated by Coleman (1988). The nature of these complementarities lie in the non-monetary terms rather than in the monetary units.

Apart from the ratio of inputs, the total production capacity might also be limited. A car factory will have a certain maximum number of cars that it can produce, as Elon Musk discovered in the case of Tesla Model 3. A computer server will be able to handle a certain number of people visiting a website. In fact, various authors argue that if Moore's law ends it will be due to thermodynamic limits. In the case of consumption there are also biological or physical thresholds. The amount of food and drink you can consume is limited by the ability of your body to digest them. The flying time from Los Angeles to New York is limited by the current aviation technology. Other limits might have to do with physical space. For example, many durable products reach saturation point in households. The demand for cars, washing machines or vacuum cleaners is not limitless. Consumption is also linked to certain phases in life. The number of nappies bought varies significantly in a lifetime. The number of Alzheimer treatments is also age-dependent.

In fact, some companies are taking into account that consumers' demand for goods has peaked. The head of sustainability of IKEA said that many familiar goods were reaching their limit: "If we look on a global basis, in the West we have probably hit 'peak stuff'. We talk about peak oil. I'd say we've hit peak red meat, peak sugar, peak stuff ... peak home furnishings."[38]

There are also limits to networks. Take, for example, company networks where there are practical or market conditions which might be restrictive. The advantage of a large network of suppliers is that you can get a good price but it is hard to maintain quality control beyond a certain limit. In the case of a monopolist, such as a supplier of rare earth metals, the network of the buyer is actually limited to one company. Similarly, the number of suppliers of airplanes or cars is not limitless. In the case of knowledge products, certain technologies are only available from certain suppliers, or by definition from only one (in the case of a patent).

These types of limits are real and have economic consequences. However, the lack of data might be the reason that such limits are rarely explored in empirical models. The SGNA should develop accounts which record these limits in non-monetary terms. Note that some limits are fixed, especially thermodynamic ones, while others are not static and may change over time. The accounts therefore need to be updated over time so that they may be used by the practitioners that model the economic systems.

FINAL THOUGHTS

Compared to the SNA, the GECA shifts attention to the global economy rather than the national economy. The GECA is also different in its use of non-monetary data and the concepts of networks and limits.

The GECA philosophy is that production, technology, innovation and consumption are understood better if non-monetary data is used in addition to monetary data.[39] Non-monetary units also offer a much better basis to model limits that may exist in an economy as well as the relationship with the environment. Basing the measurement system on a non-monetary foundation also makes it easier to use the data in modelling exercises. The availability of global input–output databases and non-monetary data has expanded rapidly in the last decade, so these accounts are currently close to becoming a reality. These global databases also provide a basis for network analysis of the economy.

The non-monetary dimensions help us understand the role which goods, services and assets play in society. These impacts are based on the quantities and characteristics of the stocks and flows. The price which is paid is not a direct measure of "value" of the product. The monetary flows which are common to the SNA (and which are also part of the GECA) are still important from a budget and transaction perspective, but the actual measurement of "value" should be left to the quality accounts.

In the 1970s a revolution took place in macroeconomic theorising by transferring "microeconomic foundations" to macroeconomic models. Welfare theoretical notions and optimisation techniques were transferred to the macro-level. Based on a foundation of non-monetary GECA data, the next generation of macro-models might introduce different micro-concepts such as networks, technology and psychological insights.[40]

9 Global Distribution Accounts (GDA)

Inequality has long been an important topic in economics. However, the last two decades have seen a surge of interest in the distribution of income and wealth in society. Symbolic is Thomas Piketty's *Capital in the Twenty-First Century*, which has become an international bestseller. The renewed interest in inequality is not surprising given developments over the last couple of decades. Figure 9.1 shows the share of the top 1 per cent of earners in the total income of the United States for the period 1913 to 2014. At the beginning of the twentieth century this share was around 20 per cent but it decreased to around 10 per cent in 1980. Subsequently, inequality returned to the 20 per cent mark quite rapidly.

The availability of inequality data has improved significantly over the last couple of decades. Many academic groups, statistical offices as well as international institutes, have improved the collection of data. Given that the SNA was revised in 1993 and 2008 one might expect this development to be reflected in the two versions of the handbook. The SNA 1993 revision process started at the end of the 1980s, and so it might seem logical that inequality was not yet on the radar. On the other hand, one might think that the SNA 2008 would have a lot to say about inequality. By then the shift in the income distribution was unmistakable.

In fact, the opposite is the case. The SNA 1993 is more ambitious in terms of inequality than the SNA 2008. The SNA 1993 includes an account called the Social Accounting Matrix (SAM). Apart from a matrix overview of the economy, the SAM also disaggregated household categories. One of the primary things that SAMs have

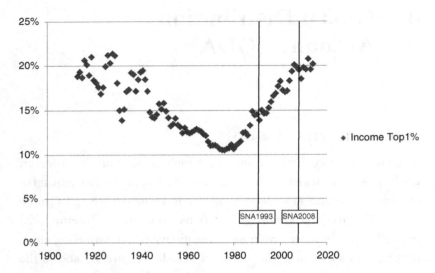

FIGURE 9.1 Share of top 1 per cent in total income (US, 1913–2014)
and timing of the SNA revisions
Source: World Inequality Database (www.wid.world)

done is to provide information about income and consumption for various household categories.

In the SNA 1993, the explanation of the SAM took up a whole chapter. The SNA 2008 could have built on this work or introduced other accounts in order to improve the understanding of inequality. In fact the opposite happened: the word "inequality" is not used in the entire SNA 2008[1] and the SAM was only discussed in the last section of chapter 28. This introduction to the SAM only includes a single paragraph on "household disaggregation" and its tone is critical. It focuses attention on the data problems and second-guesses an inequality account because it "moves beyond a rigorous accounting structure".[2]

The demotion of the SAM in the SNA 2008 is perhaps caused by the other features of this accounting matrix. The SAM was by no means perfect. It is a (overly) broad accounting matrix for the entire economy which few countries are capable (or willing) to produce on a regular basis. Given the fact that the SNA aims for global implementation, the choice to reduce attention to the SAM might have been for

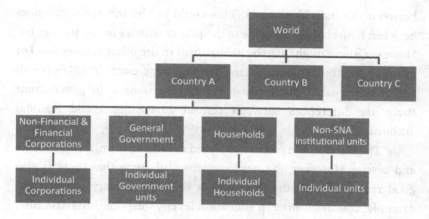

FIGURE 9.2 Multi-layered multidimensional view of global distribution

different reasons. The fact that the revision process of the SNA 2008 was completed before the financial crisis may also have been a factor. The crisis made economists and society more receptive to debates about inequality.[3]

Whatever the reason, it remains odd that the SNA 2008 hardly addresses such a crucial topic. In fact, it didn't even make it to the research agenda of the SNA.[4] Despite this missed opportunity, the interest in inequality and distributional data has only increased since the SNA 2008. It seems highly likely that a future edition of the SNA will address this topic, either in the core SNA or in a dedicated satellite account.

So what is the philosophy of the GDA? The primary feature is that it takes a multi-layered multidimensional view of global distribution. Figure 9.2 provides a representation of the structure. Given that the GDA is a global account, the first layer is inequality between nations. For example, countries are already ranked according to their GDP (in absolute terms or per capita) or financial assets.

The second layer is within a country: the distribution between institutional sectors. For example, do corporations have more financial assets than the government or the household sector? The final layer is the distribution within institutional sectors, the inequality between the individual units. This could be the income differences between households – the type of inequality which Piketty focuses on. However, there might also be inequalities in the other sectors too. For example, for the corporate sector there are differences in SMEs (small and medium-sized enterprises) and multinationals. In government there are differences between central governments and regional authorities.[5]

The distribution can be measured in monetary units (i.e. income and assets). However, the next sections will argue that there is also good reason to measure distribution of non-monetary aspects. For example, countries differ in education levels, weapons, infrastructure, generalised trust or population size.

Why should such as a broad view of distribution in society be taken? The reason is that inequalities do not appear out of thin air, they are the result of power structures in society (and what the powerful choose to do with their influence). It is therefore important to take a broad view of the global power relationships between countries, sectors and individual units. For example, since the 1980s the influence of the large corporations has increased while the role of many governments has diminished. This affects taxation, regulation and government spending, which impact on the distribution of income, wealth and non-monetary aspects in society. In order to fully understand household inequalities it is therefore important to take on board the power dynamics between countries and institutional sectors.

Note that in Figure 9.2 the first institutional sectors are from the SNA (corporations, general government and households). These are capable of holding goods and assets and taking part in economic transactions. By definition, income and wealth inequality will therefore be restricted to these sectors. So why are non-SNA sectors, which we defined in Chapter 6, included in the figure? The reason is the fact that informal groups can wield significant power in national or local communities. A protest movement, twitter network or neighbourhood watch can have significant power. For example, the "gilets jaune" protest movement (formally a non-SNA group) was able to reverse the petrol taxes of the Macron government in France in 2018. These taxes were thought to affect poorer households disproportionally and this protest therefore affected distribution in society.

Some of these non-SNA groups may evolve into formal SNA units. For example, a protest movement might end up as a political party or a twitter influencer might turn their following into a business. However, at the stage where these groups are still non-SNA units, indicators about their power can help explain societal distributions. In fact, the opposite is also true: growing inequality stimulates protest movements such as Occupy Wall Street and the "gilets jaune" to rise up against distribution in society.

THE DISTRIBUTION BETWEEN NATIONS AND INSTITUTIONAL SECTORS

Global distribution therefore starts from understanding power dynamics and inequalities between nations. For example, the size of the economy in terms of GDP and the asset wealth (including oil and other natural resources) are indications of geopolitical power. The financial interdependencies between countries, which can be seen as networks, also have geopolitical consequences. The fact that China has loaned so much money to the US makes these countries interdependent and this has an impact on their relationship.

However, there are also non-monetary factors that can be unevenly distributed and lead to different power dynamics. A country that is not rich, but nevertheless has a large population might still play an important role in geopolitics. But other non-monetary factors also play a role. North Korea is an important country geopolitically, but not because of its economy or population size. It is things like the military, specifically its nuclear threat, that makes other countries pay attention to it.

Economic relationships and trade agreements are influenced by these geopolitical power dynamics. The ability of a country to earn money from trade is therefore partially dependent on its influence in the world.[6] In some cases, such as sanctions, the income effect is even more direct. These inequalities between countries and the power dynamics underlying them are therefore part of the SGNA.

One layer deeper, there is the distribution between institutional sectors within a country. This is actually already part of the SNA, which provides monetary information in so-called sector accounts. In the SGNA, these accounts are therefore part of the distribution accounts (GDA) rather than the economic accounts. Table 9.1 shows that the sector accounts are organised around the institutional sectors of the SNA: non-financial corporations, financial corporations, general government and households.

The sector accounts include production, income generation and distribution and changes in capital and assets.[7] The production accounts are linked to the input–output tables that were discussed in Chapter 8. However, instead of industries, the data is now in institutional sectors. The balancing item of this account is Gross Domestic Product. The next account is the "generation of income", which shows which sectors create which types of income. For example, production creates wages, taxes, subsidies, depreciation of capital and mixed income.

The account for primary incomes shows which sectors receive these incomes from production. Other types of income such as property income,[8] which are not from production, are also entered into this account. The secondary distribution account shows the way in which the tax system and the system of social contributions/benefits are used to shift income from one sector to another.

The production and income accounts are so-called current accounts. In addition there are four "accumulation accounts" which record the changes in the value of assets: the capital account, the financial account, the other changes in the volume of assets account and the revaluation account. See Chapter 8 for a discussion of these items.

The SNA thus has information about the many transactions which show how income is generated, used and distributed in society.

Table 9.1 *Sector accounts*

		Non-financial corporations	Financial corporations	General government	Households
Current accounts	Production account				
	Income account (generation of income)				
	Income account (primary distribution of income)				
	Income account (secondary distribution of income)				
Accumulation accounts	Capital account				
	Financial account				
	Other changes in the volume of assets account				
	Revaluation account				

Source: Adaptation of SNA 2008 (EC at al., 2009, pp. 326–327)

The sector accounts include all types of income from production or property ownership as well as all taxes, subsidies, social contributions and benefits. In addition, it shows the changes in the value of assets, for produced capital as well as financial capital.

An overview of the ownership of assets by sectors is provided in the balance sheet of an economy. Table 9.2 shows the situation for the financial assets/liabilities and produced capital in the Netherlands, for the year 2016.[9] It reveals which sectors owned which assets at the beginning of the year.[10] In the case of the GDA, such an account would also be created although it would also have non-monetary units. For example, the cars and houses would not be measured in monetary terms (that is done in the quality accounts) but the types of car models and housing characteristics would be measured.

These tables provide ample information about the distribution on income and assets in society. However, it does not show the transfers between sectors. The network perspective needs to be brought into these accounts. The SNA itself says: "the SNA simplifies the picture it gives of the economic interrelations by not recording the 'from-whom-to-whom?' question in a fully systematic way; that is, it does not always depict the network of flows between the various types of operators".[11] In the GDA these *from-whom-to-whom?* (FWTW) tables are important.

Table 9.3 depicts such a FWTW matrix showing which flows are going from one sector to the other. It can be based on income streams, loans or other economic variables. In order to understand the dynamics of inequality it is necessary to understand the flows between the institutional sectors. The table includes the "rest of the world", which reveals the relationships of the sectors to foreign countries. The FWTW table should be expanded towards a full global account showing the relationships between all sectors in all countries.[12]

What information do Tables 9.1–9.3 provide? They show a lot about the institutional setting of a country. How "big" is the government compared to companies? What is the tax system, and what types of subsidies are paid out? What is the tax burden of the various

Table 9.2 Opening balance sheet, the Netherlands 2016 (million euros)

Asset type		Non-financial corporations sector	Financial corporations	General government	Households including NPISHs
Financial assets		1,423,395	8,277,440	243,906	2,325,310
Financial liabilities		1931176	8,351,001	529,234	830,710
Produced capital	Buildings and land	690,387	59,734	393,154	1,461,873
	Transportation equipment	50,279	271	2,727	47,809
	ICT and machines	182,184	2,003	18,333	18,026
	Oil and gas reserves	77,117		102,770	
	Intangibles		6,035	28,111	7431
	Cultivated assets and inventory	93,737			10,096
	Textiles, clothing and footwear				23,163
	Appliances and household durables				100,706

Source: Adaptation of data from Statistics Netherlands

Table 9.3 *"From-whom-to-whom?" table*

	Non-financial corporations	Financial corporations	General government	Households including NPISHs	Rest of the world
Non-financial corporations					
Financial corporations					
General government					
Households including NPISHs					
Rest of the world					
Total					

institutional units? What role does the government play in social contributions and benefits?

There is evidence that in many countries, companies have become more powerful with respect to the government. A reflection of this development is the shift in the tax burden on various sectors. The share of corporate tax in total tax revenue decreased from 30 per cent in the 1950s to under 10 per cent in 2009.[13] The taxes on households (especially employment tax, which is paid by both employers and employees) went up. Similarly the savings rates of some multinational companies have been increasing significantly. Big tech companies like Apple, Amazon, Google and Microsoft have large reserves of cash.[14]

The development which is often suggested is that powerful companies were able to reduce their tax burdens, lower certain regulatory demands and tilt the system to their advantage. The resulting profits were not automatically used to increase wages. Rather, they were paid out to shareholders. This led to increasing inequality between people who owned stock and those that did not. A second source of inequality is that the wage gap between the top earners in the firm and the lower echelons started to increase. In the 1980s, the gap between CEO salaries and average wages started to increase significantly. The underlying reason for these changes in household inequality can therefore be linked to the shift in power between the institutional sectors, government and corporations.

This power dynamics is also used in the concept of "extractive institutions", which is proposed by Acemoglu and Robinson to explain *Why Nations Fail*.[15] The idea goes that if one group is too powerful, they are able to rewrite the rules of society to their advantage. This is good for the individual group in the short run, but in the long run the society does not do as well as societies where there are countervailing powers. In the past this power struggle was between monarchs and the merchant classes. In the current setting one might argue that companies are becoming extractive institutions in the sense that they are tilting the system to their advantage. This is definitely the argument which Marianne Mazzucato makes in her book *The Value of Everything: Making and Taking the Global Economy*. She especially focuses on Big Pharma, Big Finance and Big Tech as sectors which are using their power at the expense of societal value.

Whatever side of the debate one takes on this matter, the GDA should show the distribution of income, wealth and non-monetary variables that are the end result of distributive processes in society. The GDA should also provide measures of the "power" of each sector so that scientists can analyse these dynamics. In some cases, inequality measures may at the same time reflect a variable which signals power. A sector with many assets will be able to influence the system and thereby become even richer in future. Money begets money.

THE DISTRIBUTION WITHIN NON-HOUSEHOLD SECTORS

The discussion of inequality usually focuses on the distribution of income and wealth amongst households. This topic will be covered in the next section. However, there might also be differences within other institutional sectors. For example, there is the distribution of income and wealth between the local, state and national governments. In some countries, the local or state levels are powerful, while in more centralised countries it is the federal government that has most power over taxes and government services. The GDA should therefore provide distributional data for these types of disaggregation.

Similarly, there might be inequalities in the types of companies. These may have to do with the field in which they operate. Some sectors are taxed or subsidised more heavily than others. For example, the agricultural sector in Europe and the United States receive significant subsidies. Another example is that all transportation fuels are taxed except for aviation fuel, which obviously benefits this sector.

Corporations may also differ in size. Small and medium-sized enterprises (SME) range from 1 to 200 people but there are also multinationals, which have tens of thousands or hundreds of thousands of employees worldwide. When it comes to taxation, these multinationals have a greater ability to influence their tax burden than SMEs. Multinationals are capable of reporting global profits in countries which have lower taxes. Furthermore, they are capable of negotiating a special tax status with national and state governments because of the economic and employment benefits which they can provide. An SME is less likely to use tax havens or to negotiate special taxation rules. In the SGNA, it is therefore proposed that inequalities within institutional sectors are also dealt with.

As a basis for these types of inequality measures, it would be good to look at the efforts that are being made to disaggregate the data in input–output tables. The OECD has created an expert group to look at this disaggregation.[16] The regular input–output tables typically provide data for a couple of dozen industries, but there may be large differences within an industry. For example, exporting companies might have a very different technology to companies that cater to the domestic market.[17] Therefore, the OECD ICIO database has introduced heterogeneity for China and Mexico by distinguishing the "processing" exporting companies from the non-processing firms in the input–output tables.[18]

This type of work should be expanded to reflect differences in the size and other characteristics of companies. A full account of the subsidies and taxes should be given as well as the ownership of assets. The issue of taxation also has a lot to do with globalisation. The underlying reason for low taxation of the aviation sector, large multinationals or other globally operating countries is that globalisation gives these companies leverage over national governments. Given that they operate in a global environment, they are capable of cutting the best deal possible.[19]

THE DISTRIBUTION BETWEEN HOUSEHOLDS

Despite the fact that the SNA 2008 hardly covered inequality, the topic of distribution between individuals and households has not disappeared. Most studies, such as the one by Piketty, are based on microdata such as tax records or surveys of individuals. A couple of academic groups are creating databases for a selection of countries of the world. Recently the World Inequality Database (WID) was launched, and is supported by many of the leading inequality researchers.[20] This database provides long-term income and wealth inequality statistics for fifty-eight countries sometimes back to 1891.

Branko Milanovic is responsible for the "All the Gini's" (ALG) database, which covers the period 1950–2015 and includes 166 countries. In total the ALG database has over five thousand Gini values from nationally representative household surveys. In addition to an income database, the Global Consumption and Income Project (GCIP) also produces data for consumption from the 1960s onwards for around 160 countries.

However, microdata can sometimes be inconsistent with the data from the macroeconomic accounts. There can be a couple of methodological and practical differences. One of the main practical problems is that the national accounting data does not correspond to the totals from the microdata. Therefore adjustments are needed. For example, Piketty produced US national income series from 1913 which were aligned with the national accounts totals.[21]

Certain groups have been set up to investigate these issues and they also look at approaches to combine the micro- and macro-data. The two most important groups are the Expert Group on Disparities in National Accounts (EGDNA) and the Distributional National Accounts (DINA) which is done in the context of the World Inequality Database.[22]

The EGDNA and DINA projects have some distinct approaches which have been systematically worked through by Zwijnenburg (2017), who concluded that: "whereas both the EGDNA and the DINA project aim to compile distributional results in line with national accounts aggregates, they may end up with significantly different results, due to differences in scope, the use of different concepts in measuring inequality, and possible deviations in methodology to arrive at the distributional results".

There are basically two methodological issues: the DINA project concentrates on the individual while the EGDNA focuses on the household. Second, the definitions of income differ significantly, with the EGDNA adopting a strict national accounting concept while the DINA approach has a much broader definition of income. For example, in the SNA "holding gains and losses" is not counted as income.

However, inequalities in income and assets are just part of the story.[23] People that are struggling financially are usually "poor" in other (non-monetary) domains as well. One of the most successful initiatives which looks at poverty from a broad perspective is the Multidimensional Poverty Index (MPI). The MPI, which is used in the UN Human Development Report, looks at several factors: Education (years of schooling, child school attendance), Health (child mortality, nutrition) and Living standards (electricity, improved sanitation, drinking water, flooring, cooking, fuel, asset ownership).[24] Contrary to monetary information, data in other areas such as education and health is less prevalent. The situation is, however, improving. For example, the Better Life Index of the OECD publishes data on health, education, gender and regional differences.

The SGNA is a full accounting framework which includes all aspects of life including time use, health,[25] education and social networks. Quite often these non-monetary phenomena have important impacts on well-being, but also on income and wealth. For example, the current differences in educational attainment are signals of future inequality because higher education levels generally lead to higher incomes. Networks also provide advantages in the labour market. People have widely differing social and professional networks and understanding these inequalities is vital to understand their economic performance and their well-being.

Note that not all inequality is favourable to the rich. Aguiar and Hurst (2007) found that there is a growing inequality in leisure time that is the mirror image of the growing inequality in wages and expenditures. In other words, as income and education increased, leisure time decreased. There are also large differences in time use for females and males, as we have seen in Chapter 7.

ENVIRONMENTAL IMPACT OF INEQUALITY

Inequality in consumption also leads to differences in environmental impacts. Richer household and individuals buy more products and their environmental footprint generally rises with income. The top 10 per cent global income earners are responsible for 36 per cent of the current carbon footprint of households.[26] The advantage of the SGNA is that it becomes possible to link the global input–output table (in the GECA) to the GDA accounts to calculate footprints which are specific to certain demographic groups.

To analyse the influence of consumption patterns it is possible to use the regular demographic breakdowns which are employed in inequality statistics. This might be done by splitting the population into income deciles. However, these results are generally fairly predictable: richer households have a higher footprint than poorer households. It therefore becomes interesting to look at different ways of disaggregating demographically. For example, Druckman and Jackson (2009) analyse the CO_2 emission per socioeconomic group for the UK. They split the population into a number of "super-groups" to which they give names such as "Blue collar communities", "City living", "Countryside prospering", "Suburbs", "Constrained by circumstances", "Typical traits" and "Multicultural". In another study, Baiocchi et al. (2010) link CO_2 emissions to seventeen lifestyle categories. They find that across lifestyle groups, CO_2 emissions can vary by a factor of between two and three. They conclude that the carbon footprint increases with income and decreases with education.

This type of data is also important because it allows us to analyse what would happen if global inequality was reduced. For example, what would happen if the poorest parts of the world were to achieve a slightly higher income level? Hubacek et al. (2017) finds that raising the income level from \$1.97 to \$2.97 already has a huge impact on CO_2 emissions. They conclude that "the discourse should address income distribution and the carbon intensity of lifestyles".[27]

FINAL THOUGHTS

This has been a brief chapter on the structure of the GDA. The SNA already has a lot of information that is highly relevant to understanding the determinants of household and individual inequality. These accounts will be used in the GDA. This chapter has argued that breaking up the sectors into subcomponents is important and not just for households. There can be significant inequalities between the various branches of government or corporations. For example, the onset of globalisation has meant that the tax burden on multinationals and on SMEs have developed differently.

This chapter has also explored the relationships between units from a network perspective through "from-whom-to-whom?" tables, and has stressed the importance of the power structures of society. It is the power dynamics between various countries, groups and individuals which ultimately lead to distribution in society.

This chapter has shown that there is currently ample data on income and wealth inequality. There are also groups looking at the differences between the microdata and the national accounting concepts. Data on non-monetary characteristics such as health, education and social networks is much less prevalent but is also an important component of the GDA. The data availability of these phenomena differs from country to country, depending on the statistical sources that are available. The availability of this type of data is imporving rapidly.

10 Global Quality Accounts (GQA) and Quality Indicators

The previous four chapters discussed the "system accounts" of the SGNA. They showed accounting frameworks for the environment, society and economy as well as distribution. For each of these accounts, the concepts of stocks and flows, networks and limits are useful building blocks which are applicable to each of these systems. The system accounts record the status of the systems and how they are developing over time. However, these accounts do not answer an important question: "Are things getting better or worse?" To answer this question, a quality assessment approach is needed: you need to have criteria which can evaluate whether a situation or development is good. The quality assessment approach would be based on the data from the system accounts (GENA, GSA, GECA and GDA).

This chapter will make the case that there are actually many quality assessment methods across scientific disciplines. In mainstream economics, theories such as welfare economics and the capital approach are dominant. However, there are many more ways of assessing the quality of the systems. They may for example be from other schools of thought in economics ("heterodox economics") such as happiness economics, behavioural economics or other social sciences like sociology or hedonic psychology. They may also be based on thermodynamic foundations or inspired by the assessment of complex systems, networks or limits.

The modular nature of the SGNA allows the system accounts to be linked to multiple quality assessment methods. Welfare economics and the capital approach are just two of the approaches that may be adopted, but they are not the only ones. Some argue that these mainstream economics approaches, which express developments in monetary terms, would be rejected outright. This is not the philosophy of this book. The reason to be inclusive of all quality assessment approaches is the fact that there is currently no perfect quality method and it seems plausible that this will never be the case. Each quality assessment method provides an imperfect view, which is only valid under particular restrictions and assumptions.

This chapter stresses the importance of multiple views on quality. It is not aimed at choosing "the best one" or debunking the dominant economic (or any other) theories. Different methods provide different perspectives. A multitude of imperfect perspectives provide a better picture of the situation than just looking at one imperfect approach. If a doctor only measures the temperature of their patient they might conclude that the patient is healthy, while blood pressure, MRI scan and blood test results may show that there is something seriously wrong. Used in isolation, the thermometer, sphygmomanometer, MRI scanner and blood analysis are all imperfect ways to measure the quality of a person's health but together they have a remarkable ability to diagnose disease. The underlying premise of this book is that by using mainstream economics, society is not making full use of all the instruments that exist to measure the health of our environment and society. Yet at the same time it would be foolish to discard the instruments which economists provide.

Due to the wide range of methodologies, the GQA will probably turn out to be the most contentious account of the SGNA. The system accounts are less problematic because they describe, in rather neutral terms, the functioning of the systems. On the other hand, the GQA asks a rather fundamental question about what is good and bad. Are systems deteriorating or improving? The answer to this question has profound implications for the interpretation of system developments. The question of quality might be phrased rather dramatically as quantifying "the meaning of life" or, as Herman Daly calls it, "the ultimate end".[1] Clearly there are many moral, ethical, personal and cultural dimensions to these questions. The choice of a quality assessment approach implies a choice for a worldview and will therefore provoke the most debate. To foster the multidisciplinary dialogue it is good to isolate this debate in a single account of the SGNA, the GQA.

This chapter will provide an overview of some of the ways in which quality can be assessed. We do not cover philosophical, religious or other literature which is not coupled to quantification approaches. That would not only be too daunting a task but given that in the end we want to replace GDP, it is important to look specifically at methodologies with an empirical application.

This chapter will discuss some of the benefits, assumptions, criticisms and weaknesses of each perspective. Of course, it is impossible to provide an overview of all the scientific literature behind each of these approaches. The chapter is aimed simply at showing that there are many ways in which to assess the quality of systems. Given the importance of welfare economics and the capital approach these are discussed at greater length. This does not imply that in the SGNA there will be a greater focus on these approaches.

In the beginning of the chapter, the quality approaches are discussed in isolation. However, in the long run, one might hope that there is cross-pollination between the various approaches. Multidisciplinary cooperation might lead to new insights about well-being and sustainability.[2] This chapter also explores this potential for cross-pollination.

The chapter ends with the million dollar question which the title of this book raises: What indicators(s) will replace GDP by 2030? Will GDP be replaced outright or will it still be useful in some way? We will discuss the indicators which might be derived from the system and quality accounts and how they provide a better basis to assess how society is doing.

WELFARE ECONOMICS

One of the foundations of modern economic thinking is neoclassical welfare theory. Every student of Econ 101 will be taught the basics of this theory. Welfare economics[3] is based on the concept of "utility", which has been central to economic thinking ever since it was first proposed by Bentham (1789):

> By utility is meant that property in any object, whereby it tends
> to produce benefit, advantage, pleasure, good, or happiness,
> (all this in the present case comes to the same thing) or (what comes
> again to the same thing) to prevent the happening of mischief,
> pain, evil, or unhappiness to the party whose interest is considered:
> if that party be the community in general, then the happiness of
> the community: if a particular individual, then the happiness
> of that individual.[4]

According to Sen (1985), later utilitarian economists such as Edgeworth Marshall, Pigou, Ramsey and Robertson can be divided into people who see utility as satisfaction/happiness (classical utilitarianism) or desire fulfilment (modern utilitarianism). However it is viewed, utility indicates something good and in an economic model it is something that one wants to maximise. If a person has more utility than before then they are in a better situation. If the utility experienced by society (the sum of the utilities experienced by the individuals in that society) increases then that society is better off.[5]

Economic models might start with the function: $U = f(C_1, C_2, C_3, \ldots C_n)$, where U is utility and $C_1, C_2, C_3, \ldots C_n$ stands for consumption of goods and services 1 to n. Theoretically, C is a broad concept which could include all goods or services, whether they are sold on the market or not. Utility can therefore be derived from products from a supermarket but also from non-market "goods and services" such as leisure time or walks in nature.

In the standard model consumers and producers are fully rational and all-knowing. The goal of consumers is to maximise utility, while producers are trying to maximise profits. This interplay in the market leads to an equilibrium price and quantity.[6] In the model, there is no explicit coordination between the producers and consumers; the market is self-organising. This is what Adam Smith calls "the invisible hand". If a consumer buys a product at a price which is lower than they are willing to pay, this is called the consumer surplus. For this, and other reasons, the monetary value of consumption in the SNA is not a reflection of utility.[7]

But what about the "consumption" of goods and services for which there is no market? Economists have been prolific in finding ways to value these "externalities" in terms of money.[8] Especially the field of environmental economics has provided many ways in which to value the "services" provided by the environment. Methods to estimate the value of these services have names like the travel cost method, contingent valuation method, etc. Some methods are based on "revealed preferences", where market transactions expose the value of a non-market good. For example, houses close to a park will fetch a premium, which is an expression of the added value of this facility. There are also "stated preference" approaches where respondents are asked to put a price on certain non-market services. The willingness-to-pay or willingness-to-accept (in the case of an environmental disamenity) are commonly used to assess environmental services.[9] One of the most famous (and debated) valuation studies was by Costanza and colleagues in 1997, when they estimated that the global ecosystem services amounted to $33,000,000,000,000 per year.[10]

Welfare economics and the role of supply and demand in price formation are at the core of economic thinking. This has endured for over a century and has guided policy making. It has led to useful decision tools such as cost–benefit analysis. Welfare theory can provide guidance on efficient market solutions for important environmental and social problems. One of the most enduring policy recommendations from welfare economics is that a price should be put on environmental externalities because the market will lead to an efficient solution.

However, all quality assessment methods are subject to assumptions and limitations. Without the pretence of being comprehensive, the next couple of paragraphs will cover some of them. First, there is the issue of the concepts of utility and consumption. What exactly is utility? As Amartya Sen says: "Mathematical exactness of formulation has proceeded hand in hand with remarkable inexactness of content."[11] Although many authors have philosophised about the nature of utility, the term remains quite abstract. Similarly, the concept of consumption is perhaps not as straightforward as one might expect (see Chapter 8). When are a car, a theatre ticket and life insurance "consumed"? What psychological effects do these commodities have? What role do they play in our lives?

The second point is that while methods have been created for many non-market goods and services, there are also many for which no methodology exists. The situation is especially dire in the social domain. For good reason, economists have not chosen to put a price on the "services" provided by your friends, neighbours and loved ones. Few would argue that this is a fruitful way to uncover the "value" of these relationships.[12] Even when methods exist in the social domain, they may be quite controversial. For example, economists can calculate the "value-of-life" which is lost due to premature mortality (e.g. due to pollution). However, since value-of-life calculations are based on income levels, it raises ethical concerns. Is a life in a poor country "worth" less than a life in a rich country?

Probably the most criticised part of this theory is the concept of rational perfectly informed consumers and producers which, facilitated by a perfect market (with an infinite amount of producers and consumers), are pursuing their own selfish goals (utility and profit maximisation). This representation of humans is sometimes referred to as *Homo economicus*. The motivation of humans is thus translated into a desire to obtain as much utility as possible. This theory does not hypothesise "Why" humans act this way; it simply describes "How" the behaviour can be represented mathematically. As such it reduces the "meaning of life" to a simple mechanism.

Thaler (2000), a Nobel Prize winning behavioural economist, states that this is the difference between "Econs" rather than "Humans". Later sections in this chapter will discuss other insights about human behaviour and feelings. The criticism of

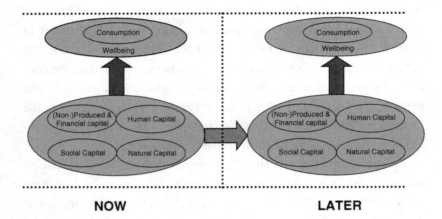

FIGURE 10.1 The capital approach
Source: Adapted from the CES recommendations (UNECE et al., 2014)

homo economicus is sometimes a bit of a strawman argument: welfare economists have created alternative models in which many of the assumptions of the standard model are relaxed.[13] Nevertheless, however complex the models become, the underlying foundation is the rather vague notion of utility and the idea that it should be maximised.[14]

THE CAPITAL APPROACH

The capital approach provides an intertemporal dimension to quality assessment. Underlying this methodology is the idea that society has the following resource types: (non-)produced and financial capital, natural capital, human capital and social capital.[15] Figure 10.1 shows these assets are needed to generate consumption and the broader notion of well-being, now and in the future.[16] The link to long-term sustainability is obvious. To ensure that future generations ("later") can achieve the same amount of well-being, the current generation ("now") should leave enough capital behind. The Stiglitz Report/CES recommendations use this extended capital approach for their frameworks.

Some of these assets are already recorded in the SNA (see Table 8.1) but the scope is limited to produced and financial capital as well as some non-produced assets such as natural resources. The SNA 2008 admits that putting a monetary value on these stocks of capital is "not a straightforward process".[17]

The estimation of the financial capital might seem the easiest. Cash, publicly traded stocks and bonds are quite easy because there are market prices which can be attached. But what about shares in non-listed companies or some of the complex financial products that exist nowadays? Some financial products are related to risks which involve complex probability calculations that might change from day to day. As any valuation expert will tell you, putting a price on these companies is not an easy task and includes many assumptions.

Produced capital refers to assets such as machines and buildings. If there are perfect second-hand markets these prices could be used to value the total assets. For example, cars have fairly good second-hand markets with which to estimate the total value of all cars. If there are market prices for new machines, but a small market for second-hand, then the Perpetual Inventory Method (PIM) can be used. In this approach, assumptions are made about the loss of value of the machine over time.[18] Another approach, the Net Present Valuation (NPV) method, quantifies the value of an asset by determining future earnings.[19] It is therefore necessary to make assumptions about how long the capital stock will survive and whether its ability to produce diminishes. The final step in valuation is to transfer all the benefits (in monetary values) to a common value by using an appropriate discount rate.[20] These approaches are explained in the OECD manual *Measuring Capital*.[21]

However, the resources of society are far broader than just financial capital, machines and buildings. The valuation of human capital has a long tradition which started with Schulz and Becker's work on education in the early 1960s.[22] These publications stressed the fact that education is an investment with a rate of return. Kendrick (1976) uses the so-called cost approach, which focused on all the investments in education, including the amount of money and time that went into childrearing. Jorgenson and Fraumeni (1989, 1992) use the so-called lifetime income approach, which is similar to the NPV method, to estimate the discounted value of all future streams of income to the present.[23]

The lifetime income approach has received the most traction in international harmonisation processes. The OECD stimulated the calculation of these human capital estimates for sixteen countries.[24] The World Bank also used this approach during the latest publication of the wealth of nations report.[25] However, these approaches take a rather narrow view of the "benefits" by only considering the incomes that are earned. As a direct result, the human capital of a retiree is automatically zero. The OECD manual stresses the importance of "non-economic" effects of human capital but there are few attempts to quantify them.

For natural capital, methods to estimate natural resources, which are owned, exist in the SNA and SEEA. To assess the value of a reserve of natural resources one needs to define an extraction rate, the cost and the benefit towards the future and then use an appropriate discount rate. However, how well equipped are scientists to predict the future price of natural resources? Despite this problem, these are the easiest of valuations for natural capital because the resources are traded on a market. But what is the value of clean air, an unchanged climate or a healthy ecosystem? Methods do not exist to measure the stocks, so efforts have concentrated on estimating *flows* of "services" using welfare economics.

Social capital is probably the most elusive asset type. In fact, there is little agreement in the literature on what social capital actually is and what "benefits" it provides. Defining the benefits would be a first step towards monetisation.[26] A stream of benefits would then have to be extrapolated to the future and then discounted. However, what is the value of the spouse, children or group of friends and what "services" do they provide? Put more broadly, what is the value of social cohesion, institutions and the networks in society? It is not hard to understand why this type of valuation is beyond the capital approach. Even if methods could be created, it is unlikely that these approaches would be in synch with what society sees as the "meaning of life".

An important point of criticism of the capital approach is theoretical: are capital stocks substitutable? When the capital approach is used for sustainability it is said that the total stock of capital should increase or stay constant over time, which implies that capital stocks are substitutable. In other words, if future generations have less natural capital then that could be compensated by more roads, machines and a better education. This is known as "weak sustainability", which is an assumption that has been criticised frequently.[27] One of the points of contention is "Critical" natural capital, which refers to environmental stocks that cannot be drawn down beyond a certain limit. This implies that the strong sustainability criterion should be adopted, i.e. there is a limit to substitutability of capital stocks.

Thus, overall, there are practical and conceptual problems associated with the capital approach. On the conceptual side the issue of the appropriate discount rates and weak/strong sustainability are important. On the practical side, I have argued that many capital stocks do not even have a method to calculate them (social capital, non-resource natural capital, marketing assets in the SNA), partial methods (human capital) or need significant assumptions (economic capital and natural resources).

Still, the capital approach provides useful information about the potential level of production in future. This is a useful measure for international comparison of economies. Taking the capital stock as a measure of sustainability is however debatable. Estimating the well-being benefits of the capital stocks is difficult enough, but projecting them towards the future and discounting them appropriately is even more daunting.[28] Add to this the issues of imperfect substitution and natural thresholds and it becomes even more problematic. The bottom line is that the capital approach might be used to say something about future income-potential but care should be taken when relating it to sustainability of well-being in a broader sense.[29]

THE CAPABILITY APPROACH

The above two methodologies are from mainstream economic thinking. They have proven to be useful, but are subject to a certain number of limitations and assumptions. There are also other economists who have suggested alternative ways of looking at the quality of people's lives. One of the most influential voices is Nobel Prize winner Amartya Sen, who created the "capability approach". In this framework, Sen (1985) is careful to identify the characteristics of a product which has objective physical properties. Sen also distinguishes the person who is using the good or service. For example, a movie is objectively the same but can be appreciated entirely differently by two people.

When a person goes to a movie or buys some other good or service, this is the *functioning* of a person. It is what actually happens and to measure it you simply need to observe this behaviour. Sen argues that looking only at functionings you are missing part of the story. He argues that it is more important to analyse what possibilities, or *capabilities*, a person has. Which possibilities are available to them? Is that person even capable of going to a movie? Do they have access to education or healthcare? A person with more choice, more freedom to choose between various options, should be considered to have greater well-being. The *potential* to live a life which one chooses is more important than assessing the actual life that someone leads.

Sen's book, *Development as Freedom*, exemplified the centrality of freedom to his thinking.[30] The capabilities approach is often admired for its philosophical analysis of utility, but it is also criticised for being hard to put into practice. Some authors have managed to provide practical application of the capability approach.[31] Most importantly, Sen's theory contributed to the creation of the Human Development Index (HDI). The HDI is a simple measure which combined health, education and GDP into a single indicator and is probably one of the best-known alternatives to GDP.[32] However, it does not do justice to the underlying philosophical framework of the capability approach.

The capability approach is particularly relevant in areas where people have few opportunities. This is why it is a popular notion in development studies because access to health, food, water and shelter is often deficient. If a population is deprived of these most basic capabilities, this is the main challenge faced by that society.

LIFE EVALUATION

Subjective well-being survey questions which elicit evaluations of a person's life situation are also examples of a quality assessment method. This self-reported well-being has already been discussed in Chapters 3 and 4. The field of happiness economics has uncovered some of the most important "drivers" of SWB. Many articles have been published which have greatly enhanced our understanding of what makes people satisfied or happy with their lives. This can be done by making comparisons between countries or looking at the microdata of individuals. The results show that poor health, separation, unemployment and lack of social contact are all strongly negatively associated with SWB.[33] However, there is contradictory evidence, potentially unobserved variables and the issue of the direction of causality. The last point is one of the main challenges in this type of research. For example, health is positively correlated to SWB, but is this because health makes people happy or happier people are healthier, or are they mutually reinforcing?

This research has provided many insights but has also provoked criticism. One of the points raised is that it is hard to formulate appropriate policies.[34] On top of that, country-level life satisfaction scores in the developed world remain fairly stable over time, so policies may affect certain subgroups, but the overall measure is fairly constant.

Life evaluations have also been criticised from a measurement perspective. Evaluating your entire life in a single digit is not an easy task for a respondent. The field of hedonic psychology[35] has looked at the underlying physiological processes that occur when answering these types of question. The OECD Handbook on Subjective

Well-being identifies more than a dozen biases.[36] Responses may be dependent on the wording of questions, scales or mood of the respondent. The order of the questions can also be of influence. Consider the following two questions: "How satisfied are you with your life?" and "Did you have a date this month?" Researchers have found that the order of these questions has a significant impact on the life satisfaction response.[37] Priming a respondent with the "date question" influences the way in which they asses their life satisfaction. Nevertheless, if attention is paid to these biases, the results are still considered robust.[38]

AFFECT EVALUATION

While the life evaluation approach asks respondents to assess their life over a longer period, other approaches measure the emotional state (or affect) of people at all various moments in time. In this approach, well-being is the result of the feelings experienced during a twenty-four-hour cycle.

The context of this theoretical apparatus is that psychological insights have had an increasing influence on economics over the last couple of decades. An influential milestone in this development was when Kahneman and Tversky proposed "prospect theory" in the late 1970s. This theory was based on human experiments which showed that people are more averse to a loss than they are to an equal gain. This directly contradicted welfare economics, which assumed that utility was the same for an equivalent increase or decrease.[39]

These psychological insights provided novel perspectives on the underlying assumptions of welfare theory and *homo economicus*. For example, the issue of altruism is one of the areas in which mainstream welfare economics does not excel.[40] Even the classic "prisoner's dilemma" has been questioned. In a creative paper, Khadjavi and Lange (2013) found that real prisoners did in fact cooperate despite the fact that the game-theoretical result would suggest that they would choose not to.

The combination of psychology and economics has blossomed into the field of behavioural economics, which has now become an important, one might even say mainstream, field in economics. The last few years have seen several Nobel Prize winners from this field: Kahnemann, Shiller and Thaler. It has deepened the understanding of the motivations, behaviour and importance of subconscious processes and biases.[41] The Wikipedia page of cognitive biases has literally dozens of ways in which the human mind is biased in decision-making processes. Knowledge of these biases has also helped to shape policies.[42] For example, Richard Thaler has written about how to "nudge" people towards desirable behaviour.[43]

Kahneman (1999) advocated that the sum over time of affect (momentary experienced happiness) should be a measure of individual welfare.[44] The combination of time-use and well-being measurement is evident in the "national time-use accounts".[45] Table 10.1 shows an example of such an account.[46]

The first three columns show the subjective affect of a person in three dimensions: positive affect, negative affect and feelings of competency. The fourth column shows the amount of time the activity takes and the fifth is a reflection of the number of people reporting a certain activity.[47] Many of the results feel intuitively plausible. "Intimate relations" seems like a logical number one (looking at "positive affect") and commuting and working are reasonably placed at the bottom of the list. But interestingly, the emotions associated with work are more complex. It scores poorly on the scale of positive/negative but when it comes to feelings of "competence" it scores relatively high. This confirms that well-being is a rather complex and multidimensional issue.

Table 10.1 also makes clear that social networks are influential.[48] The most positive affect comes from spending time with friends and loved ones;[49] so the social capital that is involved in the activities is important for the overall well-being.[50] However, this is not always the case. "Taking care of my children" scores quite low in terms of the positive affect. This might be surprising to some because the parent–child relationship is one of the closest bonds which humans have. Yet at the same time many parents will not be overly surprised

Table 10.1 *Well-being per activity*

Activities	Mean affect rating			Mean hours/ day	Proportion of sample reporting
	Positive	Negative	Competent		
Intimate relations	5.10	0.36	4.57	0.2	0.11
Socialising	4.59	0.57	4.32	2.3	0.65
Relaxing	4.42	0.51	4.05	2.2	0.77
Pray/worship/ meditate	4.35	0.59	4.45	0.4	0.23
Eating	4.34	0.59	4.12	2.2	0.94
Exercising	4.31	0.50	4.26	0.2	0.16
Watching TV	4.19	0.58	3.95	2.2	0.75
Shopping	3.95	0.74	4.26	0.4	0.30
Preparing food	3.93	0.69	4.20	1.1	0.62
On the phone	3.92	0.85	4.35	2.5	0.61
Napping	3.87	0.60	3.26	0.9	0.43
Taking care of my children	3.86	0.91	4.19	1.1	0.36
Computer/ email/internet	3.81	0.80	4.57	1.9	0.47
Housework	3.73	0.77	4.23	1.1	0.49
Working	3.62	0.97	4.45	6.9	1.00
Commuting	3.45	0.89	4.09	1.6	0.87

Source: Kahneman et al. (2004)

by this result. The actual day-to-day toil of taking care of kids is not all fun. Despite the fact that short-term happiness is not necessarily positive, many people experience long-term feelings of life fulfilment because of their children.[51] Again, this shows the complexity of well-being as a multidimensional phenomenon.

The problem with this line of research is that it is expensive and is therefore rarely applied. The surveys are difficult to fill in and therefore expensive. Some methods have been developed which make the measurement cheaper and less intrusive for respondents. However, it is likely that this approach will only become viable at the global scale if new technologies are adopted. Chapter 11 will discuss some ways in which technology might make this type of data more cost-effective to collect.

PHYSIOLOGICAL MEASUREMENT

Camerer et al. (2005) state that "The foundations of economic theory were constructed assuming that details about the functioning of the brain's black box would not be known." It has long been thought that getting to grips with the thoughts and feelings of people is only observable in indirect ways. The welfare economic strategy is to analyse the choices that people make and assume that this is a reflection of their preferences. Life satisfaction and affect evaluation ask for self-evaluations of respondents. However, as Camerer and colleagues point out, "the study of the brain and nervous system is beginning to allow direct measurement of thoughts and feelings".

"Neuroeconomics" uses techniques from neuroscience, cognitive and social psychology to analyse well-being and decision making. It uses the physical responses of the human body to assess changes in well-being.[52] This might be in the blood, brain or facial expressions. For example, Rutledge et al. (2014) confirm that MRI readings provide consistent conclusions to self-reported evaluations of well-being. Neuroscience is capable of analysing addiction, cooperation and affect and sheds light on current economic theories and may lead to new ones.

These are developments that one needs to keep in mind when thinking of the quality assessment methods which will be used in 2030. Already watches are capable of measuring heart rates and sleep patterns and the number of options to measure people's bodily functions in real time will be much greater by 2030. If these health measurements are related to well-being concepts, this will have a significant impact on our understanding of well-being.

THERMODYNAMIC/ECOLOGICAL APPROACHES

So far the methods in this chapter have been anthropocentric: they provide a human perspective on well-being. There are however also non-anthropocentric methods to assess quality. Not surprisingly, these approaches are most prevalent in the field of environmental systems, but in some cases these approaches are also applied to society or the economy.

Thermodynamic principles are sometimes used to evaluate the quality of certain systems, which could be ecosystems, economies, a production process, etc. This has led to thermodynamic concepts such as entropy and exergy, which signify the energetic wastefulness of systems. Exergy, for example, measures when work potential is lost in the system. The quality of the system is better if this loss is reduced.[53]

Energetic analysis is not just important for ecosystems and technological systems. Some authors argue that it is also fundamental when trying to understand economic growth. Traditional growth theories stress technology and institutions while Robert Ayres and co-authors propose that growth has literally been "fuelled" by the availability of cheap fossil fuels.[54]

Energy can also be used as a basis to assess the stocks of the fossil fuels using an indicator called the energy return on investment (EROI). The EROI quantifies the energy needed to extract energy and so is partially determined by the current technological capabilities.[55] As the quality of the remaining fossil fuels diminishes and the difficulty in mining grows, the EROI drops. Technological advances might, however, increase the EROI.

The biological ability to convert energy from the sun into plant biomass is known as primary production. The gross primary production is the total energy produced, but some of this is used for plant restoration and maintenance. Subtracting this, the remaining fixed energy (in mass units) is net primary production (NPP). This idea of quality is of course biased towards plant life, but an indicator has been created to identify the influence of humans (Human Appropriation of Net Primary Production (HANPP).[56]

There are also biological quality assessment approaches. For example, it is suggested that proxy species may be used to signal the quality of an entire ecosystem. A specific species provides the best indication of whether an ecosystem is doing well. For example, the farmland bird index was a measure for Eurostat's Sustainable Development Indicators set.

APPROACHES BASED ON NETWORKS AND LIMITS/BENCHMARKS

Two of the accounting building blocks of the SGNA framework are networks and limits. These concepts frame the environment, society and the economy as complex systems with many network connections. The systems perspective brings other quality assessment methods into play. If systems are viewed as networks, the quality is not equal to the sum of the individual components but rather how well the whole system functions. Taking a car as an example, if one crucial part of 1,000 engine components is not functioning, it is not correct to say that the car is working well because, on average, the components are working. Despite that fact that 999 parts of the car are functioning fine, the conclusion would be that the car, as a system (or network of components), is not functioning well. This type of reasoning also leads to notions such as "resilience",[57] which indicate the ability of a system to recover from an external shock.[58] "Adaptability" is a related term which shows the ability of the system to find a new equilibrium.

The idea of limits or thresholds plays an important role in the complex system dynamics because they indicate a boundary for the system or a point at which the system changes from one state to another. However, the concept of limits can be used in various ways. For example, a simple but effective way to measure the remaining amount of non-renewable assets such as oil reserves is to calculate the asset life. The SEEA Central Framework uses this indicator, which is defined as follows: "The asset life (or resource life) is the expected time over which an asset can be used in production or the expected time over which extraction from a natural resource can take place."[59]

Probably the most famous quality assessment measurement which is limits-based is the ecological footprint (EF).[60] The EF translates human behaviour into land area and so is capable of comparing that to the total land area on Earth. The indicator is capable of showing that society is using "more Earth" than is currently available. This allows calculation of the "overshoot day" – the day that global consumption exceeds the carrying capacity of the Earth. In 2017 this day fell on 2 August.[61]

The quality of a system can also be measured by assessing how far away it is from a certain benchmark. One such approach is called the Mean Species Abundance index, which measures the current quantity and quality and compares it to the situation before the industrial revolution.[62]

TOWARDS A MULTIDISCIPLINARY VIEW OF WELL-BEING AND SUSTAINABILITY

The previous sections have described many ways to assess the quality of environmental, societal and economic systems. While it provides a broad-brush review of methods, it is not a complete overview. The SGNA should investigate, as widely as possible, all the quality assessment criteria in the literature. Each of the generic methods also have many sub-varieties and approaches which will need to be aligned. By combining a quality assessment approach with data from the systems accounts of the SGNA, quality accounts are created.

The prime advantage of the GQA is that our perception of "quality" moves beyond welfare economics and the capital approach. The quality accounts make clear that these are just two ways to view society and the environment, but there are many more. This also raises the prospect that there will be a wider range of policy options. Economic quality assessments tend to favour market solutions such as putting a price on environmental emissions. However, other approaches might also create alternative ways of dealing with societal issues. For example, psychological approaches might help to "nudge" people towards superior outcomes. Communal arrangements which were studied by Nobel Prize winner Eleanor Ostrom might help us understand how societies come to non-market institutions to resolve social and environmental problems.

Perhaps the most important potential of the GQA is that multidisciplinary cooperation might lead to new theories. Knowledge from one field could result in improvement in another. Or two theoretical frameworks might morph into a new methodology. It is impossible to know what type of weird and wonderful ideas might emerge, but it is interesting to explore this somewhat further in this section. What multidisciplinary research agendas might emerge for well-being and sustainability?

Well-being

The anthropocentric quality approaches reviewed in this chapter have three fundamental ways of approaching utility: "decision utility" (welfare economics), "experienced utility" (life evaluation, affect and physiological measurement) and "potential utility" (capability approach). Each of these theories has merit and combining the insights might lead to new insights.

Let's just explore one avenue by taking a closer look at Table 10.1 from the various perspectives. Quite often the concept of utility is assumed to indicate pleasure or happiness. Looking at the activities in the table one might expect the most enjoyable episodes to be those in which the most expensive (or expensive public transport) products are used. However, the table shows that commuting is one of the least enjoyable activities, yet one of the most expensive tangible goods (cars) is involved. This confirms Kuznets's opinion that some components of consumption in the SNA should in fact be seen as intermediate inputs. We don't commute because we enjoy it, it is a necessary cost we incur (both time and money) to get to work.

On the other hand, some of activities that report highest positive affect, such as "intimate relations" or "pray/worship/meditate", require little in terms of consumption. Even some of the other categories such as relaxing or socialising can be done expensively (using a lot of consumption goods) but can also be fairly inexpensive (with a book and a cup of coffee). In short, the utility derived from consumption is not always equivalent to the "enjoyment value" of using them. This is does not mean that expensive goods and services do not provide utility in other ways but it confirms that it is important to be specific about the benefits of a product.[63]

Another interesting insight from Table 10.1 is about working. In mainstream economic models the hours spent at work usually do not contribute to utility. They are not part of consumption, but rather part of the production process. Becker (1965) explicitly modelled the trade-off between hours worked and hours spent on consumption.[64] This also indicates the rather binary philosophy of these models: every variable in the model has one role only. It is a discrete way of organising a model. In reality, Table 10.1 confirms that life is more of a "shades of grey" situation. The various activities in the table show that rather than 0 or 5, the experienced affect can be any number in between. In fact, for some individuals, work might actually be an enjoyable part of their lives.[65] This has implications for policy. In the standard economic model, improving working conditions and raising worker satisfaction does not contribute to utility. From a different perspective, trying to raise positive affect at work is probably one of the first areas that one would look at, given that many hours of the day are spent working (and the large potential for improvement).

Psychology could however also benefit from economic reasoning. For example, some time-use categories are not very enjoyable at the time but still worth doing because they provide advantages in the future. For example, spending time studying is generally not perceived as very pleasurable. It might be detrimental to current well-being, but people are motivated because it increases their skill levels and prospects for the future. Put to the extreme, chemotherapy is awful in the short term, but people do it for the potential health benefits in future. Similarly, the low score for "Taking care of my children" indicates that this is not always the most enjoyable "in the moment", but no one would consider stopping this activity. Thus there are many activities which do not provide instant gratification, but which never-theless are worthwhile in the long run. These types of trade-offs of scarce goods (and time) are the bread and butter of economic research.[66]

The end result would make for a powerful combination because economics is the science which understands scarcity and trade-offs while hedonic psychology understands the complexity of emotional responses and decisions of humans over time. These insights could be further enhanced by augmenting them with the concepts of networks and limits. What roles do social, professional and other networks play in well-being? Friendship, love and having your loved ones "doing well" in school or life can be a great source of well-being.[67] At the same time, comparison to your peers can make people unhappy because others are signalling a higher "status" than you.[68]

The ultimate goals of multidisciplinary cooperation would be to create some underlying theory of the motivations of humans.[69] Psychologist Abraham Maslow studied motivations in his landmark book *Motivation and Personality* in 1954. Maslow presented the "hierarchy of needs", which is a well-known psychological model in which five tiers are distinguished: physiological needs, safety needs, love and belonging, esteem and self-actualisation.[70] Other theories have also emerged which are based on motivated reasoning and beliefs.[71] Another way to approach this is to look at human behaviour through an evolutionary lens.[72]

What role might limits play? The ultimate limit to human activities is time. Our activities are confined by the fact that there are twenty-four hours in a day. And even within that time there are limits. Humans cannot choose to stay awake indefinitely. In case of addictions, this dictates the substances that are used. People cannot stop eating or drinking without consequences. One might even say that there are also limits to the amount of enjoyment one can experi-ence. For example, the three most enjoyable activities are sex, social-ising and relaxing, but it is not the case that people want to do these things 24 hours a day, 365 days a year.

Table 10.2 *Excludability and rivalry: private, common, club and public goods*

	Excludable	Non-excludable
Rivalrous	Private goods	Common goods
	Food, clothing, cars, electronics	Fish, timber, coal
Non-rivalrous	Club goods	Public goods
	Cinemas, private parks, satellite TV	Air, dykes, national defence

The concept might also be fruitfully combined with the idea of choice. Sen's capability approach shows that one might be limited in the freedom to choose certain functionings. Quite often, mainstream economic models assume that people are masters of their own destiny. They are making choices using scarce resources and all outcomes are dependent on these decisions. In reality, there are many occurrences in life that are not a matter of choice. Illness or death of loved ones, falling victim to crime, and many other occurrences are not planned, but they do happen and can have profound impacts on well-being. This might also make us rethink the questionnaire for the time-use surveys. Where are these categories in Table 10.1?[73]

One final frontier which might benefit from a multidisciplinary perspective is the concept of "ownership". A lot of economics is based on this concept. To put it in economists' terms, ownership is based on the ability to exercise "property rights".[74] In fact, environmental economists are used to thinking about goods in four categories (Table 10.2). There are two dimensions to the table. Excludability refers to the ability to stop people from benefiting from the goods or services. Rivalry refers to the phenomenon that one person's enjoyment of a good does not diminish the enjoyment of another. Growth accounting and the SNA focus on private goods. Quite understandably, the SEEA has dropped the issue of ownership because many environmental assets and "services" are not owned. Even if they are owned it might be impossible to exclude people from using them or the use might be limitless.

Many public goods are provided by government. Examples include dykes, public parks or public roads. But in many cases ownership is also a "shades of grey" situation. Many scarce resources are partially controllable.[75] Intangible capital provides a good example. Companies may have their own R&D departments and these are private assets if they are able to keep them secret (e.g. Google search engine script or Coca-Cola's recipe) or to obtain a patent. However, it would be wrong to ascribe all the productivity gains to R&D because this knowledge base can make use of the "free R&D" which is generated by the universities. This may be funded by government or by other means, but again the investor and the beneficiary are different.[76] In *The Entrepreneurial State: Debunking Public vs. Private Sector Myths*, Mariana Mazzucato makes a similar point by showing that some of the biggest companies such as Apple and Google were actually built on government-funded research.[77]

Sustainability

Future well-being is an even more difficult challenge than current well-being. How can one judge whether people in ten, thirty or a hundred years' time will be just as satisfied with their lives as people are today? Will the boundaries of our planet have been broached by that point? This is, of course, a difficult, if not impossible question. There are two certainties about the answer. First, it is not a "statistic" in the traditional sense, because it is not based on observations of the present but requires assumptions about the future. Second, to get close enough to an answer, input is required from all scientific fields. It is important to know the underlying dynamics involved in all environmental, societal and economic systems.

The Stiglitz Report says of this: "Sustainability poses the challenge of determining if at least the current level of well-being can be maintained for future generations. By its very nature, sustainability involves the future and its assessment involves many assumptions and normative choices." It goes on to say: "It is no longer a question of measuring the present, but of predicting the future."[78]

How do you measure sustainability? How do you know what well-being our children and grandchildren will be able to achieve? The only correct answer is: "who knows?" This will require some kind of assessment of the future. The SGNA provides ample data which would make it possible to deduce certain risks or may help to model future scenarios. The accounting logic of the SGNA is a valuable part of such a model.

Any projection is sensitive to the assumptions made and the time frame is also important. It seems prudent to be more specific about what the "future" means and to divide it into a shorter and longer time horizon of say one year, thirty years (one generation) and a hundred years. The longer term is more related to the planetary boundaries and environmental issue, while the shorter periods are more reflective of well-being trade-offs in a human life span.

There might of course be other ideas about how to measure future well-being. The concepts of resilience and adaptability might actually prove particularly useful in this respect. Other approaches might also be revisited. For example, Sen (2013) discussed the capability approach in the context of sustainability. Another way to approach it is to adopt a precautionary principle, i.e. to strive to reduce impacts to the extent that we do run the risk of transgressing planetary boundaries.[79]

It seems unlikely that one could arrive at a single index of sustainability. The current methodologies underlying the capital approach might be indicative of long-term income, but not of well-being. Given the uncertainties involved, perhaps a probability score is the only real way to summarise potential futures. The outcome of the modelling exercise would then yield a single estimate of the probability of continued well-being: "the chances that a person thirty years from now has the same well-being as today is X per cent". This would also enable the modellers to factor in the uncertainty of the various projections.

Table 10.3 *The modular SGNA accounts and indicators*

	Account	System indicators	Account	Quality assessment method	Quality Indicators
System accounts	Global environmental accounts		Global quality accounts	Welfare economics, Capital approach	
	Global societal accounts			Capability approach	
	Global economic accounts			Life evaluation	
				Affect evaluation	
	Global distribution accounts			Physiological measurement	
				Thermodynamic/ Biological Approaches	
				Networks/ resilience/ limits-based	
				Etc.	

REPLACING GDP: SYSTEM AND QUALITY INDICATORS

So which indicator or which indicator set will replace GDP in 2030? This book title has promised that GDP will be replaced by a better measurement system by that time. The final indicators of the process will only reveal themselves in 2030 when the common language for well-being and sustainability has been fully formalised and adopted. Yet this chapter does provide insights about the general direction of the SGNA indicators. Before we talk about them, let us first recap the structure of the SGNA.

The modular nature of the SGNA is illustrated in Table 10.3. To the left are the four system accounts which have been discussed in Chapters 6–9. The systems would be based mostly on non-monetary data. The economic system should be provided in monetary *and* non-monetary data. The various quality assessments are shown to the right of Table 10.3. Some of these methods are only useful for one of the system accounts of the SGNA. For example, the mean species abundance is only applicable to GENA accounts for ecosystems. The accounts for affect evaluation will be built on the time-use accounts of the GSA.

The system accounts provide "system indicators" which provide information about the static and dynamic aspects of the systems. The environmental system shows the major stocks/flows and networks of natural resources, climate change and biodiversity. The societal system provides an indicator of the size and growth of the population as well as the characteristics (age, education and health). The economic indicators provide the regular macroeconomic aggregates such as GDP and consumption but also non-monetary indicators about the stocks and flows.

All these systems aggregates provide important information about what is happening. However, when policy alternatives have to be prioritised an overall assessment needs to be made. For this, the quality assessment methods of the GQA are crucial because they provide criteria to assess whether things are getting better or worse. Each of the quality perspectives provides one indicator about these developments. For example:

- *Welfare economics.* This would lead to an indicator such as the Genuine Progress Indicator (GPI) which would use source data from the GENA, GSA, GECA and the GDA.[80] However, compared to the GPI it would also need to include other factors such as consumer surplus, corrections for durable goods, free electronic services and an increase in the variety of goods and services. This would be an approach which was in line with Kuznets's thinking in the 1930s and 1940s.
- *Capital approach.* This would produce indicators such as adjusted net savings and comprehensive wealth (such as the ones produced by the World Bank) which would use stock and flow data from many of the various system accounts.

- *Capability approach*. This approach already has an aggregate indicator, the Human Development Index, which would be sourced from the social and economic accounts of the SGNA. However, one might hope that the capability approach would produce a more satisfying aggregate once the full breath of SGNA data is available.
- *Life evaluation*. These surveys of people's life situation would be linked to many of the accounts of the GSA because they include many of the drivers of well-being (health, education and time use). The combination would therefore give more insights into which characteristics affect well-being.
- *Affect evaluation*. This could lead to indicators such as the "U-index", which is the percentage of time spent on unpleasant activities during a twenty-four-hour day. This would be closely connected to the time-use accounts of the GSA. Also the concept of national utility could be an option.[81]
- *Physiological measurement*. Perhaps, using neuroscientific measurements, it will become possible to provide an aggregate well-being score which can be linked to the time-use module of the GSA.
- *Thermodynamic/ecological*. These might produce exergy and entropy indicators at every system level (company, country, earth). Other thermodynamic approaches such as the Energy Return on Investment or Net Primary Production are more geared towards nature and environmental resources. Ecological science might also yield approaches to assess whether nature is doing well or not.
- *Network approaches*. The value of the network accounts of all SGNA accounts would be enhanced if this yielded aggregate indicators for the stability, resilience, adaptability or other concepts which provide insight about the various systems.
- *Limits and benchmarks*. Where there are scientifically defined limits, or benchmarks, attempts should be made to create indicators based on them. These include indicators such as ecological footprint, mean species abundance and resource life.

Each of these approaches will have to go through a harmonisation process of its own. In the context of the SGNA, the relevant scientific groups will have to converge towards a common way of measuring these indicators. The quality indicators are the alternatives which should replace GDP by 2030. However, none of these indicators is perfect. The discussion has shown that each approach is based on specific assumptions and has limitations in terms of interpretation. Well-being and sustainability are complex phenomena which can only be measured by a couple of imperfect approaches. Choosing one indicator will automatically lead to an imperfect view of society and the environment. Adopting a wide range of imperfect quality indicators is the closest we can get to a complete view of developments.

Science therefore cannot provide a definitive answer about whether the systems are going in the right or wrong direction. The political process has to weigh the information provided and the various policy options. Based on these heterogeneous insights, societies will need to decide on a course of action. These decisions should be formalised by setting targets for the system indicators. In other words, how much focus should society put on education, climate change, innovation policy or maternity leave? This set of system indicators will also replace GDP targets. Together, the set of quality indicators and the system targets should comprise the "SDG2.0" approach which will be negotiated in 2030. Such a measurement system strikes the right balance between science and politics.

What is vitally important is that all system and quality indicators are published at the same time. One of the most important legacies of economic imperialism is the fact that economic statistics are published far quicker and more frequently than social and environmental data. Currently, GDP figures are published around 30–45 days after a quarter closes. GDP is thereby always the first indication of how society is doing. Other important statistics are published months, sometimes years, after the fact. In the SGNA philosophy all indicators are provided simultaneously so that a society receives all the information from the SGNA accounts at the same time. Decisions should be reached by taking on board all relevant facts simultaneously.

So sets of quality and system indicators will replace GDP. All these indicators should also be provided for demographic breakdowns. The well-being and sustainability data should be broken down by gender, age, income, wealth, education level, background, etc. Looking at the quality of the system from an inequality perspective is important for understanding societal changes and working through policy options.

What will happen to GDP? In the SGNA philosophy, GDP is a system indicator rather than a quality indicator. GDP is a summary measure of the size of the economy. This indicator might need some methodological improvements (see Chapter 3) to resolve issues related to digitisation and globalisation. It is likely that by 2030 other macro-aggregates such as Net National Income or Net Domestic Product will become more prevalent. However, the size of the economy is not the end goal, it is a means to an end. GDP is *not* one of the quality indicators; it is simply one of the system indicators which influence well-being or sustainability.

11 Implementation of the Strategy

This book was an attempt to change the way you think about the Beyond-GDP debate. Hopefully, it has given you new ideas about the dominance of GDP and economics in society. Even better, it may have given you novel thoughts about how to move Beyond-GDP. Nevertheless, it is possible that you do not agree (even one tiny bit) with the strategy proposed. If this is the case then it will be interesting to see where the points of disagreement are. Figure 11.1 provides a step-by-step rundown of the arguments used in this book.

The first issue is whether there is a problem in the first place. This book has painted a dire picture of the Beyond-GDP situation. Some readers might make a different assessment. The ever-expanding range of Beyond-GDP initiatives could be seen as a strength. One could argue that each of these indicator systems is slowly but surely chipping away at the dominance of GDP. Clearly, this book makes the opposite argument: the plethora of Beyond-GDP initiatives is a weakness because they are competing against each other and are not providing a coherent narrative to society. Even after decades of Beyond-GDP initiatives, the dominance of GDP shows little sign of diminishing.

The second issue is whether a strategy is needed. One might take the view that the Beyond-GDP scene is a "free market" of ideas and that, in the end, the best idea will win. No intervention or strategy is needed. From this perspective the competition between the various initiatives will at some stage lead to consolidation. This book has argued against this narrative. It is definitely not what happened in the case of GDP. Although serendipity, as always, played

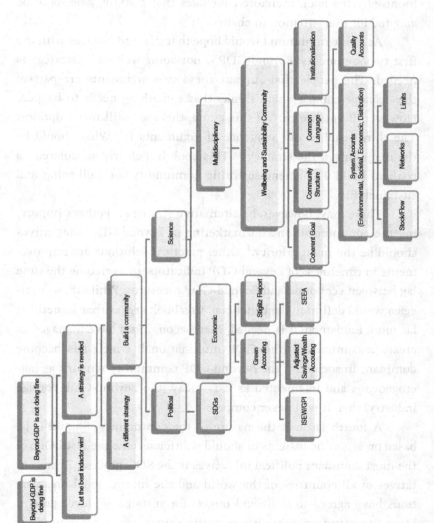

FIGURE 11.1 The argumentation of this book

239

an important role there is definitely a strategy which was set out by the United Nations and OECD, the leading countries and influential macroeconomists. Furthermore, the historical overview of Beyond-GDP does not provide much evidence that one of the perspectives is "winning". Beyond-GDP has existed now for many decades and the methodologies are becoming more heterogeneous rather than harmonised. This book therefore concludes that a strategy needs to be adopted for this situation to change.

At a bare minimum I would hope that the reader agrees with the first two arguments: Beyond-GDP is not doing well and a strategy is needed. The people that support these two arguments are part of the "change camp" which thinks that something needs to happen. However, if you are part of this group, there are still many options. The third issue in our sequence of arguments is "What should be the main aim of the strategy?" This book has clearly articulated its goal: to build a coherent scientific community for well-being and sustainability.

There may, however, be alternative strategies. Perhaps improving the communication and marketing of Beyond-GDP alternatives should be the main priority.[1] Other practical solutions are improvements in timeliness of Beyond-GDP indicators, to overcome the time lag between economic and Beyond-GDP measures. While these strategies would definitely be beneficial, this book argues that something far more fundamental is needed. Macroeconomists have managed to create a community (the GDP multinational) which has become dominant in society. If the Beyond-GDP community remains as heterogeneous and fragmented as it is today (the Beyond-GDP cottage industry) then it will never compete.

A fourth issue is the nature of the community. Should it be based on scientific insights or should politicians take the lead? One of the most dominant political initiatives is the SDG process. Representatives of all countries of the world and the international organisations have agreed to goals and targets for sustainable development. From an institutionalisation perspective this is a powerful movement which has managed to harmonise sustainable development priorities at the global level. However, the fact that the SDGs lack a scientific basis means that it is not clear what the end goal is and it is also not clear what the relationships are between the targets. This book argues that without a scientific foundation it is not possible to create coherent policies. Politicians should therefore not be in the lead.

Given that a scientific basis is required, the fifth choice is whether the community should be led by economic theory or whether it should be multidisciplinary. Given that economic imperialism has also led to the spread of economic policies and thinking in society, it might actually be easiest to go along with an economic approach. There are various candidates:

- *Green accounting.* These approaches use welfare theory and/or the capital approach to produce a single index for welfare or sustainability. Candidates are the ISEW/GPI, Adjusted Net Savings/Wealth Accounting or the SEEA depletion-adjusted aggregates.
- *Stiglitz Report.* This report is probably the most prominent in terms of its authors because a couple of Nobel Prize winners and a whole host of prominent economists contributed to it. The report has achieved a certain degree of institutionalisation.[2]

However, these approaches have existed for a long time. Green accounting has been around since the early 1970s. Welfare-based ISEW/GPI and capital-based wealth accounting have now existed for about thirty years. The Stiglitz Report was written ten years ago. There have been successes in terms of institutionalisation but, given this long time span, progress is somewhat disappointing.

More importantly, the question is whether the strategy should continue on the path of economic imperialism. This book argues against a process based on economic theory. The investigation of well-being and sustainability requires insights from many different scientific fields. Economic theory, mainstream and heterodox, is an important part of the puzzle, but should not be in the lead. The aim is to create a well-being and sustainability *science* rather than well-being and sustainability *economics*.

This brings us to the last tier: the architecture of the multi-disciplinary scientific community. This book argues that, just like macroeconomics, it should have a clear goal, a coherent structure, a common language and should be institutionalised. The *goal* of the scientific community is to understand the current well-being and future well-being (sustainability) of society. The *community structure* is a combination of a policy science (well-being and sustainability science), an accounting framework (System of Global and National Accounts) and key indicators (system and quality indicators). The SGNA should function as a *common language*. Clearly, the community will subsequently have to *institutionalise* formally through international and national institutes and academia. However, it should become informally institutionalised in the media and society.

This book has stressed the importance of the common language. The SGNA accounting framework consists of four system accounts (for the environment, society, economy and distribution). All the system accounts are based on a number of statistical building blocks: stock-flow accounting, networks and the concept of limits. In addition to the system accounts, the SGNA has quality accounts which provide indicators which show whether systems are improving or deteriorating.

A set of quality indicators and system indicators should ultimately replace GDP. This book has not yet been explicit about which indicators would emerge. What is perhaps confusing is that some proposals that were rejected at an earlier stage actually make a comeback here. For example, we rejected green accounting indicators such as the Genuine Progress Indicator (GPI) because they are symbolic of economic imperialism. Yet at this stage, the GPI is reintroduced because it is part of a broader set of quality indicators.

There is much in this argumentation that one might disagree with: the structuring of the accounts, the building blocks or the names of the science and accounting framework, for example. There are of course many conceivable improvements or potential changes that could be suggested in relation to setting up the community.

Whatever your opinion, it is clear that Figure 11.1 represents some of the most crucial choices in the debate.

Perhaps you have changed your mind about one of these questions. Perhaps you have become even more convinced about your own vision of the future of Beyond-GDP. The most important aim of this book is that a sense of urgency emerges: something needs to change. This book is meant to provoke other researchers to think about their own strategy. This might build on the one which has been formulated in the book or might be a totally different one. In either case the discussion will shift towards a more successful Beyond-GDP process.

For those who have been convinced by the (majority of) the arguments in the book it is important to have a closer look at how realistic the strategy is. The next sections will discuss various aspects of the feasibility of the strategy proposed in this book.

(NEARLY) ALL THE PIECES OF THE PUZZLE

The well-being and sustainability science can be viewed as a giant jigsaw puzzle. In recent decades a vast amount of knowledge, methods and data has been collected in a wide variety of scientific fields. Each area of knowledge can be seen as a piece of the puzzle. The various chapters have shown that a huge amount of this knowledge and data already exists (and it is by no means a complete overview). The strategy proposed in this book is simply providing a plan for how the pieces in the giant jigsaw puzzle might fit together.

Nevertheless, this book has also uncovered a number of important areas for further research: not all the pieces of the jigsaw puzzle are currently present. Without attempting to be comprehensive, a number of topics of the research agenda are discussed below.

Multidisciplinary View of Well-being and Sustainability

One of the greatest challenges would be to get a multidisciplinary view of well-being and sustainability. Well-being could be based on psychological, economic, philosophical and sociological insights and should also take on board the importance of networks and limits.

Ultimately a model should emerge of human motivations and behaviour. In the case of sustainability, this is a question about the future which should be tackled by natural scientists and social scientists together. Notions such as complex systems and the resilience of these networks should become even more important. The concept of limits will also play a more significant role in managing the future of our planet and society.

Multidisciplinary Policies

The multidisciplinary view should lead to a more diverse set of policy options. Market-based solutions such as pricing externalities will remain an important policy tool, but other strategies should also emerge: for example, policies that are based on psychology will help to nudge behaviour while other behavioural insights might be used to overcome "free rider" behaviour. Other policies might emerge from the field of political science which focus on the role of communities in solving problems.

ICT and Globalisation

ICT and globalisation have had profound impacts on society and the economy. They affect production processes and have led to defragmentation into global value chains. They have also led to new products and many free services and different business models. Social interactions have changed dramatically over the last few decades. These phenomena have profound impacts on well-being and sustainability and should be a field of intensive research.

This book has stressed that these concepts cannot be fully comprehended if it relies only on monetary data. Physical units are vital to understand technology and units such as time are vital for understanding the impact of ICT on our daily lives.

Networks

The concepts of networks and limits are universal across the environment, society and the economy. In all fields from ecology to economics, networks are considered important to understanding the dynamics of the system.[3] Classification schemes of the various networks (the nodes and edges) of the environmental, societal and economic systems will have to be categorised.[4] The networks should include individuals but also networks of institutional units such as companies, governments, neighbourhoods and groups of friends. The end result should be that these various systems are viewed as complex networks.[5]

Limits

This book has argued that systems are restricted by various limits such as technological, thermodynamic, biological, practical or time restrictions. Environmental limits, or planetary boundaries, are cited most often but system limits exist everywhere. These limits need to be categorised in terms of the various categories. Statistics should be collected so that models increasingly take on board limits in their methodologies.

Spatial and Temporal Scales

The spatial and time scales of the various systems can vary significantly.[6] Some developments change in a day, a minute or a second (emotions) while other processes take decades or centuries (climate change and nuclear waste). For some systems it is important to have a local perspective (a small ecosystem or neighbourhood) while in other cases a more global perspective is required (biodiversity). The borders of the systems might not adhere to political borders. For example, the borders of ecosystems do not follow national boundaries.

   Sometimes the scale of the problem is different to the scale of the policy solution. Many global environmental problems such as climate change need to be solved at the national level, but also locally or even at the level of individual polluters. Well-being and sustainability science needs to find appropriate aggregations in order to report the relevant indicators, but it also needs to allow for spatial and temporal disaggregation. Geo-referencing and time stamping of all microdata would provide a solid basis for this type or flexibility.

Alignment

The SGNA provides a macro-societal perspective of development. However, there are currently many companies that are active in measuring sustainability, corporate social responsibility (CSR), impact measurement (Integrated Profit and Loss accounting), and so on. The situation at the company level is just as chaotic as at the national level: there is a "financial accounting multinational" which is competing against the "corporate sustainability cottage industry". Harmonisation at the macro-level might also contribute to convergence at the company levels.

STRUCTURED MULTIDISCIPLINARITY

Cooperation within scientific disciplines is a difficult task, but meaningful collaboration across disciplines is even more daunting. It is good to be frank on this matter: multidisciplinary research sounds good on paper but quite often disappoints in practice. This is why one of the problems of the strategy will be to create a collaborative framework in which many scientific disciplines contribute. There is a danger that a chaotic process will provide few results and much frustration. Because of this it is important to explicitly structure the collaboration.

The System of Global and National Accounts provides such a structure. Table 11.1 shows some of the scientific disciplines which may contribute to the various accounts. It shows that the multidisciplinary science is not an unstructured free-for-all in which all sciences cover all areas. The development of the environmental accounts should be led by natural scientists, economic accounts by economists and societal accounts by the other social sciences.

Given that there needs to be coherence between the various accounts, there are also scientific disciplines which connect various fields.[7] For example, environmental and ecological economists combine environmental and societal/economic knowledge. An even broader field is "sustainability science" which, out of the existing

Table 11.1 *Structured multidisciplinarity*

	Account	Science	Generic sciences
System accounts	GENA	Climatologists, geologists, chemistry, meteorology, biology, ecology	Network theory, complexity science, resilience theory, data science
	GSA	Demography, sociology, political science	
	GECA	Macroeconomics, labour economics, innovation economics, trade economics, network economics	
	GDA	Inequality economists, sociologists	
Quality account	GQA	Many natural and social sciences	

Account links	Linking sciences
GENA-GECA/ GSA	Ecological economist, environmental economists, sustainability science
GSA-GECA-GDA	Institutional economics, economic sociology, political economy

scientific fields, probably comes closest to the well-being and sustainability science proposed in this book.[8] The scientific disciplines that link different fields are vitally important to facilitate dialogue between the various schools of thought. There are also generic sciences which transcend a single field such as network science, resilience, complexity science or data science.

There is only one account in which the multidisciplinarity is explicit and no school of thought has the lead. The Global Quality Accounts (GQA) is the only case where there is no logical dominant school. This is because quality assessment methods are provided by many natural and social sciences as well as some of the generic sciences such as network and complexity science.

For multidisciplinary collaboration on the GQA to work it is important to populate it with scientists who are capable of this type of cooperation. The philosophy of the GQA should not be to choose "the best" quality assessment tool but rather to provide a full range of imperfect methods. For each individual quality approach, the relevant experts will have to agree on how to harmonise the accounts/indicators. Also the links between the system accounts and the GQA have to be formalised.

Assuming that well-being and sustainability science is rooted in this structured multidisciplinary process, this seems a feasible route. The most exciting prospect would be that it leads to cross-fertilisation between disciplines that results in new theories and policies.

THE AGE OF DATA ABUNDANCE

When the United Nations Statistical Division was created, just after the war, its first two projects were the System of National Accounts and methodological advancement of survey theory. These were mutually reinforcing endeavours. Improvements in survey methodology meant that more accurate economic statistics could be produced at a lower cost. The advances in survey methodology thereby contributed significantly to the proliferation of the SNA.

In the case of the SGNA there is an opportunity to capitalise on a new phase of data collection: the era of "big data". The onset of ICT in society has caused the availability of electronic data to explode. Companies and governments have started creating all types of "registers" in which data is collected in a structured way. Furthermore, the internet has added even more information which is available on countless websites.

Data itself is becoming a commodity that is commercially important. There are computers, sensors and other electronic devices which are collecting and storing data in historically unprecedented amounts. As *The Economist* said in 2010: "Information has gone from scarce to superabundant."[9] These new sources are sometimes referred to as "big data", although a precise definition of this term is elusive. Big data might not just contribute to cost savings, but also provide data which surveys are unable to generate. Although it is impossible to envisage all the ways in which electronic data sources may be used in the SGNA, it is good to list some of the data types which are already being employed.

- *Registers*. Before the ICT revolution, administrative records would be kept on paper. Nowadays, electronic databases are being set up by governments and companies which record a vast amount of information. These are sometimes known as registers, and in the case of government databases, administrative registers. Increasingly, these systems are becoming harmonised because they are linked to accounting standards or other classification schemes. These registers can also be linked if they have some kind of unique variable such as a social security number.[10] Statistical offices are increasingly using this data rather than sending out questionnaires.[11]
- *Internet*. The internet has a multitude of data, although this is less structured than in registers. It is possible to harvest public data from websites by using webcrawlers/internet robots. Some statistical offices are starting to use these methods to collect prices and other data from websites. Academic groups also created pioneering efforts such as the Billion Prices Projects (BPP) of MIT. By 2010, it was collecting five million prices every day from over three hundred retailers in fifty countries.[12] This data is used to create daily information figures. Even national sentiments can be measured through twitter posts.[13] Apart from the published data, companies are also registering information about how people use the internet by installing so-called cookies. In addition, the data from social networking applications is being used to create psychological profiles of users.
- *Internet of things*. Not only computers, tablets and smartphones are collecting data. Many other electronic appliances and machines, such as

cars and household appliances, are storing and transmitting data. Some cars are equipped with a transponder that tracks where they are. Electricity meters and digital television sets are transmitting data to the providers without citizens realising it. In the longer term, the "internet of things" idea is that all electronic equipment will communicate with each other. It will be like a network of machines in houses which cooperate to the benefit of consumers. It could also provide statistical agencies with a whole lot of additional data which could be used in the SGNA.

- *Satellite data, mobile devices and sensors.* The availability of satellite data has improved in terms of cost, availability and granularity in the last couple of decades. This provides GIS data from which land use patterns, ecosystems and infrastructure can be derived. Most ecosystem accounting is now done based on satellite images. Furthermore, society has also installed many sensors such as the ones that track the traffic densities on roads or air quality. Also personal sensors for people have become much more sophisticated. People can wear watches which track their heart rates and sleeping patterns and in a laboratory setting researchers can track physiological developments. This will be a big boost to fields such as neuro-economics, which uses physiological measurements.

These are just some of the ways in which electronic data is transforming the information landscape. Of course, the issue of privacy is already a big problem which is constantly being revisited as the era of big data evolves. Especially linking data from different datasets can provide powerful personal profiles. It is sometimes jokingly said that Google knows more about you than you do yourself. In the hands of companies or governments, this data may be misused. At the same time, scientifically speaking, they have the ability to provide a much better understanding of human behaviour. A healthy balance will have to be found.

The electronic data will lead to significant cost reductions or even make new observations possible. In Boxes 11.1 and 11.2, two specific SGNA accounts are discussed which would benefit greatly from using electronic data.

By 2030, official statistics are likely to be a combination of surveys, registers and other big data. The use of big data in official

BOX 11.1   **New ways of measuring time use**

The SGNA stresses the importance of time-use accounts. Yet the current time-use surveys are expensive and are carried out rarely. Innovation is needed to make this viable. There are groups that are working on innovative ways to improve the quality and cost-effectiveness of time-use measurement using accelerometry and wearable cameras.[14] Simply asking people for the GPS and time data from a mobile phone (or other wearable GPS device) tells you exactly where someone was at what time. Combined with information from Google Maps it is probably possible to identify the activity. The travel speed probably tells you whether you were on foot, on a bike, in a car or train. All this information can be filled into a time-use account before asking the respondent specific questions to verify and enhance the data using questionnaires. In future, it might become possible to give respondents a device which measures physiological data so that a profile of well-being over time can be composed. The starting point for this innovation is to think of all the places where a digital footprint of our daily lives is created or to see how electronic devices might help us to track our daily activities.

BOX 11.2   **New ways of measuring networks**

The SGNA stresses the importance of networks when thinking about ecosystems and societal and economic systems. However, capturing information about networks through surveys is difficult and will, by definition, be incomplete. A survey approaches only a small portion of the population and it is not practical to ask a respondent to list their entire social and professional network. Given the proliferation of social networking platforms it is now becoming far easier to record the networks of a person. The interactions even provide some indication of the quality of the different network relationships. Similarly, the networks of companies are becoming more visible because of big data sources.[15]

252 THE NEW STRATEGY

statistics obviously requires a new mindset,[16] and raises issues related to privacy.[17] It might also lead to a shift in responsibilities related to the production of (official) statistics. Currently, this data is produced mostly by official statistical agencies. The collection and harmonisation of national data are done by international institutes but also by academic consortia. It is conceivable that in future data will, even more than today, become a marketable commodity. If this is the case, companies will also be part of the mix of providing data.[18]

The importance of data in society is symbolised by the demand for data scientists. Hal Varian, chief economist of Google, said: "I keep saying the sexy job in the next ten years will be statisticians. People think I'm joking, but who would've guessed that computer engineers would've been the sexy job of the 1990s?"[19]

THE COST OF THE STRATEGY

An important barrier to adopting this strategy could be its cost. It is not possible to come up with a number for the total amount of money required for the implementation. The scope of the exercise needs to be worked out further and the potential role of big data is still too unclear. Nevertheless, it is possible to provide some context on this matter by splitting the work into a number of component parts.

Firstly, a group of scientists and statisticians needs to work together on this common accounting framework. In relative terms this will not be expensive because the scientists have more than enough knowledge and literature to build on. Of course, creating a synthesis and fostering collaboration between scientific disciplines takes time and dedication, but there is ample experience in setting up these kinds of processes.

The second phase of the strategy, the implementation of the SGNA and SWW research, is a different matter. Implementing data collection, dissemination and quality control of the SGNA requires additional resources. In the rich countries countless databases on globalisation, inequality, environmental accounts and demography are already funded and maintained by various projects or institutes.

The biggest challenge will be implementation in developing countries. Given that the ambition of the SGNA is to provide a worldwide accounting framework, the statistical capacity of developing nations will have to be upgraded significantly.

Currently, there is great inequality in the statistical capacity of countries. Even the implementation of the SNA or other important accounts such as censuses are weak in many countries.[20] Some of these deficiencies have been addressed in the book *Poor Numbers*, which painted a bleak picture of African economic statistics.[21] In many cases the situation with respect to the source statistics is dire. Numerous countries lack a good business register or even knowledge of their population. Any statistical institute should at least know which people and companies reside in their country.

Poor Numbers emphasises the need to invest in the statistical capacity of poorer countries. This call will become even more pressing in the context of the SDGs. Already the UN, World Bank and IMF are investing money in statistical capacity in weaker statistical systems of the world. An independent Expert Advisory Group for the UN has called for a "data revolution", which will be needed to make monitoring of the SDGs work.[22]

THE CHALLENGE: INSTITUTIONALISATION

Around seventy years ago, the UN and the OECC/OECD embarked on a crucial process which led to the SNA. Without this initiative, it is unlikely that GDP or macroeconomics would have been as successful as they are today. But the current coordination of SGNA is far more difficult than the SNA situation because after the war there were only 10–20 countries that were actively doing national accounting. There were also a number of dominant figures (such as Keynes and Stone) who had the clout to get their approach adopted by the OEEC and later the UN. The current situation for Beyond-GDP is different. There are hundreds of systems and no one system, academic theory or scientist dominates the field. Also the range of issues (e.g. inequality, environment, economy) that are within the scope of Beyond-GDP is broad. Thus harmonisation is a far greater challenge.

On the bright side, the UN and other international institutes have been through these types of harmonisation processes before. Literally dozens of statistical handbooks and guidelines have been created on sub-domains that have to do with Beyond-GDP. The SNA and the SEEA are just the most successful. They were made possible by cooperation between important institutes such as the UN, OECD, European Commission, IMF and World Bank. Apart from statistical coordination, the UN also has experience in galvanising scientific knowledge such as the IPCC for climate science. The international institutes have the ability to engage the very best in the scientific community in a way few national institutes can.[23]

There are five roles for international institutes. First, they need to coordinate the handbooks which will define the SGNA and the core accounts described at the beginning of this chapter. Second, they will have to also work on the items of the research agenda together. Third, they have a role to play in the creation of the globally comparable datasets. Fourth, they have a role in statistical work that goes beyond national boundaries, such as the measurement of multinationals and the global commons. Finally, the international organisations have a crucial role to play in disseminating the data.

So why has this harmonisation process not emerged? The problem is that institutes have their own priorities and interests, so that cooperation is not automatic. Each institute has its own "Beyond-GDP" flagship. The OECD has the Better Life Initiative, the European Commission has its Beyond-GDP workstream. The UN has many initiatives, of which the SDG process is the most prominent.[24]

The international organisations might start to work together on this topic; or one of the international institutes might take the lead. This is what happened in the case of the SNA. The SNA 1953 and SNA 1968 were UN documents.[25] The OECD actually maintained its own manuals up to 1977 and only officially became co-author together with the other institutes for the SNA 1993.

One might think that some kind of mandate is needed for this process to start. The SNA process formally started when, in 1939, the statistical body of the League of Nations requested a harmonisation process for national accounts. So where is the mandate to start working on Beyond-GDP? In actuality, the mandate has been there for a long time. Take a look at these two statements:

> Commonly used indicators such as the gross national product (GNP) and measurements of individual resource or pollution flows do not provide adequate indications of sustainability. Methods for assessing interactions between different sectoral environmental, demographic, social and developmental parameters are not sufficiently developed or applied. Indicators of sustainable development need to be developed to provide solid bases for decision-making at all levels and to contribute to a self-regulating sustainability of integrated environment and development systems. (UN, 1992)

> We recognize the need for broader measures of progress to complement GDP in order to better inform policy decisions, and in this regard, we request the UN Statistical Commission in consultation with relevant UN System entities and other relevant organizations to launch a programme of work in this area building on existing initiatives. (UN, 2012)

The first is from the outcome document of the Earth Summit in 1992 and the second is from the Rio+20 document in 2012. The UN response after 1992 was to create the CSD indicators, but these have since been discontinued (see Chapter 4). The UN response to the 2012 mandate seems to concentrate on the SDGs. However, these lack the conceptual basis necessary for a scientific community. The most powerful approach would be to link the SDGs to the process proposed in this book. The SGNA might even be framed as a research agenda for the SDGs, which would uncover the relationship between the SDG goals. In this way, the political momentum is coupled to a conceptual foundation.[26] The SGNA could also provide a template by which to redesign the SDGs in 2030.[27]

One problem is that the global statistical system is rather fragmented. Eurostat and the OECD have powerful statistical bodies but they cater to only a portion of the world. The IMF and World Bank also have their own statistical programmes. Within the UN system, the production of statistics is decentralised to organisations such as the ILO, WHO, UNFCCC, UNEP and many other agencies. Statistics are located in the UN department with the most knowledge of the phenomenon. For example, labour statistics are produced mostly by the International Labour Organization.[28] In fact the UN Statistical Division is responsible for only a small part of the puzzle: SNA, SEEA and trade statistics. Given the broad scope of the SGNA this is a major hurdle because it will require a large amount of coordination.

Overall, there are challenges for institutionalisation. The international institutes are not collaborating in a coherent manner on this issue. This is reminiscent of the argument made by Thomas Hale and David Held in their books *Gridlock* and *Beyond Gridlock*. They consider that some of the policy challenges of the twenty-first century are inherently transnational but that international institutions often fail to address them appropriately. This type of barrier will have to be overcome.

WILL IT HAPPEN?

> "The real difficulty in changing any enterprise lies not in developing new ideas, but in escaping from the old ones..."
>
> John Maynard Keynes in the preface of The General Theory of Employment, Interest and Money (1936)

This quotation by Keynes is relevant to this book on two levels. First, Keynes stresses the inertia of old ideas. This book has also argued that macroeconomic ideas will be difficult to replace. Second, Keynes stresses that the problem is not a lack of new ideas. Again, this book has provided an overview, which is by no means exhaustive, of the plethora of initiatives and methods to go Beyond-GDP.

To overcome this "difficulty", it is important to analyse the problem at hand. The core issue is that macroeconomists have formed a coherent and powerful community. The field of well-being and sustainability has not. There are now hundreds of alternative to GDP yet the Beyond-GDP cottage industry is no match for the GDP multinational.

Without a strategy, the situation will not improve. The number of alternatives will continue to rise unabated in future without it having any major impact. The new strategy proposed in this book is simple in its aim: to create a powerful community for well-being and sustainability.

Overall, this book has shown that the strategy is feasible. There is decades-worth of scientific research and data initiatives to build on. If the process capitalises on the big data revolution it is likely to become more cost-effective. The challenge is like a giant jigsaw puzzle that needs putting together: most of the pieces are there, but the puzzle will not self-assemble.

The greatest challenge is institutionalisation. There has been a UN mandate to work on this topic since 1992. So far, the international institutes have failed to produce a comprehensive and compulsory scientific process. One or more of the international bodies might initiate this strategy. They might start such a process of their own accord, or governments, scientists or the general public might implore them to do it. Whatever the motive, the chance that this happens is greatest if a large group stands up and advocates a change in strategy. If the "change group", which demands a new strategy, grows then the implementation of a strategy becomes more likely.

On an optimistic note, the international institutes have done this before. The SNA, the IPCC, SDGs and the SEEA are all examples of successful community-building processes. The fact that the SNA and the SDGs will probably be revised in the period 2025–2030 provides ample opportunity to align this WSS/SGNA strategy to existing powerful institutional processes.

This book is a plea to start such a process. Currently society and governments are looking at the world through a GDP lens. Society deserves a more balanced multidisciplinary perspective with which to guide society towards well-being and sustainability. It is time to make this transition. By 2030, at the latest.

#ReplaceGDPby2030

Annex: Beyond-GDP Milestones and Measurement Systems

The tables below provide information about the Beyond-GDP milestones and measurement systems shown in Table 2.1 and discussed in Chapter 4.

Table A1 *Influential conferences/initiatives*

Period	Year	Name	Institute	Location	Final Report/website	Link to measurement system
1945–1969	1968–1974	Problems of Modern Society	OECD			
1970–1974	1972	Stockholm Conference – United Nations Conference on the Human Environment	UN	Stockholm, Sweden		
1980–1984	1983–1987	World Commission on Environment and Development (WCED)	UN		WCED (1987)	
1990–1994	1992	Rio Earth Summit – United Nations Conference on Environment and Development (Earth Summit)	UN	Rio de Janeiro, Brazil	UN (1992)	
	1992–2012	Commission for Sustainable Development (CSD)	UN			CSD indicators
2000–2004	2000–2015	Millennium Development Goals (MDG)	UN		un.org/millenniumgoals	MDGs
	2002	Rio+10 – World Summit on Sustainable Development	UN	Johannesburg, South Africa		
	2003	Global Footprint Network (GFN)	GFN		footprintnetwork.org	Ecological footprint

Year	Event	Organization	Location	Reference	Output
2004	World Forum 2004 – 1st OECD World Forum on "Statistics, Knowledge and Policy"	OECD	Palermo, Italy		
2004–2008	Working Group for Statistics of Sustainable Development (WGSSD)	UN/OECD/EC		UNECE et al. (2008)	WGSSD indicators
2005–2009 2007	World Forum 2007 – 2nd OECD World Forum on "Statistics, Knowledge and Policy"	OECD	Istanbul, Turkey		
2007	Beyond-GDP Conference – Beyond-GDP: Measuring Progress, True Wealth, and the Well-being of Nations	EC	Brussels, Belgium		
2008–2009	Commission on the Measurement of Economic Performance and Social Progress (CMEPSP)	France		Stiglitz et al. (2009)	
2009	World Forum 2009 – 3rd OECD World Forum on "Statistics, Knowledge and Policy"	OECD	Busan, Korea		
2009–2014	Task Force on Measuring Sustainable Development (TFSD)	UN/OECD/EC		UNECE et al. (2014)	CES recommendations
2010–2011	Sponsorship Group on Measuring Progress, Well-being and Sustainable Development	EC		ESS (2011)	

Table A1 (*cont.*)

Period	Year	Name	Institute	Location	Final Report/website	Link to measurement system
2010–2014	2011	Better Life Initiative	OECD		oecdbetterlifeindex.org	Better Life Index
	2011–2014	Bringing Alternative Indicators into Policy (BRAINPOoL)	EC		Whitby (2014)	
	2012	World Forum 2012 – 4th OECD World Forum on "Statistics, Knowledge and Policy"	OECD	New Delhi, India		
	2012	Rio+20 – United Nations Conference on Sustainable Development	UN	Rio de Janeiro, Brazil	UN (2012)	
	2012–	UN Sustainable Development Solutions Network (UN-SDSN)	UNSG		unsdsn.org	
	2012–2014	e-Frame – European Framework for Measuring Progress	EC		eframeproject.eu	
	2013–2018	High-Level Expert Group on the Measurement of Economic Performance and Social Progress (HLEG)	OECD			
2015–2019	2015	World Forum 2015 – 5th OECD World Forum on "Statistics, Knowledge and Policy"	OECD	Guadalajara, Mexico		

| 2015–2030 | Sustainable Development Goals (SDG) | UN | | UN (2015) | SDGs |
| 2018 | World Forum 2018 – 6th OECD World Forum on "Statistics, Knowledge and Policy" | OECD | Incheon, Korea | | |

UN – United Nations, OECD – Organisation of Economic Development, World Commission on Environment and Development

Table A2 *Influential Beyond-GDP publications*

Period	Year	Title	Institute	Reference
1945–1969	1953	SNA53 – A System of National Accounts and Supporting Tables	UN	UN (1953)
	1958	Affluent Society	Academic	Galbraith (1958)
	1962	Silent Spring	Academic	Carson (1962)
	1968	SNA68 – A System of National Accounts	UN	UN (1968)
	1968	Population Bomb	Academic	Ehrlich (1968)
	1968	The Tragedy of the Commons	Academic	Hardin (1968)
1970–1974	1972	The Limits to Growth	Club of Rome	Meadows et al. (1972)
	1974	Easterlin Paradox – Does Economic Growth Improve the Human Lot?	Academic	Easterlin (1974)
1985–1989	1987	Our Common Future (Brundtland Report)	WCED	WCED (1987)
1990–1994	1990–onwards	Human Development Report	UNDP	UNDP (1990)
	1993	SNA 1993 – System of National Accounts 1993	EC/IMF/OECD/ UN/World Bank	EC et al. (1993)
	1993	SEEA 1993 – Integrated Environmental and Economic Accounting	UN	UN (1993)
2000–2005	2003	SEEA 2003 – Integrated Environmental and Economic Accounting 2003	UN	UN et al. (2003)
2005–2009	2006	Wealth of Nations 2006 – Where is the Wealth of Nations?	World Bank	World Bank (2006)
	2008	SNA 2008 – System of National Accounts 2008	EC/IMF/OECD/ UN/World Bank	EC et al. (2009)

	Year	Title	Institution	Reference
	2008	Measuring Sustainable Development	UN/OECD/EC	UNECE et al. (2008)
	2009	Report by the Commission on the Measurement of Economic Performance and Social Progress		Stiglitz et al. (2009)
2010–2014	2010	Wealth of Nations 2010 – The Changing Wealth of Nations	World Bank	World Bank (2010)
	2012	SEEA 2012 – System of Environmental-Economic Accounting 2012– Central Framework	UN	UN et al. (2014)
	2012/2014	Inclusive Wealth Report (2012 and 2014)	UNU-IHDP	UNU-IHDP and UNEP (2012, 2014)
	2012–onwards	World Happiness Report (2012, 2013, 2015–2018)	UNSDSN	Helliwell et al. (2018)
	2012	SEEA 2012 – System of Environmental-Economic Accounting 2012 – Experimental Ecosystem Accounting	UN	EC et al. (2013)
2014–2019	2013	Guidelines on Subjective Well-being	OECD	OECD (2013)
	2014–onwards	Global Sustainable Development Report (2014, 2015, 2016 and 2019)	UN	UN (2016)
	2014	CES Recommendations – Conference of European Statisticians Recommendations on Measuring Sustainable Development	UN/OECD/EC	UNECE et al. (2014)
	2017	Wealth of Nations 2017 – The Changing Wealth of Nations 2018	World Bank	Lange et al. (2017)
	2018	Stiglitz II		
	2018	Inclusive Wealth Report	Academic	Cobb et al. (1995)

Table A3 *Beyond-GDP indicators by type*

	Period	Year	Country	Reference/Source
TYPE 1. **Subjective** **wellbeing**	**World Happiness** **Database**			First data point for this country in the World Happiness Database Veenhoven (2017)
	1945–1969	1946	US – USA	
		1948	MX – Mexico	
		1958	JP – Japan	
		1962	IN – India	
		1965	UK – United Kingdom	
		1966	FI – Finland	
	1970–1974	1972	NO – Norway	
		1973	BE – Belgium	
		1973	DK – Denmark	
		1973	FR – France	
		1973	DE – Germany	
		1973	IE – Ireland	
		1973	IT – Italy	
		1973	LX – Luxemburg	
		1973	NL – Netherlands	
	1975–1979	1975	AT – Austria	
		1979	KR – South Korea	
	1980–1984	1981	AR – Argentina	
		1981	GR – Greece	
	1985–1989	1985	PT – Portugal	
		1985	ES – Spain	
		1989	RU – Russia	

1990–1994	1990	BG – Bulgaria
	1990	CH – China
	1990	PO – Poland
	1991	SV – El Salvador
1995–1999	1997	BR – Brazil
	1997	CO – Colombia
	1997	EC – Ecuador
	1998	RO – Romania
2000–2004	2000	EG – Egypt
	2001	CZ – Czech republic
	2001	EE – Estonia
	2001	HU – Hungary
	2001	JO – Jordan
	2001	LV – Latvia
	2001	LT – Lithuania
	2001	SK – Slovakia
	2001	SI – Slovenia
	2001	ZW – Zimbabwe
	2002	SA – Saudi Arabia
Gallup	2005–2009	2005	Gallup (27 countries)
		2006	Gallup (89 countries)
		2007	Gallup (102 countries)
		2008	Gallup (110 countries)
		2009	Gallup (114 countries)

Derived from the dataset of Chapter 2 of the World Happiness report Helliwell et al. (2018)

Table A3 (*cont.*)

	Period	Year	Country	Reference/Source
	2010–2014	2010	Gallup (124 countries)	Information obtained from file on GESIS website. https://dbk.gesis.org/dbksearch/file.asp?file=ZA4804_EVS-WVS_ParticipatingCountries.pdf
		2011	Gallup (146 countries)	
		2012	Gallup (142 countries)	
		2013	Gallup (137 countries)	
		2014	Gallup (145 countries)	
	2015–2019	2015	Gallup (143 countries)	
		2016	Gallup (142 countries)	
		2017	Gallup (141 countries)	
European/World Value Survey (EVS/WVS)	1980–1984	1981	EVS1 (16 countries)	
		1981	WVS1 (8 countries)	
	1985–1989	1989	WVS2 (18 countries)	
	1990–1994	1990	EVS2 (29 countries)	
		1994	WVS3 (152 countries)	
	1995–1999	1999	EVS3 (33 countries)	
		1999	WVS4 (40 countries)	
	2000–2004	2004	WVS5 (58 countries)	
	2005–2009	2008	EVS4 (41 countries)	
	2010–2014	2010	WVS6 (60 countries)	
	2015–2019	2017	WVS7 (70–80 countries)	
Other	2005–2009	2006	U-Index	Kahneman and Krueger (2006)

TYPE 1. Green accounting

1970–1974	1970	Total Income System of Accounts (TISA)	See Eisner (1988) for references
	1972	Measure of Economic Welfare (MEW)	Nordhaus and Tobin (1972)
	1974	Sustainable National Income (SNI)	Hueting (1974)
1975–1979	1976	Adjusted GNP	See Eisner (1988) for references
1980–1984	1981	Economic Aspects of Welfare (EAW)	See Eisner (1988) for references
	1982	Integrated Economic Accounts (IEA)	See Eisner (1988) for references
1985–1989	1987	Gross Private Domestic Product	See Eisner (1988) for references
	1989	Index of Sustainable Economic Welfare (ISEW)	Daly and Cobb (1989)
1990–1994	1993	Genuine Savings	Pearce and Atkinson (1993)
1995–1999	1995	Genuine Progress Indicator (GPI)	Cobb et al. (1995)
	1999	Sustainable Net Benefits Index (SNBI)	Lawn and Sanders (1999)
2005–2009	2006	Total/Comprehensive Wealth	World Bank (2006)
2010–2014	2010	Adjusted Net Saving (ANS)	World Bank (2010)
	2012	Inclusive Wealth Index (IWI)	UNU-IHDP and UNEP (2012)

Table A3 (cont.)

	Period	Year	Country	Reference/Source
TYPE 1. Other	1990–1995	1994	Ecological Footprint (EF)	Wackernagel (1994)
TYPE 2.	1970–1974	1974	Life Situation Index (LSI)	SCP (1974)
Composite	1990–1994	1990	Human Development Index (HDI)	UNDP (1990)
indicators				
	1995–1999	1998	Living Planet Index (LPI)	WWF (1998)
		1998	Index of Economic Well-being (IEWB)	Osberg and Sharpe (1998)
		1999	Environmental Vulnerability Index (EVI)	
	2000–2004	2000	Environmental Sustainability Index (ESI)	
		2001	Well-being Index (WI)	Prescott-Allen (2001)
	2005–2009	2005	Environmental Performance Index (EPI)	
		2006	Happy Planet Index (HPI)	NEF (2006)
		2007	Legatum Prosperity Index	Legatum (2007)
		2008	Sustainable Society Index (SSI)	Van de Kerk and Manuel (2008)
		2009	Fondazione Eni Enrico Mattei Sustainability Index (FEEM)	

Type		Period	Year	Name	Reference
		2010–2014	2010	Multidimensional Poverty Index (MPI)	Alkire and Santos (2010)
			2011	Canadian Index of Wellbeing (CIW)	Michalos et al. (2011)
			2014	Social Progress Index (SPI)	Stern et al. (2014)
		2015–2019	2015	SDG index	Kroll (2015)
			2016	Sustainable Wellbeing Index (SWI)	Costanza et al. (2016)
TYPE 3. Non-conceptual indicator set	Other	1970–1974	1972	Gross National Happiness	grossnationalhappiness.com/
		1995–1999	1996	Commission for Sustainable Development (UN-CSD)	UN (1996)
		2000–2004	2000	Millennium Development Goals (MDG)	un.org/millenniumgoals
		2005–2009	2005	Eurostat – Sustainable Development Indicators	European Communities (2005)
		2010–2014	2010	Wheel of Well-being	ons.gov.uk/peoplepopulationandcommunity/wellbeing
		2015–2019	2015	Sustainable Development Goals (SDG)	UN (2012)

Table A3 (cont.)

	Period	Year	Country	Reference/Source
Country indicators sets for sustainable development	1995–1999	1996	UK – United Kingdom	These are the first publications for Sustainable Development Indicators in these countries. The years are derived from data underlying Figure 1 in Schoenaker et al. (2015) and own additional research.
	2000–2004	2000	RO – Romania	
		2000	FI – Finland	
		2000	MX – Mexico	
		2002	DK – Denmark	
		2002	AU – Australia	
		2002	KZ – Kazakhstan	
		2003	FR – France	
		2003	LV – Latvia	
		2004	DE – Austria	
		2004	BR – Brazil	
	2005–2009	2005	AR – Argentina	
		2005	BE – Belgium	
		2006	CZ – Czech Republic	
		2006	LX – Luxemburg	
		2006	MO – Morocco	
		2006	KO – South Korea	
		2007	ME – Montenegro	
		2007	SB – Serbia	
		2007	TR – Turkey	
		2008	BU – Bulgaria	
		2009	EE – Estonia	
		2009	ES – Spain	

Type	Category	Period	Year	Indicator / Country	Reference
		2010–2014	2010	IS – Israel	
			2010	LT – Lithuania	
			2010	MT – Malta	
			2010	SV – Slovenia	
			2011	HU – Hungary	
			2011	PO – Poland	
			2011	ZA – South Africa	
			2012	PT – Portugal	
			2012	SV – Sweden	
			2012	VN – Vietnam	
			2013	IR – Ireland	
			2013	IT – Italy	
TYPE 4. Conceptual Indicator Set	Country indicators sets for sustainable development	2000–2004	2002	CH – Switzerland	
			2003	NZ – New Zealand	
		2005–2009	2005	NO – Norway	
			2009	NL – Netherlands	
		2015–2019	2015	BE – Belgium	
	Other	2005–2009	2009	Measuring Sustainable Development	UNECE et al. (2008)
		2010–2014	2011	Green Growth Indicators	oecd.org/greengrowth/green-growth-indicators/
			2011	Better Life index (BLI)	oecdbetterlifeindex.org/
			2014	CES Recommendations	UNECE et al., (2014)

Notes

PREFACE

1 The beginning of Chapter 4 includes a brief discussion on the number of Beyond-GDP indicator systems.
2 Smits et al. (2014).
3 I can vividly remember reading about the conceptual debates in the early days of national income accounting in Lintott (1996).
4 The PhD thesis was later published as Bos (2009).

I REPLACING THE MOST INFLUENTIAL INDICATOR IN THE WORLD

1 For further details of the BEA "lock-up" procedures see Moyer (2016).
2 Vavreck (2009).
3 EC et al. (2009).
4 The EU's legal guidelines on national accounts refer to the European System of Accounts (ESA), which is based on the SNA.
5 The monarch of Bhutan decided in the 1970s to run his society on the principle of Gross National Happiness. However, more recently, the Prime Minister was becoming more critical. See "Index of Happiness? Bhutan's New Leader Prefers More Concrete Goals", *New York Times*, 4 October 2013.
6 Costanza et al. (2017) argue that societies' focus on growth, without consideration of the long-term consequences, is similar to an addiction. It might therefore be treated using therapies that have been created for individuals.
7 Kuznets (1934a, p. 7).
8 EC et al. (2009, p. 12).
9 There are already two suggestions in the literature to create an index from the SDGs (Costanza et al., 2016; Sachs et al., 2017).
10 As quoted in Landefeld (2000).
11 Schumpeter (1939).

12 Schumpeter (1942).

13 Kate Raworth makes a similar point her book *Doughnut Economics*, in which she stresses the communicative power of visualisations. She argues that economists have proposed seven powerful figures which have helped them to communicate their theories and policies to society.

14 There are macroeconomists that are critical of the common language laid down in the national accounts (see also Chapter 4). Nevertheless, the criticisms are usually formulated in terms of changes that should be made to the accounts. The SNA therefore still remains the foundation of this line of reasoning.

15 Parris and Kates (2003) make a similar point: "A major step in reducing such confusion would be the acceptance of distinctions in terminology, data, and methods."

16 Costanza et al. (2014a).

17 2030 is interesting from another standpoint. It is the 100-year anniversary of a famous prediction by Keynes. In 1930, in an essay entitled "Economic Possibilities for our Grandchildren" (printed in Keynes, 1931), Keynes predicted that 100 years later, in 2030, mankind would have solved "the economic problem", the need for humans to work hard to make a living and survive. His most famous prediction was that humans would only need to work about fifteen hours per week, having the rest of their time for leisure and higher pursuits such as arts and literature.

2 WHY IS GDP SUCCESSFUL?

1 A phrase borrowed from Schmelzer (2016).

2 Karabell (2014) discusses a full range of key indicators such as unemployment, inflation and consumer confidence but also sees GDP as the most influential.

3 The chapter draws on these references (Coyle, 2014; Philipsen, 2015; Fioramonti, 2013; Masood, 2016; Schmelzer, 2016; Pilling, 2018; Mazzucato, 2018) as well as more formal academic overviews of the national accounts, such as *The Income of Nations, The Accounts of Nations, The History of National Accounting* and *National Accounts for Analysis and Policy* as well as older references and scientific articles (Bos, 2009, 2017; Kendrick, 1970; Kenessey, 1994; Studenski, 1958; Vanoli, 2005).

4 World Bank (2010) sees the Domesday Book, commissioned by William
the Conqueror in 1058/1059, as one of the first efforts to measure
"wealth". They quote the Anglo-Saxon Chronicle, which says that the aim
was to measure "what, or how much, each man had, who was an occupier
of land in England, either in land or in stock, and how much money it
were worth".
5 The British efforts were by William Petty and Gregory King. The first
efforts in France were by De Boisguillebert and Vauban.
6 These data are from Studenski (1958). The year for the Netherlands is
corrected based on information from Bos (2009).
7 Studenski (1958).
8 Studenski (1958) distinguishes mercantilists, dissenters from
mercantilism, physiocratic concept, material production concept,
comprehensive production concept, Marxian national income theory and
Keynesian dynamic approach.
9 The Studenski line in Figure 2.1 shows how many countries had
experience in national accounting up to that point. The line is therefore
always increasing. England would be present since 1665 because of the
Petty estimates, irrespective of whether England actually did national
accounting in a given year. For the UN figures it simply shows the
number of countries submitting data to the official UN publication.
The UN data shows that the number of countries sometimes decreases.
Also, Studenski includes all estimates, whether they are from individual
researchers or from official government sources. The United Nations only
asks for "official statistics" from its member states which are produced
by government institutes. Finally, it is also important to note that the
number of countries and regions have varied significantly over the years.
For example, the break-up of the Soviet Union or Yugoslavia in the 1990s
increased the number of states significantly.
10 In fact there are even more countries and regions in the UN statistical
database, because the UN actually estimates these for countries that do
not themselves provide figures.
11 Studenski (1958, p. 158).
12 The demise of the Bretton Woods agreement was a process which took a
couple of years.
13 *Science* devoted a special section to the problems of the "postfactual era"
(Malakoff, 2017).

14 Kuznets (1934b).

15 The history of the measurement of unemployment data is covered by Karabell (2014).

16 Philipsen (2015).

17 Keynes (1936).

18 Leontief (1936).

19 The full text of Tinbergen's Dutch paper of 1936 is available in English in Klaassen et al. (1959).

20 In *The Economic Consequences of the Peace* Keynes wrote: "If we aim at the impoverishment of Central Europe, vengeance, I dare say, will not limp. Nothing can then delay for very long the forces of Reaction and the despairing convulsions of Revolution, before which the horrors of the later German war will fade into nothing, and which will destroy, whoever is victor, the civilisation and the progress of our generation" (Keynes, 1920).

21 Philipsen (2015).

22 Other economists also contributed to the war effort and the demobilisation after the war. For example, Wasilly Leontief worked at the US's Office of Strategic Services (head of the Russian Economic Subdivision) during the Second World War. An input–output table was used to determine the necessary steel capacity in the post-war US economy (Polenske, 2004). Another example is Tjalling Koopmans, the 1975 Nobel laureate, who joined the Allied war effort as a statistician for the British Merchant Shipping Mission in Washington in order to optimise the logistical streams necessary for the war effort.

23 Many of the names mentioned in this section were both economists and good statisticians. Arguably some leaned more towards economics and some more towards statistics, but most were proficient in both modelling and data compilation. Kuznets, Tinbergen, Meade, Stone and Leontief were Nobel Prize economists, but were also empirically savvy. Nowadays, data producers and academic economists are separate specialised disciplines.

24 Science in a broader sense also thrived in the war. The war had produced scientific breakthroughs that proved to be extremely powerful, in a positive and negative sense.

25 Schmelzer (2016) and Ward (2004).

26 Debreu (1991); Mirowski (1991, 2002); Weintraub (2002).

27 Weintraub (2002) recounts in some detail the peer review process of this classic Arrow and Debreu (1954) paper. The associate editor for *Econometrica* was Georgescu Roegen, who is discussed later in this book because of his work on thermodynamics in economics. The two reviewers were William Baumol, an economist, who favoured publication and Cecile Glenn Phipps, a mathematician, who was emphatically against publication (Weintraub, 2002, p. 195).

28 Solow (1956).

29 Desrosières (2001); Duncan and Shelton (1978).

30 This phenomenon did not happen equally fast in all countries. Christensen (2017) analyses four country cases to better understand the institutional conditions which led to proliferation of economic thinking in taxation policy.

31 Education as human capital (Becker, 1962, 1964), health as human capital (Becker, 2007), social interactions (Becker, 1974a), time allocation (Becker, 1965), advertising (Becker and Murphy, 1993) and insurance (Ehrlich and Becker, 1972) marriage (Becker, 1974b). Becker also wrote on the "the quantity and quality of life and world inequality" (Becker et al., 2005).

32 All these quotes are from Schmelzer (2016).

33 Schmelzer (2016).

34 Lucas (2003).

35 Galbraith (1958).

36 Schmelzer (2016).

37 Carson (1962); Ehrlich (1968); Hardin (1968).

38 Arndt (1978); Schmelzer (2016).

39 Cropper and Oates (1992).

40 Hordijk (1991).

41 WCED (1987).

42 Krugman (2009).

43 Solow (2008) also critically discusses the "state of macroeconomics". Skidelsky (2010) argues for the relevance of Keynesian theories after the financial crisis.

44 Sapienza and Zingales (2013).

45 "France to count happiness in GDP" (15 September 2009).

46 See also *The Future of Productivity* (OECD, 2015).

47 So far efforts to create a daily alternative for GDP have failed. Google tried to develop something based on Google searches but discontinued that

project. Yet by 2030 it would seem likely that there will be an indicator of this sort.

48 This chronology is based mostly on Bos (2009) and Vanoli (2005).

49 UN (1947).

50 The relationship seems to have been civil in terms of scientific debates (see for example Gilbert et al. (1948) and the response by Kuznets (1948).

51 Stone (1942).

52 Denison (1947).

53 UN (1953).

54 The first official estimates were produced in 1880 in Australia (Bos, 2009).

55 EC et al. (1993, 2009); UN (1968b).

56 It is thought that North Korea still uses the MPS.

57 Even between major nations there can be differences. The United States still uses a slightly different system, called National Income and Product Accounts (NIPA). Although NIPA is becoming increasingly similar to the SNA, it still is not fully consistent in its accounting scheme (McCulla et al., 2015). In the European setting, there are also fundamentally differing views about whether the illegal economy should be part of the accounts.

3 WHAT DOES GDP MEASURE (AND WHAT NOT)?

1 Van den Bergh (2009).

2 See van den Bergh (2009) for a good overview.

3 Kenessey (1994).

4 There are many areas which may fall under "non-observed or hidden economy". These are aspects such as illegal production or the barter economy, which officially fall under the SNA production boundary. At the same time, they may not be covered by official government surveys or may remain hidden for other reasons. Practical differences in survey approaches may therefore also lead to problems when comparing countries.

5 In the case of home cooking, the cost of all vegetables, meat and utensils are included in the national accounts. In the case of cleaning, all cleaning products are included. It is only the labour effort which is excluded from national accounts.

6 Health and education are two important areas of government services where productivity analysis has progressed.

7 Mazzucato (2018).

8 Big Mac index, *The Economist* (January 2017).

9 Deaton (2010) and Deaton and Heston (2008).

10 From a different perspective Schwartz (2004) actually argues that this increased choice actually leads to stress.

11 Bean (2016) and Boskin Commission (1996).

12 Manski (2015) and Morgenstern (1950).

13 This does not include revisions of the quarterly figures because of things like benchmark revisions.

14 Jerven (2013).

15 For a discussion of Moore's Law see chapter 3 in Brynjolfsson and McAfee (2014). Schuster (2016) asks whether Moore's law is coming to an end.

16 DeCanio (2016) presents a model that suggests that robots will depress wages.

17 Baldwin (2016).

18 Timmer et al. (2014).

19 The Economist (2015)

20 Rodrik (2011) and Stiglitz (2003).

21 Autor et al. (2016).

22 See Chapter 6 and Copeland and Taylor (2004).

23 Sturgeon (2013) and UNECE (2015).

24 This position is echoed in an OECD paper by Ahmad and Schreyer (2016). They do however point to the difficulties of measuring prices and transboundary flows.

25 Kuznets (1946).

26 Easterlin (1974).

27 Source: Web of science, search term "Easterlin paradox". Deaton (2012) found that the financial crisis had only a short-lived effect on SWB.

28 Various overviews have been written (Diener and Biswas-Diener, 2008; Frey and Stutzer, 2002; Layard, 2005).

29 The influences are income, personal characteristics (who we are, our genetic makeup and age, gender, ethnicity, personality), socially developed characteristics (education, health, type of work, unemployment), how we spend our time (the work and activities we engage in), attitudes and beliefs

towards self/others/life (including marriage and intimate relationships, having children, seeing family and friends), and the wider economic, social and political environment (such as income inequality, unemployment rates, inflation, welfare system and public insurance, degree of democracy, climate and the natural environment, safety and deprivation of the area, and urbanisation).

30 Piketty (2014).

31 Piketty (2014, p. 14).

32 Elsby et al. (2013); Karabarbounis and Neiman (2014).

33 Pfister (2010).

34 Ehrlich and Holdren (1971).

35 When environmental pressures grow, but not as fast as the economy, it is known as relative decoupling. When environmental pressures fall while GDP increases, it is called absolute decoupling.

36 Stern (2004).

37 Martínez-Alier et al. (2010).

38 Van den Bergh (2017) and Raworth (2017) argue for an agnostic perspective on the growth debate.

39 The Elfstedentocht is a traditional 200 km ice-skating race in Fryslân (North of the Netherlands) which can only be held when the winters are extremely cold. It has only been held three times in the last fifty years and because of climate change, the frequency is likely to reduce even further.

40 Some economists have tried to argue that GDP and social welfare are in fact conceptually equivalent. Using mathematical proof, Weitzman (1976) shows that Net National Product is a measure of social welfare. However, to prove this, as Weitzman himself says, "We abstract heroically in more ways than one". Most striking is that social welfare is assumed to be equivalent to consumption ("ultimate end"). In the model the aim is to maximise consumption because this leads to the highest utility or welfare.

41 The Geary-Khamis dollar is a method to make long-term intertemporal comparisons of GDP.

42 Given that this is a global average, it masks the specific economic boom periods (and collapse) that some countries went through.

43 Source of all figures in this section: CLIO-INFRA.

44 Van Zanden et al. (2014).

45 Kubiszewski et al. (2013).

4 WHY IS BEYOND-GDP NOT SUCCESSFUL?

1 Some feel that GDP should not be replaced at all, but rather that indicators are needed, *in addition* to GDP. The latter group prefers the term to be "GDP and Beyond" rather than "Beyond-GDP".

2 IISD (2017).

3 Wikiprogress.org (2017).

4 It is hard to estimate but other authors have come to similar conclusions. Sirgy (2011) says: "There are literally hundreds (maybe thousands) of indicators projects that are not published in scholarly journals." Parris and Kates (2003) mention over 500 efforts. Other overviews include Bleys (2012), who provides a classification scheme and identifies twenty-three Beyond-GDP indicators (but no indicator sets are included). Volkery et al. (2006) look at seventeen national sustainable development strategies. Steurer and Hametner (2013) review twenty-four SDI sets in Europe. Three hundred community indicator systems are listed at www.community indicators.net/. Hagerty et al. (2001) review twenty-two of the most-used Quality of Life indexes.

5 https://seea.un.org/content/global-assessment-environmental-economic-accounting

6 In fact, estimates can even be made for countries that do not have their own measurement programmes. For example, Abdallah et al. (2008) estimated life satisfaction scores for 178 countries by bringing together subjective well-being data from four surveys and using stepwise regression to estimate scores for nations where no subjective data is available.

7 Various international environmental agreements/treaties have also been instrumental in stimulating data collection. In 1979, the Convention on Long-Range Transboundary Air Pollution was adopted by the UNECE, which led to many protocols on air pollution. In 1987, the Montreal Protocol on Substances that Deplete the Ozone Layer was agreed upon. In 1992, the United Nations Framework Convention on Climate Change (UNFCCC) was launched and followed by the Kyoto Protocol in 1997, where countries agreed to reductions in greenhouse gases to counter global climate change. All these developments added to the pressure to get more environmental data. One of the first tasks set by the UNFCCC was that nations establish national inventories of greenhouse gas emissions and

removals. These were used to create the benchmark levels for 1990. They need to be updated by all the countries that have agreed to targets under the Kyoto Protocol.

8 Galbraith (1958).

9 Carson (1962); Ehrlich (1968); Galbraith (1958) and Hardin (1968).

10 Masood (2016).

11 Pearce (2002); Røpke (2004) and Sandmo (2015).

12 Schmelzer (2016).

13 The term "sustainable development" was actually coined earlier in the *World Conservation Strategy*, published by the International Union for the Conservation of Natural Resources in 1980. The document did not, however, contain the definition of sustainable development as it was later defined in the Brundtland Report.

14 UN (1992).

15 Most recent publication: Lange et al. (2017).

16 OECD (2013).

17 See the World Happiness Database (WHD) by Veenhoven (2017).

18 Another subjective indicator actually did far better than SWB: the consumer confidence index started in the 1950s. This indicator asked respondents how confident people are about the economic conditions. George Katona at the University of Michigan started this line of research to study the relationship between the economy and the mindset of people (Karabell, 2014). He believed that if consumers felt confident about economic conditions then this would be good for the economy. Measuring consumer attitudes therefore helped in understanding the economic cycle. At first these efforts were frowned upon by the (then) mainstream economists, but later they turned out to generate valuable information; so much so that these surveys are nowadays done by commercial firms.

19 See Schmelzer (2016) for the discussions in the OECD about the social indicator movement. The UN perspective is provided in UN (1989) and Ward (2004).

20 This is based on the World Happiness Report 2018. In total there is data for 156 countries but not all of them are surveyed each year.

21 Ecological Monetary Assessment (EMA) (see the chapter by Stone in Kahneman et al., 1999) and the Day Reconstruction Method (DRM).

22 Nordhaus and Tobin (1972).

23 Note that other elements are corrected for as well. For example, the utility of the durable goods is spread over the lifetime of the product.

24 For example, Lawn (2007) adopts the term green accounting although it is also sometimes referred to as "extended accounting" (Eisner, 1988).

25 Eisner (1988) provides a good overview of the efforts up to the mid-1980s.

26 Daly and Cobb (1989).

27 (Cobb et al., 1995).

28 Bagstad et al. (2014).

29 Talberth and Weisdorf (2017).

30 Hueting (1974).

31 The method requires estimating technology cost curves, sustainability limits and also requires assumption about how an economy might react to imposing the technology. In its most recent application this was done using a general equilibrium model (Gerlagh et al., 2002). The method received support from Nobel Laureate Jan Tinbergen (Tinbergen and Hueting, 1991).

32 Hicks (1939).

33 Pearce and Atkinson (1993).

34 We have not discussed studies that investigate relative comparisons of "welfare" measures that go beyond GDP (Becker et al., 2005; Jones and Klenow, 2016). These approaches include aspects such as health and leisure time in their welfare measurement This provides a method for country comparison of welfare as well as growth rates but does not generate absolute values.

35 SCP (1974). See Boelhouwer (2010) for details of Life Situation Index.

36 Sen (1985, 1999).

37 This is quoted in Masood (2014).

38 Composite indicators are less suited to growth analysis because the growth figure has no theoretical interpretation.

39 The author was a member of this working group and there were significant differences of opinion. Some advocated Type 1 while a large group advocated Type 3.

40 Another Type 4 indicator set of the OECD are the Green Growth Indicators.

41 Edens (2013).

42 Vanoli (2005).

43 According to the OECD a satellite accounts "provide a framework linked to the central accounts and which enables attention to be focused on a certain field or aspect of economic and social life in the context of national accounts; common examples are satellite accounts for the environment, or tourism, or unpaid household work".

44 UN (1993).

45 The way to measure environmental damage is a matter of considerable debate in the SEEA 1993.

46 In fact the SEEA 1993 even includes a discussion about household work.

47 UN et al. (2003).

48 UN et al. (2014).

49 Note that the SEEA, just like the SNA, is part of a process which is constantly evolving. Things which are not considered part of the Central Framework now, such as degradation, might be part of future versions of the SEEA. Apart from the central framework there are also a number of separate SEEA manuals related to water, energy and materials. Some environmental problems, such as biodiversity loss, have not been dealt with fully in the SEEA Central Framework, which is why "experimental ecosystem accounts" were published related to ecosystem services (EC et al., 2013). Just like the national accounts, it is likely that the SEEA accounts will continue to develop in order to cater to new issues. In practice, statistical offices tend to focus on the physical accounts. There are other monetary accounts in the SEEA which are popular. For example, there is an account which quantifies the economic importance of the environmental goods and services sector (EGSS) for the economy. But these are not the same as green accounting aggregates.

50 https://seea.un.org/content/global-assessment-environmental-economic-accounting

51 Bleys and Whitby (2015) identify four opportunities: "harmonizing and updating the methodological framework, extending macroeconomic models to include a wider range of welfare-related items, improving the communication around these indicators and promoting indicator and researcher entrepreneurship".

52 It is also important to note that in some cases, Beyond-GDP indicators provide different conclusions about how things are developing thereby adding to societal confusion (Nourry, 2008; Wilson et al., 2007).

5 OUTLINE OF THE STRATEGY

1 Schmelzer (2016).

2 Granovetter (2017).

3 Sustainable National Income (SNI) is not included in this list, not because it does not have intellectual merit, but rather because it has achieved little institutional traction.

4 Bagstad et al. (2014).

5 It was proposed in the SDG setting (target 17.19) but did not manage to make it to the final resolution (UN, 2017).

6 However, in the case of the capital approach, the most often heard criticism is related to the substitutability of capital (weak versus strong sustainability).

7 Stiglitz has continued to work on this issue as part of the High-Level Expert Group on the Measurement of Economic Performance and Social Progress (HLEG). A new report (Stiglitz II) was released in November 2018 but the impact of this report is not yet clear.

8 Glaser (2012) is one of the many authors that suggested a scientific approach, arguing that: "A major difficulty is the interdisciplinary nature of sustainable development. It cuts across economic, environmental and social dimensions in ways that are not well understood. An understanding of climate change, for example, will be necessary to define measures across water, food and energy security. The working group will need to draw on the best available knowledge to analyse these linkages, possible synergies and trade-offs."

9 To assist in the quantification of SDGs, the UN Statistical Commission set up the Inter-agency Expert Group on SDG Indicators. One of their tasks was to make an inventory of potential indicators for each target. The recent report by the IAEG-SDG categorised them into three tiers:

- Tier 1: Indicator conceptually clear, established methodology and standards available and data regularly produced by countries.
- Tier 2: Indicator conceptually clear, established methodology and standards available but data is not regularly produced by countries.
- Tier 3: Indicator for which there is no established methodology and standards or methodology/standards are being developed/tested.

The report makes clear that there is a great statistical challenge. The status on 21 December 2016 was: 83 Tier I indicators, 59 Tier II indicators and 83 Tier III indicators. Five indicators have multiple tiers; different components of the indicator are classified into different tiers (IAEG, 2016).

10 For example, Statistics Netherlands (which is an advanced statistical office) published their first SDG report and found that there were still many SDGs for which data did not exist (CBS, 2017).

11 OECD (2017).

12 Note that it is rather striking that in the SDG process, the influence of economists is actually quite small, at least in terms of the conceptual framework.

13 Daniel Kahneman, originally a psychologist, was a member. He had won the Nobel Prize for Economics by then.

14 The full name of the Stiglitz Commission is the "Commission on the Measurement of Economic Performance and Social Progress", which also implies that the economy is the primary issue with social progress was of secondary concern.

15 Richard Stone, the main architect of the SNA, contributed greatly to the idea of satellite accounts. In the early half of the 1970s, as a UN consultant, he published *Towards a System of Social and Demographic Statistics*, which was based on earlier work that he had done for the OECD (Stone, 1971, 1975). In these accounts he extended the accounting ideas to population, education and time use. Ruggles and Ruggles (1973) also had proposals about how to create social accounts. More recent attempts were focused on measuring productivity better (Jorgenson, 2009; Nordhaus et al., 2006), human capital (UNECE, 2016) or intangible capital (Corrado et al., 2009). Antolini (2016). argues that it will be inevitable for the SNA to include happiness in future.

16 Campagna et al. (2017) also argue that economic terminology masks the real environmental damage.

17 These are all methods which fall neatly under the overall definition of economics which Lionel Robins gave: "Economics is a science which studies human behaviour as a relationship between ends and scarce means which have alternative uses."

18 Van den Bergh and Botzen (2015).

19 Quoted in Silk (1976, p. 208).

20 Hopwood et al. (2005), Kates et al. (2005) and Redclift (2005).

21 This is also more popularly known as "People–Planet–Profit".

22 Terminology from the CES recommendations (UNECE et al., 2014).

23 Raworth (2017).

24 Scientifically neutral is used in the sense that a single science, economics, does not dominate the terms and theory. Of course, a term like "neutral" is problematic because no theory can be seen as 100 per cent objective.

25 www.nobelprize.org/uploads/2018/06/stone-lecture.pdf

26 For a wonderful description of the history of double-entry bookkeeping for companies and economies see Gleeson-White (2012).

27 In fact, it is not just the direct links between people that are important but also the second or third tier connections, which Mark Granovetter calls the "strength of weak ties" (Granovetter, 1973).

28 For overviews of network theory see Newman (2003) and Strogatz (2001).

29 This type of thinking is also similar to the *Tipping Point* narrative of Gladwell (2000).

6 GLOBAL ENVIRONMENTAL ACCOUNTS (GENA)

1 The 8.7 million comes from Mora et al. (2011). The number is disputed and is seen by some as an underestimate (see for a discussion www.nytimes.com/2011/08/30/science/30species.html).

2 The term was first used by Nobel Prize winner (Chemistry) Paul Crutzen in an article in *Nature* in 2002 (Crutzen, 2002). A highly cited follow-up is Steffen et al. (2007). See also Vitousek et al. (1997).

3 Looking at the matter even more fundamentally, the number of genes per species can conceptually be captured in a stock/flow account. This would give insights into genetic drift and the influence of monocultures on genetic diversity.

4 The SEEA does cover depletion of natural resources, which is the reduction in *quantity* of environmental assets. Degradation is the reduction in *quality*, which is not covered.

5 In the SNA 2008 (EC et al. 2009, p. 42).

6 The SNA does include some natural assets and motivates it as such (EC et al., 2009, p. 7): "However, the ownership criterion is important for determining which natural resources are treated as assets in the SNA.

Natural resources such as land, mineral deposits, fuel reserves, uncultivated forests or other vegetation and wild animals are included in the balance sheets provided that institutional units are exercising effective ownership rights over them, that is, are actually in a position to be able to benefit from them. Assets need not be privately owned and could be owned by government units exercising ownership rights on behalf of entire communities. Thus, many environmental assets are included within the SNA. Resources such as the atmosphere or high seas, over which no ownership rights can be exercised, or mineral or fuel deposits that have not been discovered or that are unworkable, are not included as they are not capable of bringing any benefits to their owners, given the technology and relative prices existing at the time."

7 www.nature.com/articles/d41586-018-05984-3

8 The fact that the word "may" is used does not make this part of the definition very clear anyway.

9 Earlier versions of the SEEA (1993 and 2003) were far more forceful in arguing that all natural capital should be included.

10 Note that certain system boundaries are adopted. For example the IPCC does not include all carbon in the core of the earth. From a conceptual point of view, these are part of the carbon stock on earth, but given that they don't play an active role in the carbon cycle measuring these values are not relevant.

11 It is argued that negative emissions technologies should be adopted to recapture the CO_2 in the air. There are however serious limitations to these technologies (see Anderson and Peters (2016) and Smith et al. (2016)).

12 Botzen et al. (2008) and Friman and Hjerpe (2015) discuss the issue of historical responsibility of countries for their CO_2 emissions.

13 Note that total emissions in Table 6.1 and Table 6.2 are not the same (354 PgC vs. 365 PgC) because they are from different databases and there are some methodological differences.

14 However, the table on industry-level emissions only exists for years from 1990 onwards.

15 Nowadays the PIOT focuses on the physical flows in the economy. In future, if you look at the intellectual predecessors of the PIOT, it was an accounting framework for the economy *and* the environment (Daly, 1968; Victor, 1972). Those frameworks were similar in scope to the GENA.

16 Davis and Caldeira (2010); Jakob and Marschinski (2013); Peters (2008); Peters et al. (2011).

17 This is a term coined by Baldwin (2006).

18 Zhou and Wang (2016) provide an overview of the literature and methods. Marques et al. (2012) propose the so-called income-based responsibility where the ownership of the emitting factories is taken as the criterion for responsibility. For example, many of the factories in China are owned by companies from the developed countries.

19 See also Levin (1992) on the relationship between population and ecosystem dynamics.

20 From an accounting perspective, the concept of an ecosystem is more difficult to delineate than a species because the boundary between two types of ecosystems is not always obvious.

21 www.worldwildlife.org/pages/rhino-facts-and-species

22 This is an adaption of Table 4.7 of the SEEA-EEA.

23 Sala et al. (2000) create scenarios for biodiversity up to 2100. They find that for terrestrial ecosystems, the main pressures come from land-use change as well as climate change, nitrogen deposition, biotic exchange and elevated carbon dioxide concentration. See also Hooper et al. (2005), Nelson et al. (2006) and Srinivasan et al. (2008).

24 See also Norgaard (2010) and (Chee, 2004).

25 Wilson (1998). A review is provided by Tylianakis and Morris (2016).

26 See Paine (1966) for early work in this field. There were also preliminary attempts to link ecosystems functioning to the economic input–output framework in the late 1960s–1970s (Daly, 1968; Isard, 1972; Isard et al., 1968). The line of research later developed under the name Ecosystem Network Analysis (ENA) (Fath et al., 2007; Hannon, 1973; Lenzen, 2007).

27 According to Strogatz (2001).

28 Suh (2005) uses mass and energy to synthesise the work of ecologists and economists.

29 Groffman et al. (2006); Holling (1973); and Holling et al. (2009).

30 Malthus (1798).

31 Ehrlich (1968) and Meadows et al. (1972).

32 Boulding is reputed to have said this during hearing for the Energy Reorganization Act of 1973 (Hearings, Ninety-third Congress, first session, on H.R. 11510, p. 248).

33 Arrow et al. (1995).

34 Scheffers et al. (2016) describe the effects of climate change on biodiversity.

35 Barnosky et al. (2011), Ceballos et al. (2015) and Pimm and Raven (2000).

7 GLOBAL SOCIETAL ACCOUNTS (GSA)

1 UNDESA (2008).

2 De Haas (2010); Greenwood (1975); Lee (1966); Massey (1990); and Massey et al. (1993).

3 UNDESA (2008, p. 102) states: "In general, 'usual residence' is defined for census purposes as the place at which the person lives at the time of the census, and has been there for some time or intends to stay there for some time." The SNA also has a similar criterion but it stresses the economic aspects more. Chapter 19 (paragraph 19.10) states: "persons are resident in the country where they have the strongest links thereby establishing a centre of predominant economic interest. Generally, the criterion would be based on their country of residence for one year or more. In most cases, the concept of residence is straightforward, being based on the dwelling a person occupies on a permanent basis, although there are some borderline cases discussed further in chapter 26."

4 Stone (1971, 1975).

5 Schutlz (1961) and Becker (1962, 1964).

6 A good overview of all human capital methods, monetary and non-monetary, can be found in Wößmann (2003).

7 OECD (2001a, p. 18).

8 Hanushek and Woessmann (2008).

9 WHO (1948).

10 "Non-profit institutions serving households (NPISHs) are legal entities that are principally engaged in the production of non-market services for households or the community at large and whose main resources are voluntary contributions."

11 EC et al. (2009, p. 2).

12 Having a good grasp on the population and institutional units is essential for a country's statistical system. If a country does not know the number of people, households, companies and government units, it will never be able to produce good national statistics.

13 For overviews of the literature see Woolcock (1998) and Durlauf and Fafchamps (2004), which discuss many of the important source such as Bourdieu (1986); Dasgupta (2005); Fukuyama (1995, 2000); Grootaert (1998); Knack and Keefer (1997); Portes (1998); Putnam (2000); Sobel (2002).
14 Groot et al. (2007) and Helliwell and Putnam (2004).
15 Kawachi et al. (1997).
16 Pretty and Ward (2001).
17 Nannestad (2008).
18 North (1991, p .97).
19 Simon (1991).
20 An overview of social networks is provided by Girvan and Newman (2002).
21 Williams et al. (2016) discuss the various ways in which time poverty is defined in the literature.
22 Goodin et al. (2005).
23 The Dutch East India Company is often seen as one of the first shareholder funded multinationals.
24 UNDESA (2008).
25 UNDESA (2015).
26 The data is obtained in the OECD's Programme for International Student Assessment (PISA) and Programme for the International Assessment of Adult Competencies (PIAAC).

8 GLOBAL ECONOMIC ACCOUNTS (GECA)

1 Gordon (2016).
2 This does not mean that the SNA should not improve or change. Chapter 3 has already discussed many aspects on the research agenda such as intangibles, ICT and globalisation.
3 Bernstein and Baker (2013).
4 Data on R&D expenditures (i.e. investments) are collected in most OECD countries and can therefore be recorded in the production accounts as investments.
5 EC et al. (2009, p. 237).
6 UNDESA (2008, Table 2, pp. 188–189).
7 Formally, the SNA and SEEA are based on Supply and Use Tables (SUT) which split the input–output thinking into two separate tables. However, this distinction is not important for the purpose of this book.

8 Input–output tables are either industry-by-industry or commodity-by-commodity in scope. The intermediate inputs and outputs are shown using either of these two types. Supply and use tables have an industry-by-commodity layout.

9 Global input–output tables can be seen as networks (Fagiolo et al., 2010; Maluck and Donner, 2015). This is also why non-economists with knowledge of network theory are publishing papers in journals such as *Physics Review E* based on these international input–output tables (Serrano and Boguñá, 2003). In some cases economic models (gravity models) are combined with engineering network models (Hübler, 2016). Network theory has also been used to investigate international relations (Hafner-Burton et al., 2009).

10 Coe (2011); Gereffi (2014); Timmer et al. (2014); Baldwin (2006, 2016).

11 For an overview of databases see Tukker and Dietzenbacher (2013).

12 Sturgeon, (2013); UNECE (2015).

13 The Economist (2011).

14 Smith (1776).

15 Chang (2014).

16 Merciai and Schmidt (2018); The European Commission has also financed a follow-up project called PANORAMA.

17 Grübler et al. (1999) provides long-term assessment of energy technologies in non-monetary units.

18 The current PIOT are focused on mass and only report the total weight of products such as cars. In future it would be highly beneficial to add a third dimension to this type of accounting to show the underlying material composition of products (Hoekstra and van den Bergh, 2006). For example, a car will be split into the metals, plastics and rubber and all other material components. This will then enable us to tackle topics such as substitution or recycling in the context of the circular economy.

19 Acemoglu and Autor (2010).

20 Physical inputs can be used for many different things: fossil fuels may be used for their energy, but may also be used to produce chemical or plastics (Hoekstra and van den Bergh, 2006). Services are even more difficult: insurance, business consulting services or transportation services provide different functions in the production process. Wallis and North (1988) showed that a sizeable part of the economy is actually composed of "transactions costs".

294 NOTES TO PAGES 179–182

21 Timmer et al. (2018).

22 This is the premise of the so-called endogenous growth theory that links R&D and innovations to economic growth. See for example the work of Nobel Prize winner Paul Romer.

23 For 2016, durables amounted to €54,252 million. The total consumption of goods was €132,206 million and the total consumption of goods and services €310,196 million (Statistics Netherlands, 2017).

24 The only exception is the treatment of houses. The purchase of a house is not recorded as consumption (see Chapter 3). The SNA "imputes" a value for the housing services which home-owners "produce" for themselves.

25 Petrol use and repairs, car leasing services and train tickets are also recorded per year. This makes comparison of annual costs of the various modalities on the basis of national accounts data impossible without knowing the length of the life of cars.

26 There are also some fairly controversial categories in "miscellaneous". For example, the consumption of prostitution is included, which means that increases in these expenditures contribute to the economy.

27 Life insurance is a bit of a paradox. The benefits of this service only kick in when the purchaser is dead. In that respect life insurance is an odd thing to buy for a *homo economicus* trying to maximise personal utility. Of course, if you would expand the utility function to "caring about loved ones", this might be modelled.

28 The COICOP categories show the consumption of the household. However, there are other forms of consumption. The first type is by non-profit institutions serving households (NPISHs). These can be for housing, health, recreation and culture, education, social protection or other services). These will also benefit individual consumers. "Government consumption" occurs when services are provided by governments which benefit individuals or are public goods. The purposes of these consumption types are governed by the COPNI and COFOG classifications respectively.

29 Apart from these adjustments to consumption, economists have also suggested other ways of improving the theoretical notion of utility and consumption. For example, some economists explicitly included the characteristics of the products in their model (Gorman, 1980; Lancaster, 1966, 1971). Lancaster developed a model in which it was the characteristics of the consumer good that led to utility.

30 Grzeskowiak et al. (2014) argues that the durable goods have different psychological effects during various stages in the product life-cycle: purchase, preparation, ownership, consumption and maintenance experiences.

31 Quotes are from the SNA 2008 (EC et al., 2009, pp. 216 and 608).

32 EC et al. (2009, p. 608).

33 "[T]he number of users, their willingness to pay, and their trust in peers and the platform as the key value drivers." This is the conclusion of Enders et al. (2008) about what drives the value of social networks.

34 Adler and Seok-Woo Kwon (2002), Nahapiet and Ghoshal (1998) and Tsai and Sumantra Ghoshal (1998) take the concept of social capital and relate it to firms. Durlauf (2012), Foster (2005) and Rosser (1999) explored the issue of complexity and economics. The relationships between corporate boards were used to analyse the spread of "poison pills" and "golden parachutes" in companies (Davis and Greve, 1997). Vitali and Battiston (2014) and Vitali et al. (2011) analysed the network of corporate control in the world. Networks are not exclusive to persons or institutional units. Goods can also be linked in a network. So-called network effects are defined by Birke (2009) as "Network effects, the increase in value of consuming a product if many other consumers use the same product, are a feature of many markets and in particular of many high-technology products". Many companies try and create a suite of products which are all interconnected. Especially in the realm of computers, an operating system or some other kind of standard (Apple i-tunes store, or Google search engine) gives a company network power.

35 On the financial crisis, networks and trade see Saracco et al. (2016).

36 For a survey of network economics see Shy (2011).

37 Autor et al. (2003); Goldin and Katz (1998); Griliches (1969).

38 The Guardian (2016). Redmond (2001) also looks at the limits to consumption.

39 In both cases, production and consumption, more thought needs to be given to the concept of "benefits" of the inputs. The concept of "benefits" is referred to a couple of times in the SNA but a classification is not supplied.

40 In the field of financial markets behavioural economics is already having a major impact. See for example the work of Nobel Prize winner Robert Shiller.

9 GLOBAL DISTRIBUTION ACCOUNTS (GDA)

1 It is mentioned four times in the SNA 1993.
2 EC et al. (2009, p. 520).
3 Note that in the past the SNA process has been receptive to new phenomena. During the SNA 1993 the revision process was sensitive to the discussion on environmental issues which eventually led to the development of the SEEA. This did not happen in the case of inequality.
4 See annex 4 of the SNA 2008.
5 Figure 9.2 could also be organised differently. For example, Lakner and Milanovic (2016) and Milanovic (2016) discuss the famous "elephant chart" in which the growth rate (1988–2008) of incomes of all countries are ranked. He does not stratify according to individual countries. He thereby can show that the global rich (the 95th–100th percentiles) did extremely well, wherever they lived (this is the trunk of the elephant). The people in the world who were around the 50th percentile also did well (the back of the elephant). The bottom percentile (global poor) and the 80th–90th percentiles (which is suggested are the western lower and middle classes) were however subject to much lower growth rates.
6 Rodrik (2011).
7 There is another sector which is defined in the SNA: the "rest of the world". For Tables 9.1 and 9.2 this has been dropped but it will be discussed further in Table 9.3.
8 "Property income accrues when the owners of financial assets and natural resources put them at the disposal of other institutional units. The income payable for the use of financial assets is called investment income while that payable for the use of a natural resource is called rent. Property income is the sum of investment, income and rent" (EC et al., 2009, p. 150).
9 The underlying data of Statistics Netherlands provides more information about detailed asset categories. For example, the financial assets range from gold to pensions to shares. There is also disaggregation to around twenty-nine different types of produced assets.
10 Currently the balance sheets of corporations have assets. However, in terms of ultimate ownership, either governments or households have the

shares in these entities. Note that these assets can also be held by foreign governments and households.

11 EC et al. (2009, p. 16).

12 The G-20 Data Gaps Initiative also aims to improve the availability of from-whom-to-whom tables.

13 Joint Committee on Taxation (2010).

14 www.wsj.com/graphics/apple-cash/

15 Acemoglu and Robinson (2012).

16 OECD Expert Group on Extended Supply-Use Tables.

17 See Michel et al. (2018) for the role of exporters and domestic producers in global value chains.

18 Yang et al. (2015).

19 The OECD plays an important role in trying to avoid unwanted tax structure though a programme called "Base erosion and profit shifting (BEPS)". As the OECD says: "This refers to tax avoidance strategies that exploit gaps and mismatches in tax rules to artificially shift profits to low or no-tax locations. Under the inclusive framework, over 100 countries and jurisdictions are collaborating to implement the BEPS measures and tackle BEPS." See www.oecd.org/tax/beps/

20 www.WID.world

21 Piketty et al. (2016).

22 Alvaredo et al. (2017) and Zwijnenburg et al. (2016).

23 Note that income and wealth are different to most other scarce resources in the sense that they are transferable. Through taxes, income can be shifted from one unit to another. Some of the other scarce resources cannot be shifted from one person to another. For example, you cannot transfer your education level to someone else.

24 UNDP (2015).

25 There are various studies related to health inequalities, including Allison and Foster (2004), Deaton (2003), Gakidou et al. (2000) and Pradhan et al. (2003).

26 Hubacek et al. (2017).

27 Druckman et al. (2012) link carbon emissions to time use rather than to goods and services. This might also be an interesting perspective in a distributional setting.

10 GLOBAL QUALITY ACCOUNTS (GQA) AND QUALITY INDICATORS

1 Daly (1992).

2 The SGNA takes well-being and sustainability as a basis. There are other terms such as "quality of life" which might also been used (see Sirgy et al., 2006, for an overview).

3 See Hicks (1975) for a historical overview of welfare economics.

4 This quote was taken from Kimball et al. (2006).

5 There has been a long debate about whether utility of individuals can be aggregated. Cardinal utility assumes that absolute satisfaction levels exist and that it is therefore possible to add them up. Ordinal utility theory implies that it is only meaningful to indicate the preference for one option over another. However, one cannot say how much better. Ordinal utility took over economic thinking after the 1930s (see for example Hicks and Allen, 1934). Another problem in aggregation of individual preferences into social welfare is known as Arrow's impossibility theorem (Arrow, 1950). This social choice theory shows that under certain assumptions it is impossible to satisfy the preferences of all citizens simultaneously. See also Ng (1997, 2003), who argues for a return of cardinal thinking.

6 Alfred Marshall, introduced the notion that market price is determined by both supply and demand of commodities. Before Marshall there were other theories of value which thought that the price of a product was equal to the cost of the inputs. The supply of commodities is defined by the supply function, which generally shows that producers will provide a greater quantity of products if the price rises. The demand curve typically shows that consumers are willing to buy many goods at a low price but that demand drops as the price rises. This demand for goods and services is determined by the utility that people derive from them.

7 Slesnick (1998) provides an overview of the theoretical aspect of the relationship between consumer surplus and utility.

8 In theory, the concept of utility is not measured in money. The goal in economic models is simply to generate the maximum amount of "utils" per period.

9 Freeman et al. (2014) provide a comprehensive overview of the theoretical and practical methodologies involved in measuring environmental and resource values.

10 See Costanza et al. (1997) for the original study and Constanza et al.
    (2014b) for an update. This type of accounting was later also pursued in
    The Economics of Ecosystem and Biodiversity (TEEB, 2010). Later still,
    the SEEA process created experimental accounts for ecosystem services
    (EC et al., 2013). De Groot et al. (2012) provide a meta-analysis of several
    hundred studies about ecosystems services from around the world.

11 Sen (1985).

12 Gary Becker did analyse marriage from a welfare perspective
    (Becker, 1972).

13 Dani Rodrik (2015), in his book *Economics Rules*, explains that
    economists do not make these assumptions (such as *Homo economicus*)
    because they believe they are true. Economists use mathematical
    simplification in order to illustrate mechanisms. Rodrik argues that it is
    not a problem if economic models have unrealistic assumptions. It is only
    a problem if these use simplistic *critical* assumptions, which means that
    if you changed these assumptions, the model mechanisms would be
    different.

14 See also other discussions on *homo economicus*: Anderson (2000); Bowles
    and Gintis (1993); Henrich et al. (2001); Ng and Tseng (2008).

15 Other types of capital have been suggested as well (see for example Arrow
    et al., 2012).

16 For the "here and now", the Stiglitz Report stresses that consumption
    and income are to be preferred above production indicators such as GDP.

17 EC et al. (2009, p. 416).

18 The valuation of some of the specific economic and financial capital
    stocks from the SNA still do not have robust methods. For example,
    valuation of intellectual property rights and non-produced assets such as
    marketing assets and goodwill are problematic.

19 The SNA describes the difference between the PIM and NPVs method as
    follows: "There are thus two sorts of questions that may be posed about
    the value of an asset; (i) how much would it fetch if sold, and (ii) how much
    will it contribute to production over its useful life. The first of these is the
    traditional question asked by national accountants; the second is basic
    to studies of productivity" (EC et al., 2009, p. 416).

20 See for example Weitzman (1998), which discusses the discount rate to be
    used for the very distant future.

21 OECD (2001b).

22 Schultz (1961) and Becker (1962, 1964).

23 Le et al. (2003) provide a comparison of the two approaches. The economic aspects of health were incorporated into the human capital approach by Becker (2007) and Grossman (1972).

24 Boarini et al. (2012); Liu (2011).

25 Lange et al. (2017).

26 The process of defining the services provided by natural capital was already undertaken in the 1970s, but has not so far been systematically attempted for social capital.

27 Ayres (2007).

28 Vemuri and Costanza (2006) is a rare example where the contributions of capital stocks to life satisfaction are estimated.

29 The latest version of the *Changing Wealth of Nations* of the World Bank seems to follow this interpretation too. In its executive summary it states that "Wealth indicates the prospects of maintaining that income over the long run" (Lange et al., 2017).

30 Sen (1999). Fleurbaey (2009, 2015) provides a theoretical synthesis of utility, capabilities and subjective well-being.

31 For further reading on the capability approach see Anand et al. (2009); Robeyns (2005, 2006); Nussbaum (2000).

32 Sen was opposed to reducing well-being to a single indicator. When Mahbub ul Haq, the initiator of the HDI at the UN Development Programme, tried to get Sen on board, Masood (2016, p. 158) quotes Sen as saying: "Look, you are sophisticated enough guy to know that to capture complex reality in one number is just vulgar, like GDP." Ul Haq is then reputed to have replied: "Amartya, I want you to create something as vulgar as GDP."

33 Dolan et al. (2008).

34 Austin (2016) argues that the policy decision would be much better served by the capability approach rather than the "hegemony of happiness".

35 Kahneman et al. (1999).

36 OECD (2013, table 2.1).

37 Strack et al. (1988).

38 Diener et al. (2013).

39 Kahneman and Tversky (1979; Tversky and Kahneman (1992).

40 Fehr and Fischbacher (2003); Fehr and Gachter (2002); Fehr and Schmidt (1999).

41 Kahneman (2011).

42 https://en.wikipedia.org/wiki/List_of_cognitive_biases

43 Thaler (2015).

44 Veenhoven (1996) proposes something similar: the happy life expectancy. This combines life evaluation, rather than affect, with the number of years that people live.

45 The data is taken from Kahneman et al. (2004). See also Krueger et al. (2009).

46 See also Gershuny (2012).

47 Note that the survey was done amongst 909 employed women. Therefore all respondents were recorded as "working" so it is not a representative sample of society.

48 Ecosystem networks also contribute to human well-being (Naeem et al., 2016).

49 This can also lead to unhappiness, such as the relationship between workers and their boss. Technical competence of bosses is the single most important predictor of worker satisfaction according to Artz et al. (2016).

50 Note that time-use accounts do not provide insights into traumatic experiences or life events that might have long-lasting impacts on well-being. Kendler et al. (1999), for example, find that assault, rape, mugging, divorce/separation, financial problems, serious housing problems, serious illness or injury, job loss, legal problems, loss of a confidant, serious marital problems, having been robbed and serious difficulties at work fall into that category. They also looked at network impacts such as when people have trouble getting along with an individual, a social network, a serious personal crisis of someone in your network or death/illness of an individual who is close. Luhmann et al. (2012) look at life events in general.

51 Dolan et al, (2008, p. 107).

52 Camerer et al. (2005); Glimcher and Fehr (2014); McCabe and Houser (2008).

53 These principles have led to multiple approaches with names such as "emergy", "exergetic life-cycle analysis" and "net-exergy consumption".

54 Ayres and Voudouris (2014); Ayres et al. (2013); Warr and Ayres (2012); Warr et al. (2010).

55 Fizaine and Court (2016); Hall et al. (2014).

56 Haberl et al. (2007); Vitousek et al. (1986).

57 Folke et al. (2002, 2004); Holling (1973); Holling et al. (2009); Scheffer et al. (2001).
58 Linkov et al. (2014).
59 UN et al. (2012, p. 155).
60 Wackernagel (1994); Rees (2017).
61 www.footprintnetwork.org/our-work/earth-overshoot-day/
62 Wilting et al. (2017).
63 Sirgy et al. (2013) address the varying views of whether materialism contributes to happiness.
64 Becker (1965) formalised this into a model which includes a trade-off of time and consumption. He splits the time that a person has into the time spent on work and the time spent on consumption. By optimising their time use, an optimal consumption bundle is created. The theory does not however specify exactly how the consumption time is filled in.
65 To complicate matters even more, we know that being unemployed is one of the factors which affects life satisfaction negatively (Dolan et al. 2008).
66 On scarcity and value, see Shah et al. (2015).
67 On the other hand, having a child who is a drug addict, criminal or estranged might overshadow one's life significantly. Alesina et al. (2004) also look at the effect of inequality on happiness.
68 Brekke and Howarth (2000); Brekke et al. (2003).
69 Kenrick et al. (2010).
70 These are not equal needs; they are hierarchical in the sense that the first needs are to be satisfied first. This is why it is also sometimes depicted as a pyramid, although Maslow did not in fact do this in his 1954 publication. In many cases Maslow's needs can be linked to consumption categories (food, shelter, health). However, many of the higher goals are more personal and less covered by the consumption categories (esteem). Max-Neef (1992; Max-Neef et al., 1991) adapted Maslow's framework and developed a fundamental human needs and human development scale. The human needs are subsistence, protection, affection, understanding, participation, leisure, creation, identity and freedom, and Max-Neef also introduced a second dimension with existential categories of being, having, doing and interacting. A thirty-six-cell matrix is derived from the two dimensions.

71 Bénabou and Tirole (2016) and Epley and Gilovich (2016) discuss how the field of motivated reasoning and beliefs fulfils important psychological and functional needs of the individual.

72 For an extensive overview of evolutionary thinking in economics see van den Bergh (2018). Evolutionary thinking is applied to production activities but it is increasingly also used in consumption (Collins et al., 2016; Gao and Edelman, 2016; Nelson and Consoli, 2010; Nelson and Winter, 1982; Rayo and Becker, 2007a, 2007b).

73 For example, what about the activity "in bed with an illness", "fighting with my spouse", "undergoing a crime", "committing a crime", "high on drugs", "attending a funeral", "in jail" or "compulsory socialising with people I don't like". These are unlikely to get good response rates in time-use surveys. Yet they are all things which happen in the real world. They are not necessarily episodes that take much time (although illness can actually take up a lot of working and leisure time) but it is definitely the case that some of these activities have profound and long-lasting influence on well-being.

74 These are just some of the ways in which new insights might emerge from the GQA. Sometimes these synergies are already tried in the literature. For example, Jackson and Marks (1999) link goods and services to Max-Neef's characterisation of human needs. Costanza et al. (2007) also present an integrative approach which includes subjective well-being, capital and time.

75 Hodson (2015).

76 Freeman and Soete (2009); Martin (2016).

77 Mazzucato (2013).

78 Stiglitz et al., (2009, p. 61).

79 The Sustainable National Income is also based on the idea of the precautionary principle. This method has the advantage that it uses only information from the present (Tinbergen and Hueting, 1991). It uses the environmental sustainability limits as a basis for the calculation and then calculates how much it would cost to remain within those limits (using current technologies). Gerlagh et al. (2002) calculated SNI within the setting of a General Equilibrium Model.

80 Note that we had rejected the GPI as being too economic at an earlier stage. However, in this context the GPI is part of a broader set of quality indicators.

81 Gershuny (2012).

11 IMPLEMENTATION OF THE STRATEGY

1 Current web-based visualisations of Beyond-GDP indicators (e.g. the Better Life Index) are already far more communicative than any bar chart of GDP growth.

2 See the discussion about the *CES recommendations for measuring sustainable development* in Chapter 4.

3 See Strogatz (2001) for an impressive overview.

4 Milo et al. (2002) looks at the "basic building blocks of networks".

5 Durlauf (2012); Foster (2005); Holling (2001).

6 The spatial and temporal scales are the basis of the concept of Panarchy (Allen et al., 2014).

7 Cash et al. (2003).

8 For overviews of sustainability science see Bettencourt and Kaur (2011); Kates, (2011) and Kates et al. (2001). This an eclectic field of varied studies that has exploded since the 1990s.

9 www.economist.com/special-report/2010/02/25/data-data-everywhere

10 For example, if there is a register on employment and a register on residence, the distance to work or advantages of moving house or changing jobs can be calculated (Mervis, 2017).

11 In fact, it is not permitted for Statistics Netherlands to put out a questionnaire if there is a government register which could provide the same information.

12 Cavallo and Rigobon (2016).

13 Mitchell et al. (2013).

14 Kelly et al. (2015).

15 For example, in Belgium the transactions between companies are available because the tax authorities have a VAT data file which shows the deliveries between companies (Dhyne et al., 2015).

16 ICT will not only affect the availability of data but will have other benefits. For example, the statistical process is already becoming far more automated. Methods for now-casting may be developed to create more timely data. One of the biggest improvements should be expected in the presentation of the data. The availability of websites in particular makes it possible to create interactive data visualisations.

17 Much of the data is highly sensitive and private. This tension between privacy and statistics is not new but in the big data era it is already

getting more pronounced. Citizens and countries view this trade-off differently. Some cultures are open to the use of sensitive information while others are highly protective of data. In addition to government data, the data held by commercial companies is now causing concern. In many cases companies like Google and Facebook or internet providers have highly sensitive information about people. The issue of privacy will be an enduring feature of the big data era. Some kind of common ground will need to be found over what is admissible and what is not. Protecting the microdata and making sure that it is used only for statistical purposes is an important part of the implementation of the strategy.

18 If anything, statistical offices are lagging behind in this development. In some cases this might lead to collaboration. For example, many statistical offices these days have business registers which are created from Chambers of Commerce or other sources. At the same time companies like Google have data for 100 million companies sorted into nearly 100 categories of companies (see the "Places API" of Google). For countries that do not have a business register, or that wish to check their data, this is a pretty good place to start.

19 *The McKinsey Quarterly*, January 2009.

20 Note that even developed nations do not publish all the accounts of the SNA. What all countries have in common is that they calculate the "current accounts", and more precisely the accounts that calculate income and production (GDP).

21 Jerven (2013).

22 IEAG (2014).

23 It is important that the job is not given to economists alone. If the UN creates a Stiglitz-type commission, it should have people from various disciplines. A multidisciplinary accounting framework should be developed by a multidisciplinary team.

24 These include the Inclusive Wealth Index, Green Economy Initiative, Human Development Index and the Global Sustainable Development Report.

25 The OECD did take part in these SNA processes and the OEEC national accounts were very influential at the time.

26 Such as global network of statistics under the SDG flag was also suggested by (Lu et al., 2015).

27 The UN has even created a scientific community for sustainable development which might take up the challenge. Currently it produces the Global Sustainable Development Report, which is a quadrennial report aiming to bring together scientific evidence in a multidisciplinary report (UN, 2016).

28 The UN statistical system is highly decentralised. There is a lot of work being done outside of the UN Statistical Division (UNSD). The IAEG report on SDGs names possible "Custodian Agencies and Partner Agencies" in the statistical process including DESA Population Division, FAO, IFAD, ILO, ITU, UNDP, UNEP, UN-Habitat, UNICEF, UNISDR, UNSD, UN-Women, UPU, World Bank in addition to national governments and the Global Donor Working Group on Land. This might already seem like a long list, but this is just the first page, which covers the first seven SDG targets!

References

Abdallah, S., Thompson, S., and Marks, N. (2008). Estimating Worldwide Life Satisfaction. *Ecological Economics 65*, 35–47.

Acemoglu, D., and Autor, D. (2010). Skills, Tasks and Technologies: Implications for Employment and Earnings. National Bureau of Economic Research Working Paper Series *No. 16082*.

Acemoglu, D., and Robinson, J.A. (2012). *Why Nations Fail: The Origins of Power, Prosperity and Poverty* (New York: Crown).

Adler, P. S., and Kwon, S.-W. (2002). Social Capital: Prospects for a New Concept. *The Academy of Management Review 27*, 17–40.

Aguiar, M., and Hurst, E. (2007). Measuring Trends in Leisure: The Allocation of Time over Five Decades. *The Quarterly Journal of Economics 122*, 969–1006.

Ahmad, N., and Schreyer, P. (2016). Are GDP and Productivity Measures Up to the Challenges of the Digital Economy? *International Productivity Monitor 30* (www.csls.ca/ipm/30/ahmadandschreyer.pdf).

Alesina, A., Di Tella, R., and MacCulloch, R. (2004). Inequality and Happiness: Are Europeans and Americans Different? *Journal of Public Economics 88*, 2009–2042.

Alkire, S., and Santos, M. E. (2010). *Acute Multidimensional Poverty: A New Index for Developing Countries* (Oxford: OPHI, University of Oxford).

Allen, C. R., Angeler, D. G., Garmestani, A. S., Gunderson, L. H., and Holling, C. S. (2014). Panarchy: Theory and Application. *Ecosystems 17*, 578–589.

Allison, R. A., and Foster, J. E. (2004). Measuring Health Inequality Using Qualitative Data. *Journal of Health Economics 23*, 505–524.

Alvaredo, F., Atkinson, A., Chance, L., Piketty, T., Saez, E., and Zucman, G. (2017). Distributional National Accounts (DINA) Guidelines : Concepts and Methods Used in WID.world.

Anand, P., Hunter, G., Carter, I., Dowding, K., Guala, F., and Van Hees, M. (2009). The Development of Capability Indicators. *Journal of Human Development and Capabilities 10*, 125–152.

Anderson, E. (2000). Beyond Homo Economicus: New Developments in Theories of Social Norms. *Philosophy & Public Affairs 29*, 170–200.

Anderson, K., and Peters, G. (2016). The Trouble with Negative Emissions. *Science 354*, 182.

Antolini, F. (2016). The Evolution of National Accounting and New Statistical Information: Happiness and Gross Domestic Product, Can We Measure It? *Social Indicators Research 129*, 1075–1092.

Arndt, H. W. (1978). *The Rise and Fall of Economic Growth* (Melbourne, Australia: Longman Chesire).

Arrow, K. J. (1950). A Difficulty in the Concept of Social Welfare. *Journal of Political Economy 58*, 328–346.

Arrow, K. J., and Debreu, G. (1954). Existence of an Equilibrium for a Competitive Economy. *Econometrica 22*, 265–290.

Arrow, K. J., Bolin, B., Costanza, R., Dasgupta, P., Folke, C., Holling, C. S., Jansson, B.-O., Levin, S., Mäler, K.-G., Perrings, C., et al. (1995). Economic Growth, Carrying Capacity, and the Environment. *Science 268*, 520.

Arrow, K. J., Dasgupta, P., Goulder, L. H., Mumford, K. J., and Oleson, K. (2012). Sustainability and the Measurement of Wealth. *Environment and Development Economics 17*, 317–353.

Artz, B. M., Goodall, A. H., and Oswald, A. J. (2016). Boss Competence and Worker Well-Being. ILR Review 0019793916650451.

Austin, A. (2016). On Well-Being and Public Policy: Are We Capable of Questioning the Hegemony of Happiness? *Social Indicators Research 127*, 123–138.

Autor, D. H., Levy, F., and Murnane, R. J. (2003). The Skill Content of Recent Technological Change: An Empirical Exploration. *The Quarterly Journal of Economics 118*, 1279–1333.

Autor, D. H., Dorn, D., and Hanson, G. (2016). The China Shock: Learning from Labor Market Adjustment to Large Changes in Trade. *Annual Review of Economics 8*, 205–240.

Ayres, R. U. (2007). On the Practical Limits to Substitution. *Ecological Economics 61*, 115–128.

Ayres, R. U., and Kneese, A. V. (1969). Production, Consumption, and Externalities. *The American Economic Review 59*, 282–297.

Ayres, R. U., and Voudouris, V. (2014). The Economic Growth Enigma: Capital, Labour and Useful Energy? *Energy Policy 64*, 16–28.

Ayres, R. U., van den Bergh, J. C. J. M., Lindenberger, D., and Warr, B. (2013). The Underestimated Contribution of Energy to Economic Growth. *Structural Change and Economic Dynamics 27*, 79–88.

Bagstad, K. J., Berik, G., and Gaddis, E. J. B. (2014). Methodological Developments in US State-Level Genuine Progress Indicators: Toward GPI 2.0. *Ecological Indicators 45*, 474–485.

Baiocchi, G., Minx, J., and Hubacek, K. (2010). The Impact of Social Factors and Consumer Behavior on Carbon Dioxide Emissions in the United Kingdom. *Journal of Industrial Ecology 14*, 50–72.

Baldwin, R. (2006). *Globalisation: The Great Unbundling(s)* (Helsinki: Economic Council of Finland).

Baldwin, R. (2016). The World Trade Organization and the Future of Multilateralism. *Journal of Economic Perspectives 30*, 95–116.

Barnosky, A. D., Matzke, N., Tomiya, S., Wogan, G. O. U., Swartz, B., Quental, T. B., Marshall, C., McGuire, J. L., Lindsey, E. L., Maguire, K. C., et al. (2011). Has the Earth's Sixth Mass Extinction Already Arrived? *Nature 471*, 51–57.

Bean, C. (2016). Independent Review of UK Economic Statistics (www.gov.uk/government/publications/independent-review-of-uk-economic-statistics-final-report).

Becker, G. S. (1962). Investment in Human Capital: A Theoretical Analysis. *Journal of Political Economy 70*, 9–49.

Becker, G. S. (1964). *Human Capital: A Theoretical and Empirical Analysis, with Special Reference to Education* (New York: National Bureau of Economic Research (NBER)).

Becker, G. S. (1965). A Theory of the Allocation of Time. *The Economic Journal 75*, 493–517.

Becker, G. S. (1974a). A Theory of Social Interactions. *Journal of Political Economy 82*, 1063–1093.

Becker, G. S. (1974b). *A Theory of Marriage. In Economics of the Family: Marriage, Children, and Human Capital* (Theodore W. Schultz, Ed.) (Chicago: University of Chicago Press).

Becker, G. S. (2007). Health as Human Capital: Synthesis and Extensions. *Oxford Economic Papers 59*, 379–410.

Becker, G. S., and Murphy, K. M. (1993). A Simple Theory of Advertising as a Good or Bad. *The Quarterly Journal of Economics 108*, 941–964.

Becker, G. S., Philipson, T. J., and Soares, R. R. (2005). The Quantity and Quality of Life and the Evolution of World Inequality. *The American Economic Review 95*, 277–291.

Bénabou, R., and Tirole, J. (2016). Mindful Economics: The Production, Consumption, and Value of Beliefs. *Journal of Economic Perspectives 30*, 141–164.

Bentham, J. (1789). *An Introduction to the Principles of Morals and Legislation* (London: T. Payne and Son).

Berndt, E. R., and Wood, D. O. (1979). Engineering and Econometric Interpretations of Energy-Capital Complementarity. *The American Economic Review 69*, 342–354.

Bernstein, J., and Baker, D. (2013). What Is 'Seinfeld' Worth? *New York Times*, 31 July.

Bettencourt, L. M. A., and Kaur, J. (2011). Evolution and Structure of Sustainability Science. *Proceedings of the National Academy of Sciences 108*, 19540–19545.

Birke, D. (2009). The Economics of Networks: A Survey of the Empirical Literature. *Journal of Economic Surveys 23,* 762–793.

Bleys, B. (2012). Beyond GDP: Classifying Alternative Measures for Progress. *Social Indicators Research 109,* 355–376.

Bleys, B., and Whitby, A. (2015). Barriers and Opportunities for Alternative Measures of Economic Welfare. *Ecological Economics 117,* 162–172.

Boarini, R., Mira d'Ercole, M., and Liu, G. (2012). *Approaches to Measuring the Stock of Human Capital: A Review of Country Practices* (Paris: OECD).

Boelhouwer, J. (2010). *Wellbeing in the Netherlands: The SCP Life Situation Index since 1974* (The Hague: The Netherlands Institute for Social Research).

Bos, F. (2009). *The National Accounts as a Tool for Analysis and Policy* (Saarbrücken: VDM Verlag Dr. Muller).

Bos, F. (2017). Uses of National Accounts from the 17th Century till Present and Three Suggestions for the Future. *EURONA: Eurostat Review on National Accounts and Macroeconomic Indicators 1,* 41–61.

Boskin Commission (1996). Toward a More Accurate Measure of the Cost of Living (Advisory Commission to Study the Consumer Price Index). Washington, DC, 4 December.

Botzen, W. J. W., Gowdy, J. M., and van den Bergh, J. C. J. M. (2008). Cumulative CO_2 Emissions: Shifting International Responsibilities for Climate Debt. *Climate Policy 8,* 569–576.

Boulding, K. E. (1966). The Economics of the Coming Spaceship Earth. In H. Jarrett (Ed.) *Environmental Quality in a Growing Economy* (Baltimore: Resources for the Future/Johns Hopkins University Press), pp. 3–14.

Bourdieu, P. (1986). The Forms of Capital. In J. Richardson (Ed.) *Handbook of Theory and Research for the Sociology of Education* (New York: Greenwood), pp. 241–258.

Bowles, S., and Gintis, H. (1993). The Revenge of Homo Economicus: Contested Exchange and the Revival of Political Economy. *The Journal of Economic Perspectives 7,* 83–102.

Brekke, K. A., and Howarth, R. B. (2000). The Social Contingency of Wants. *Land Economics 76,* 493–503.

Brekke, K. A., Howarth, R. B., and Nyborg, K. (2003). Status-seeking and Material Affluence: Evaluating the Hirsch Hypothesis. *Ecological Economics 45,* 29–39.

Brown, J. H., Gillooly, J. F., Allen, A. P., Savage, V. M., and West, G. B. (2004). Toward a Metabolic Theory of Ecology. *Ecology 85,* 1771–1789.

Brynjolfsson, E., and McAfee, A. (2014). *The Second Machine Age Work, Progress, and Prosperity in a Time of Brilliant Technologies* (New York: W. W. Norton).

Brynjolfsson, E., Hu, Y., and Smith, M. D. (2003). Consumer Surplus in the Digital Economy: Estimating the Value of Increased Product Variety at Online Booksellers. *Management Science 49*, 1580–1596.

Camerer, C., Loewenstein, G., and Prelec, D. (2005). Neuroeconomics: How Neuroscience Can Inform Economics. *Journal of Economic Literature 43*, 9–64.

Campagna, C., Guevara, D., and Le Boeuf, B. (2017). Sustainable Development as Deus ex Machina. *Biological Conservation 209*, 54–61.

Carson, R. (1962). *Silent Spring* (Boston: Houghton Mifflin; Cambridge, MA: Riverside Press).

Cash, D. W., Clark, W. C., Alcock, F., Dickson, N. M., Eckley, N., Guston, D. H., Jäger, J., and Mitchell, R. B. (2003). Knowledge Systems for Sustainable Development. *Proceedings of the National Academy of Sciences 100*, 8086–8091.

Cavallo, A., and Rigobon, R. (2016). The Billion Prices Project: Using Online Prices for Measurement and Research. *The Journal of Economic Perspectives 30*, 151–178.

CBS (2017). *Measuring the SDGs: An Initial Picture for the Netherlands* (The Hague: Statistics Netherlands).

Ceballos, G., Ehrlich, P. R., Barnosky, A. D., García, A., Pringle, R. M., and Palmer, T. M. (2015). Accelerated Modern Human-Induced Species Losses: Entering the Sixth Mass Extinction. *Science Advances 1*, 19 June.

Chang, H.-J. (2014). *Economics: The User's Guide* (New York: Bloomsbury Press).

Charmes, J. (2015). Time Use across the World: Findings of a World Compilation of Time Use Surveys. UNDP Human Development Report Office. Background Paper.

Chee, Y. E. (2004). An Ecological Perspective on the Valuation of Ecosystem Services. *Biological Conservation 120*, 549–565.

Christensen, J. (2017). *The Power of Economists within the State* (Stanford, CA: Stanford University Press).

Ciais, P., Sabine, C., Bala, G., Bopp, L., Brovkin, V., Canadell, J., Chhabra, A., DeFries, R., Galloway, J., Heimann, M., et al. (2013). Carbon and Other Biogeochemical Cycles. In T. F. Stocker, D. Qin, G.-K. Plattner, M. Tignor, S. K. Allen, J. Boschung, A. Nauels, Y. Xia, V. Bex and P. M. Midgley (Eds.) *Climate Change 2013: In The Physical Science Basis. Contribution of Working Group I to the Fifth Assessment Report of the Intergovernmental Panel on Climate Change, 2013*(Cambridge: Cambridge University Press), pp. 465–570.

Clark, A. E., Frijters, P., and Shields, M.A. (2008). Relative Income, Happiness, and Utility: An Explanation for the Easterlin Paradox and Other Puzzles. *Journal of Economic Literature 46*, 95–144.

Cobb, C., Rowe, J., Halstead, T., and Progress, R. (1995). *The Genuine Progress Indicator: Summary of Data and Methodology* (San Francisco, CA: Redefining Progress).

Coe, N. M. (2011). Geographies of Production II. *Progress in Human Geography 36*, 389–402.

Cohen, J., Briand, F., and Newman, C. (1990). *Community Food Webs: Data and Theory* (Berlin: Springer-Verlag).

Coleman, J. S. (1988). Social Capital in the Creation of Human Capital. *American Journal of Sociology 94*, S95–S120.

Collins, J., Baer, B., and Weber, E. J. (2016). Evolutionary Biology in Economics: A Review. *Economic Record 92*, 291–312.

Copeland, B. R., and Taylor, M. S. (2004). Trade, Growth, and the Environment. *Journal of Economic Literature 42*, 7–71.

Corrado, C., Hulten, C., and Sichel, D. (2009). Intangible Capital and U.S. Economic Growth. *Review of Income and Wealth 55*, 661–685.

Costanza, R., d'Arge, R., de Groot, R., Farber, S., Grasso, M., Hannon, B., Limburg, K., Naeem, S., O'Neill, R. V., Paruelo, J., et al. (1997). The Value of the World's Ecosystem Services and Natural Capital. *Nature 387*, 253–260.

Costanza, R., Fisher, B., Ali, S., Beer, C., Bond, L., Boumans, R., Danigelis, N. L., Dickinson, J., Elliott, C., Farley, J., et al. (2007). Quality of Life: An Approach Integrating Opportunities, Human Needs, and Subjective Well-being. *Ecological Economics 61*, 267–276.

Costanza, R., Kubiszewski, I., Giovannini, E., Lovins, H., McGlade, J., Pickett, K. E., Ragnarsdóttir, K. V., Roberts, D., De Vogli, R., and Wilkinson, R. (2014a). Time to Leave GDP Behind. *Nature 505*, 283–285.

Costanza, R., de Groot, R., Sutton, P., van der Ploeg, S., Anderson, S. J., Kubiszewski, I., Farber, S., and Turner, R. K. (2014b). Changes in the Global Value of Ecosystem Services. *Global Environmental Change 26*, 152–158.

Costanza, R., Daly, L., Fioramonti, L., Giovannini, E., Kubiszewski, I., Mortensen, L. F., Pickett, K. E., Ragnarsdottir, K. V., De Vogli, R., and Wilkinson, R. (2016). Modelling and Measuring Sustainable Wellbeing in Connection with the UN Sustainable Development Goals. *Ecological Economics 130*, 350–355.

Costanza, R., Atkins, P. W. B., Bolton, M., Cork, S., Grigg, N. J., Kasser, T., and Kubiszewski, I. (2017). Overcoming Societal Addictions: What Can We Learn from Individual Therapies? *Ecological Economics 131*, 543–550.

Coyle, D. (2014). *GDP: A Brief but Affectionate History* (Princeton, NJ: Princeton University Press).

Cropper, M. L., and Oates, W. E. (1992). Environmental Economics: A Survey. *Journal of Economic Literature 30*, 675–740.

Crutzen, P.J. (2002). Geology of Mankind. *Nature 415*, 23–23.

Daly, H. E. (1968). On Economics as a Life Science. *Journal of Political Economy 76*, 392–406.

Daly, H. E. (1992). *Steady-State Economics* (London: Earthscan).

Daly, H. E., and Cobb, J. B. (1989). *For the Common Good: Redirecting the Economy toward Community, the Environment, and a Sustainable Future* (Boston, IL: Beacon Press).

Dasgupta, P. (2005). Economics of Social Capital. *Economic Record 81*, S2–S21.

Davis, G. F., and Greve, H. R. (1997). Corporate Elite Networks and Governance Changes in the 1980s. *American Journal of Sociology 103*, 1–37.

Davis, S. J., and Caldeira, K. (2010). Consumption-based Accounting of CO_2 Emissions. *Proceedings of the National Academy of Sciences 107*, 5687–5692.

Deaton, A. (2003). Health, Inequality, and Economic Development. *Journal of Economic Literature 41*, 113–158.

Deaton, A. (2010). Price Indexes, Inequality, and the Measurement of World Poverty. *The American Economic Review 100*, 3–34.

Deaton, A. (2012). The Financial Crisis and the Well-being of Americans 2011 OEP Hicks Lecture. *Oxford Economic Papers 64*, 1–26.

Deaton, A., and Heston, A. (2008). Understanding PPPs and PPP-based National Accounts. *National Bureau of Economic Research Working Paper Series* No. 14499.

Debreu, G. (1991). The Mathematization of Economic Theory. *The American Economic Review 81*, 1–7.

DeCanio, S. J. (2016). Robots and Humans – Complements or Substitutes? *Journal of Macroeconomics 49*, 280–291.

Dedrick, J., Kraemer, K. L., and Linden, G. (2010). Who Profits from Innovation in Global Value Chains? A Study of the iPod and Notebook PCs. *Industrial and Corporate Change 19*, 81–116.

De Groot, R., Brander, L., van der Ploeg, S., Costanza, R., Bernard, F., Braat, L., Christie, M., Crossman, N., Ghermandi, A., Hein, L., et al. (2012). Global Estimates of the Value of Ecosystems and Their Services in Monetary Units. *Ecosystem Services 1*, 50–61.

De Haas, H. (2010). Migration and Development: A Theoretical Perspective. *The International Migration Review 44*, 227–264.

Denison, E. F. (1947). *Report on Tripartite Discussions of National Income Measurement* (New York: National Bureau of Economic Research).

Desrosières, A. (2001). Statistics, History of A2 – Smelser, Neil J. In P. B. Baltes (Ed.) *International Encyclopedia of the Social & Behavioral Sciences* (Oxford: Pergamon), pp. 15080–15085.

Dhyne, E., Magerman, G., and Rubínová, S. (2015). *The Belgian Production Network 2002–2012* (Brussels: National Bank of Belgium).

Diener, E., and Biswas-Diener, R. (2008). *Happiness: Unlocking the Mysteries of Psychological Wealth* (Malden: Blackwell Publishing).

Diener, E., Inglehart, R., and Tay, L. (2013). Theory and Validity of Life Satisfaction Scales. *Social Indicators Research* 112, 497–527.

Dolan, P., Peasgood, T., and White, M. (2008). Do We Really Know What Makes Us Happy? A Review of the Economic Literature on the Factors Associated with Subjective Well-being. *Journal of Economic Psychology* 29, 94–122.

Drews, S., and van den Bergh, J. C. J. M. (2016). Public Views on Economic Growth, the Environment and Prosperity: Results of a Questionnaire Survey. *Global Environmental Change* 39, 1–14.

Druckman, A., and Jackson, T. (2009). The Carbon Footprint of UK Households 1990–2004: A Socio-economically Disaggregated, Quasi-multi-regional Input–output Model. *Ecological Economics* 68, 2066–2077.

Druckman, A., Buck, I., Hayward, B., and Jackson, T. (2012). Time, Gender and Carbon: A Study of the Carbon Implications of British Adults' Use of Time. *Ecological Economics* 84, 153–163.

Duncan, J. W., and Shelton, W. C. (1978). *Revolution in U.S. Government Statistics, 1926–1976* (Washington, DC: US Department of Commerce).

Durlauf, S. N. (2012). Complexity, Economics, and Public Policy. *Politics, Philosophy & Economics* 11, 45–75.

Durlauf, S. N., and Fafchamps, M. (2004). Social Capital. *National Bureau of Economic Research Working Paper Series* No. 10485.

Easterlin, R. A. (1974). Does Economic Growth Improve the Human Lot? Some Empirical Evidence. In P. A. David and M. W. Reder (Eds.) *Nations and Households in Economic Growth: Essays in Honor of Moses Abramovitz* (New York: Academic Press), pp. 89–125.

EC, IMF, OECD, UN, and World Bank (1993). *System of National Accounts 1993* (Brussels: European Commission; New York: International Monetary Fund; Paris: Organisation for Economic Co-operation and Development; Washington, DC: United Nations and the World Bank).

EC, IMF, OECD, UN, and World Bank (2009). *System of National Accounts 2008* (Brussels: European Commission; New York: International Monetary Fund; Paris: Organisation for Economic Co-operation and Development; Washington, DC: United Nations and the World Bank).

EC, OECD, UN, and World Bank (2013). *System of Environmental-Economic Accounting 2012 Experimental Ecosystem Accounting*. White cover publication, pre-edited text subject to official editing (Brussels: European Commission;

Paris: Organisation for Economic Co-operation and Development; Washington, DC: United Nations and the World Bank).

Edens, B. (2013). Depletion: Bridging the Gap between Theory and Practice. *Environmental and Resource Economics 54*, 419–441.

Ehrlich, P. (1968). *The Population Bomb* (New York: Sierra Club/Ballantine Books).

Ehrlich, I., and Becker, G. S. (1972). Market Insurance, Self-Insurance, and Self-Protection. *Journal of Political Economy 80*, 623–648.

Ehrlich, P. R., and Holdren, J. P. (1971). Impact of Population Growth. *Science 171*, 1212.

Eisner, R. (1988). Extended Accounts for National Income and Product. *Journal of Economic Literature 26*, 1611–1684.

Elsby, M. W. L., Hobijn, B., and Şahin, A. (2013). The Decline of the U.S. Labor Share. *Brookings Papers on Economic Activity* Fall, 1–52.

Enders, A., Hungenberg, H., Denker, H.-P., and Mauch, S. (2008). The Long Tail of Social Networking: Revenue Models of Social Networking Sites. *European Management Journal 26*, 199–211.

Epley, N., and Gilovich, T. (2016). The Mechanics of Motivated Reasoning. *Journal of Economic Perspectives 30*, 133–140.

ESS (2011). *Sponsorship Group on Measuring Progress, Well-being and Sustainable Development* (Luxemburg: European Statistical System).

European Communities (2005). *Measuring Progress Towards a More Sustainable Europe: Sustainable Developement Inidcators for the European Union* (Luxemburg: Office for Official Publications of the European Communities).

Fagiolo, G., Reyes, J., and Schiavo, S. (2010). The Evolution of the World Trade Web: A Weighted-network Analysis. *Journal of Evolutionary Economics 20*, 479–514.

Fath, B. D., Scharler, U. M., Ulanowicz, R. E., and Hannon, B. (2007). Ecological Network Analysis: Network Construction. *Ecological Modelling 208*, 49–55.

Fehr, E., and Fischbacher, U. (2003). The Nature of Human Altruism. *Nature 425*, 785.

Fehr, E., and Gachter, S. (2002). Altruistic Punishment in Humans. *Nature 415*, 137.

Fehr, E., and Schmidt, K. M. (1999). A Theory of Fairness, Competition, and Cooperation. *The Quarterly Journal of Economics 114*, 817–868.

Fioramonti, L. (2013). *Gross Domestic Problem: The Politics Behind the World's Most Powerful Number* (London: Zed Books).

Fizaine, F., and Court, V. (2016). Energy Expenditure, Economic Growth, and the Minimum EROI of Society. *Energy Policy 95*, 172–186.

Fleurbaey, M. (2009). Beyond GDP: The Quest for a Measure of Social Welfare. *JEL 47*, 1029–1075.

Fleurbaey, M. (2015). On Sustainability and Social Welfare. *Journal of Environmental Economics and Management 71*, 34–53.

Folke, C., Carpenter, S., Elmqvist, T., Gunderson, L., Holling, C. S., and Walker, B. (2002). Resilience and Sustainable Development: Building Adaptive Capacity in a World of Transformations. *AMBIO: A Journal of the Human Environment 31*, 437–440.

Folke, C., Carpenter, S., Walker, B., Scheffer, M., Elmqvist, T., Gunderson, L., and Holling, C. S. (2004). Regime Shifts, Resilience, and Biodiversity in Ecosystem Management. *Annual Review of Ecology, Evolution, and Systematics 35*, 557–581.

Foster, J. (2005). From Simplistic to Complex Systems in Economics. *Cambridge Journal of Economics 29*, 873–892.

Freeman, C., and Soete, L. (2009). Developing Science, Technology and Innovation Indicators: What We Can Learn from the Past. *Research Policy 38*, 583–589.

Freeman, A. M., Herriges, J. A., and Kling, C. L. (2014). *The Measurement of Environmental and Resource Values: Theory and Methods* (New York: RFF Press).

Frey, B. S., and Stutzer, A. (2002). What Can Economists Learn from Happiness Research? *Journal of Economic Literature 40*, 402–435.

Frey, C. B., and Osborne, M. A. (2017). The Future of Employment: How Susceptible Are Jobs to Computerisation? *Technological Forecasting and Social Change 114*, 254–280.

Friman, M., and Hjerpe, M. (2015). Agreement, Significance, and Understandings of Historical Responsibility in Climate Change Negotiations. *Climate Policy 15*, 302–320.

Fukuyama, F. (1995). *Trust : The Social Virtues and the Creation of Prosperity / Francis Fukuyama* (New York: Free Press).

Fukuyama, F. (2000). *Social Capital and Civil Society*. Working Paper No. 00/74 (Washington, DC: International Monetary Fund).

Gakidou, E. E., Murray, C. J., and Frenk, J. (2000). Defining and Measuring Health Inequality: An Approach Based on the Distribution of Health Expectancy. *Bulletin of the World Health Organization 78*, 42–54.

Galbraith, J.K. (1958). *Affluent Society* (Boston: Houghton Mifflin).

Gao, Y., and Edelman, S. (2016). Between Pleasure and Contentment: Evolutionary Dynamics of Some Possible Parameters of Happiness. *PLOS ONE 11*, e0153193.

Georgescu-Roegen, N. (1971). *The Entropy Law and the Economic Process* (Cambridge, MA: Harvard University Press).

Gereffi, G. (2014). Global Value Chains in a Post-Washington Consensus World. *Review of International Political Economy 21*, 9–37.

Gerlagh, R., Dellink, R., Hofkes, M., and Verbruggen, H. (2002). A Measure of Sustainable National Income for the Netherlands. *Ecological Economics 41*, 157–174.

Gershuny, J. (2012). National Utility: Measuring the Enjoyment of Activities. *European Sociological Review 29*, 996–1009.

Gilbert, M., Jaszi, G., Denison, E. F., and Schwartz, C. F. (1948). Objectives of National Income Measurement: A Reply to Professor Kuznets. *The Review of Economics and Statistics 30*, 179–195.

Girvan, M., and Newman, M. E. J. (2002). Community Structure in Social and Biological Networks. *Proceedings of the National Academy of Sciences 99*, 7821–7826.

Gladwell, M. (2000). *The Tipping Point: How Little Things Can Make a Big Difference* (New York: Little, Brown and Company).

Glaser, G. (2012). Policy: Base Sustainable Development Goals on Science. *Nature 491*, 35–35.

Gleeson-White, J. (2012). *Double Entry: How the Merchants of Venice Created Modern Finance* (New York: W. W. Norton & Co.).

Glimcher, P. W., and Fehr, E. (2014). *Neuroeconomics: Decision Making and the Brain* (Amsterdam: Academic Press).

Goldin, C., and Katz, L. F. (1998). The Origins of Technology-Skill Complementarity. *The Quarterly Journal of Economics 113*, 693–732.

Goodin, R. E., Rice, J. M., Bittman, M., and Saunders, P. (2005). The Time-Pressure Illusion: Discretionary Time vs. Free Time. *Social Indicators Research 73*, 43–70.

Gordon, R. J. (2016). *The Rise and Fall of American Growth: The U.S. Standard of Living since the Civil War* (Princeton, NJ: Princeton University Press).

Gorman, W. M. (1980). A Possible Procedure for Analysing Quality Differentials in the Egg Market. *The Review of Economic Studies 47*, 843–856.

Goyal, S., and Galeotti, A. (2012). Special Issue Introduction: Social Networks and Economics. *Review of Network Economics 11*.

Granovetter, M. S. (1973). The Strength of Weak Ties. *American Journal of Sociology 78*, 1360–1380.

Granovetter, M. S. (2017). *Society and Economy: Framework and Extensions* (Cambridge, MA: The Belknap Press of Harvard University Press).

Greenwood, M. J. (1975). Research on Internal Migration in the United States: A Survey. *Journal of Economic Literature 13*, 397–433.

Griliches, Z. (1969). Capital-Skill Complementarity. *The Review of Economics and Statistics 51*, 465–468.

Groffman, P. M., Baron, J. S., Blett, T., Gold, A. J., Goodman, I., Gunderson, L. H., Levinson, B. M., Palmer, M. A., Paerl, H. W., Peterson, G. D., et al. (2006). Ecological Thresholds: The Key to Successful Environmental Management or an Important Concept with No Practical Application? *Ecosystems 9*, 1–13.

Groot, W., van den Brink, H. M., and van Praag, B. (2007). The Compensating Income Variation of Social Capital. *Social Indicators Research 82*, 189–207.

Grootaert, C. (1998). *Social Capital: The Missing Link?*, Social Capital Initiative Working Paper Series 3 (Washington, DC: The World Bank).

Grossman, M. (1972). On the Concept of Health Capital and the Demand for Health. *Journal of Political Economy 80*, 223–255.

Grübler, A., Naki⊠enovi⊠, N., and Victor, D. G. (1999). Dynamics of Energy Technologies and Global Change. *Energy Policy 27*, 247–280.

Grzeskowiak, S., Lee, D.-J., Yu, G. B., and Sirgy, M. J. (2014). How Do Consumers Perceive the Quality-of-Life Impact of Durable Goods? A Consumer Well-Being Model Based on the Consumption Life Cycle. *Applied Research in Quality of Life 9*, 683–709.

Guiso, L., Sapienza, P., and Zingales, L. (2006). Does Culture Affect Economic Outcomes? *The Journal of Economic Perspectives 20*, 23–48.

Haberl, H., Erb, K. H., Krausmann, F., Gaube, V., Bondeau, A., Plutzar, C., Gingrich, S., Lucht, W., and Fischer-Kowalski, M. (2007). Quantifying and Mapping the Human Appropriation of Net Primary Production in Earth's Terrestrial Ecosystems. *Proceedings of the National Academy of Sciences 104*, 12942–12947.

Hafner-Burton, E. M., Kahler, M., and Montgomery, A. H. (2009). Network Analysis for International Relations. *International Organization 63*, 559–592.

Hagerty, M. R., Cummins, R. A., Ferriss, A. L., Land, K., Michalos, A. C., Peterson, M., Sharpe, A., Sirgy, J., and Vogel, J. (2001). Quality of Life Indexes for National Policy: Review and Agenda for Research. *Social Indicators Research 55*, 1–96.

Hall, C. A. S., Lambert, J. G., and Balogh, S. B. (2014). EROI of Different Fuels and the Implications for Society. *Energy Policy 64*, 141–152.

Hannon, B. (1973). The Structure of Ecosystems. *Journal of Theoretical Biology 41*, 535–546.

Hanushek, E. A., and Woessmann, L. (2008). The Role of Cognitive Skills in Economic Development. *Journal of Economic Literature 46*, 607–668.

Hardin, G. (1968). The Tragedy of the Commons. *Science 162*, 1243–1248.

Hayden, A., and Wilson, J. (2016). Is It What You Measure That Really Matters? The Struggle to Move Beyond GDP in Canada. *Sustainability 8*, 623–641.

Heede, R. (2014). Tracing Anthropogenic Carbon Dioxide and Methane Emissions to Fossil Fuel and Cement Producers, 1854–2010. *Climatic Change 122*, 229–241.

Helliwell, J. F., and Putnam, R. D. (2004). The Social Context of Well-being. *Philosophical Transactions of the Royal Society B: Biological Sciences 359*, 1435–1446.

Helliwell, J. F., Layard, R., and Sachs, J. D. (2018). *World Happiness Report 2018* (New York: Sustainable Development Solutions Network).

Henrich, J., Boyd, R., Bowles, S., Camerer, C., Fehr, E., Gintis, H., and McElreath, R. (2001). In Search of Homo Economicus: Behavioral Experiments in 15 Small-Scale Societies. *The American Economic Review 91*, 73–78.

Hicks, J. R. (1939). *Value and Capital: An Inquiry into some Fundamental Principles of Economic Theory* (Oxford: Clarendon Press).

Hicks, J. R. (1975). The Scope and Status of Welfare Economics. *Oxford Economic Papers 27*, 307–326.

Hicks, J. R., and Allen, R. G. D. (1934). A Reconsideration of the Theory of Value. Part I. *Economica 1*, 52–76.

Hodson, G. M. (2015). Much of the "Economics of Property Rights" Devalues Property and Legal Rights. *Journal of Institutional Economics 11*, 683–709.

Hoekstra, R., and van den Bergh, J. C. J. M. (2006). Constructing Physical Input–Output Tables for Environmental Modeling and Accounting: Framework and Illustrations. *Ecological Economics 59*, 375–393.

Hoekstra, R., Michel, B., and Suh, S. (2016). The Emission Cost of International Sourcing: Using Structural Decomposition Analysis to Calculate the Contribution of International Sourcing to CO_2-Emission Growth. *Economic Systems Research 28*, 151–167.

Holling, C. S. (1973). Resilience and Stability of Ecological Systems. *Annual Review of Ecology and Systematics 4*, 1–23.

Holling, C. S. (2001). Understanding the Complexity of Economic, Ecological, and Social Systems. *Ecosystems 4*, 390–405.

Holling, C. S., Allen, C. R., and Gunderson, L. H. (2009). *Foundations of Ecological Resilience* (Washington, DC: Island Press).

Hooper, D. U., Chapin, F. S., Ewel, J. J., Hector, A., Inchausti, P., Lavorel, S., Lawton, J. H., Lodge, D. M., Loreau, M., Naeem, S., et al. (2005). Effects of Biodiversity on Ecosystem Functioning: A Consensus of Current Knowledge. *Ecological Monographs 75*, 3–35.

Hopwood, B., Mellor, M., and O'Brien, G. (2005). Sustainable Development: Mapping Different Approaches. *Sustainable Development 13*, 38–52.

Hordijk, L. (1991). Use of the RAINS Model in Acid Rain Negotiations in Europe. *Environmental Science and Technology 25*, 596–603.

Howarth, R. B., and Norgaard, R. B. (1992). Environmental Valuation under Sustainable Development. *The American Economic Review 82*, 473–477.

Hubacek, K., Baiocchi, G., Feng, K., and Patwardhan, A. (2017). Poverty Eradication in a Carbon Constrained World. *Nature Communications 8*, 912.

Hübler, M. (2016). A New Trade Network Theory: What Economists Can Learn from Engineers. *Economic Modelling 55*, 115–126.

Hueting, R. (1974). *Nieuwe Schaarste en Economische Groei* (Amsterdam: Agon Elsevier).

IEAG (2014). *A World that Counts: Mobilising the Data Revolution for Sustainable Development* (New York: United Nations Secretary-General's Independent Expert Advisory Group on a Data Revolution for Sustainable Development (IEAG)).

IEAG (2016). *Tier Classification for Global SDG Indicators* (New York: Inter-agency Expert Group on SDG Indicators).

IISD (2017). Compendium: A Global Directory to Indicator Initiatives. Online database which is no longer available.

Isard, W. (1972). *Ecologic-Economic Analysis for Regional Development: Some Initial Explorations with Particular Reference to Recreational Resource Use and Environmental Planning* (New York: The Free Press; Collier-MacMillan).

Isard, W., Bassett, K., Choguill, C., Furtado, J., Izumita, R., Kissin, j., Romanoff, E., Seyfarth, R., and Tatlock, R. (1968). On the Linkage of Socio-economic and Ecological Systems. *Papers in Regional Science 21*, 79–99.

Jackson, T. (2017). *Prosperity Without Growth: Foundation for the Economy of Tomorrow* (London: Routledge).

Jackson, T., and Marks, N. (1999). Consumption, Sustainable Welfare and Human Needs – With Reference to UK Expenditure Patterns between 1954 and 1994. *Ecological Economics 28*, 421–441.

Jakob, M., and Marschinski, R. (2013). Interpreting Trade-related CO2 Emission Transfers. *Nature Climate Change 3*, 19–23.

Jerven, M. (2013). *Poor Numbers How We Are Misled by African Development Statistics and What to Do about It* (Ithaca, NY: Cornell University Press).

Joint Committee on Taxation (2010). Present Law and Historical Overview of the Federal Tax System (Scheduled for a Public Hearing before the Senate Committee on Finance on 2 December 2010).

Jorgenson, D. W. (2009). A New Architecture for the U.S. National Accounts. *Review of Income and Wealth 55*, 1–42.

Jorgenson, D. W., and Fraumeni, B. M. (1989). The Accumulation of Human and Nonhuman Capital, 1948–1984. In R. E. Lipsey and H. S. Tice (Eds.) *The Measurement of Savings, Investment and Wealth*, (Chicago, IL: The University of Chicago Press), pp. 227–282.

Jorgenson, D. W., and Fraumeni, B. M. (1992). The Output of the Education Sector. In Z. Griliches (Ed.) *Output Measurement in the Services Sector* (Chicago, IL: The University of Chicago Press), pp. 303–338.

Kahneman, D. (1999). Objective Happiness. In D. Kahneman, E. Diener and N. Schwartz (Eds.) *Well-Being: The Foundations of Hedonic Psychology* (New York: Russell Sage Foundation), pp. 3–25.

Kahneman, D. (2011). *Thinking, Fast and Slow* (London: Penguin Books).

Kahneman, D., and Krueger, A. B. (2006). Developments in the Measurement of Subjective Well-Being. *Journal of Economic Perspectives* 20, 3–24.

Kahneman, D., and Tversky, A. (1979). Prospect Theory: An Analysis of Decision under Risk. *Econometrica* 47, 263–291.

Kahneman, D., Krueger, A. B., Schkade, D. A., Schwarz, N., and Stone, A. A. (2004). A Survey Method for Characterizing Daily Life Experience: The Day Reconstruction Method. *Science* 306, 1776.

Kahneman, D., Diener, E., and Schwarz, N. (1999). *Well-Being: The Foundations of Hedonic Psychology* (New York: Russell Sage Foundation).

Karabarbounis, L., and Neiman, B. (2014). The Global Decline of the Labor Share. *The Quarterly Journal of Economics 129*, 61–103.

Karabell, Z. (2014). *The Leading Indicators: A Short History of the Numbers that Rule Our World* (New York: Simon and Schuster Paperbacks).

Kates, R. W. (2011). What Kind of a Science is Sustainability Science? *Proceedings of the National Academy of Sciences 108*, 19449–19450.

Kates, R. W., Clark, W. C., Corell, R., Hall, J. M., Jaeger, C. C., Lowe, I., McCarthy, J. J., Schellnhuber, H. J., Bolin, B., Dickson, N. M., et al. (2001). Sustainability Science. *Science 292*, 641.

Kates, R. W., Parris, T. M., and Leiserowitz, A. A. (2005). What is Sustainable Development? Goals, Indicators, Values, and Practice. *Environment: Science and Policy for Sustainable Development 47*, 8–21.

Kawachi, I., Kennedy, B. P., Lochner, K., and Prothrow-Stith, D. (1997). Social Capital, Income Inequality, and Mortality. *American Journal of Public Health* 87, 1491–1498.

Kelly, P., Thomas, E., Doherty, A., Harms, T., Burke, Ó., Gershuny, J., and Foster, C. (2015). Developing a Method to Test the Validity of 24 Hour Time Use Diaries Using Wearable Cameras: A Feasibility Pilot. *PLOS ONE 10*, e0142198.

Kendler, K. S., Karkowski, L. M., and Prescott, C. A. (1999). Causal Relationship Between Stressful Life Events and the Onset of Major Depression. *American Journal of Psychiatry 156*, 837–841.

Kendrick, J. (1970). The Historical Development of National-Income Accounts. *History of Political Economy 2*, 284–315.

Kendrick, J. (1976). *The Formation and Stocks of Total Capital* (New York: Columbia University Press for NBER.).

Kenessey, Z. (1994). *The Accounts of Nations* (Amsterdam: IOS Press).

Kenrick, D. T., Griskevicius, V., Neuberg, S. L., and Schaller, M. (2010). Renovating the Pyramid of Needs: Contemporary Extensions Built Upon Ancient Foundations. *Perspectives on Psychological Science 5*, 292–314.

Keynes, J. M. (1920). *The Economic Consequences of the Peace* (New York: Harcourt, Brace and Howe).

Keynes, J. M. (1931). Economic Possibilities for our Grandchildren. In *Essays in Persuasion* (London: Macmillan), pp. 321–332.

Keynes, J. M. (1936). *The General Theory of Employment, Interest and Money* (London: MacMillan and Cambridge University Press).

Khadjavi, M., and Lange, A. (2013). Prisoners and Their Dilemma. *Journal of Economic Behavior & Organization 92*, 163–175.

Kimball, M., Willis, R., Rangel, A., Rayo, L., Shapiro, M., Silverman, D., Stutzer, A., and Tsutsui, Y. (2006). Utility and Happiness. University of Michigan, 30 October.

Klaassen, L. H., Koyck, L. M., and Witteveen, H. J. (1959). *Jan Tinbergen Selected Papers* (Amsterdam: North-Holland).

Knack, S., and Keefer, P. (1997). Does Social Capital Have an Economic Payoff? A Cross-Country Investigation. *The Quarterly Journal of Economics 112*, 1251–1288.

Krausmann, F., Gingrich, S., Eisenmenger, N., Erb, K.-H., Haberl, H., and Fischer-Kowalski, M. (2009). Growth in Global Materials Use, GDP and Population during the 20th Century. *Ecological Economics 68*, 2696–2705.

Kroll, C. (2015). *Sustainable Development Goals: Are the Rich Countries Ready?* (New York: Bertelsmann Stiftung and Sustainable Development Solutions Network (SDSN)).

Krueger, A. B., Kahneman, D., Fischler, C., Schkade, D., Schwarz, N., and Stone, A. A. (2009). Time Use and Subjective Well-Being in France and the U.S. *Social Indicators Research 93*, 7–18.

Krugman, P. (2009). How Did Economists Get It So Wrong? *New York Times*, 2 September.

Kubiszewski, I., Costanza, R., Franco, C., Lawn, P., Talberth, J., Jackson, T., and Aylmer, C. (2013). Beyond GDP: Measuring and Achieving Global Genuine Progress. *Ecological Economics 93*, 57–68.

Kuznets, S. (1934a). *National Income, 1929–1932* (Washington, DC: 72nd US Congress).

Kuznets, S. (1934b). *National Income, 1929–1932: NBER Bulletin* (New York: NBER).

Kuznets, S. (1946). *National Income: A Summary of Findings* (New York: NBER).

Kuznets, S. (1948). National Income: A New Version. *The Review of Economics and Statistics 30*, 151–179.

Lakner, C., and Milanovic, B. (2016). Global Income Distribution: From the Fall of the Berlin Wall to the Great Recession. *The World Bank Economic Review 30*, 203–232.

Lancaster, K. J. (1966). A New Approach to Consumer Theory. *Journal of Political Economy 74*, 132–157.

Lancaster, K. J. (1971). *Consumer Demand: A New Approach* (New York: Columbia University Press).

Landefeld, J. S. (2000). GDP: One of the Great Inventions of the 20th Century. *Survey of Current Business 80*, 6–14.

Lange, G.-M., Carey, K., and Wodon, Q. (2017). *The Changing Wealth of Nations 2017* (Washington, DC: World Bank).

Lawn, P. (2007). A Stock-Take of Green National Accounting Initiatives. *Social Indicators Research 80*, 427–460.

Lawn, P. A., and Sanders, R. D. (1999). Has Australia Surpassed Its Optimal Macro-economic Scale? Finding Out with the Aid of "Benefit" and "Cost" Accounts and a Sustainable Net Benefit Index. *Ecological Economics 28*, 213–229.

Layard, R. (2005). *Happiness: Lessons from a New Science* (London: Allen Lane Penguin Books).

Le, T., Gibson, J., and Oxley, L. (2003). Cost- and Income-based Measures of Human Capital. *Journal of Economic Surveys 17*, 271–307.

Lee, E. S. (1966). A Theory of Migration. *Demography 3*, 47–57.

Legatum (2007). *The 2007 Legatum Prosperity Index A Global Assessment of Wealth and Wellbeing* (Dubai: Legatum).

Lélé, S. M. (1991). Sustainable Development: A Critical Review. *World Development 19*, 607–621.

Lenzen, M. (2007). Structural Path Analysis of Ecosystem Networks. *Ecological Modelling 200*, 334–342.

Leontief, W. W. (1936). Quantitative Input and Output Relations in the Economic Systems of the United States. *The Review of Economics and Statistics 18*, 105–125.

Levin, S. A. (1992). The Problem of Pattern and Scale in Ecology: The Robert H. MacArthur Award Lecture. *Ecology 73*, 1943–1967.

Linkov, I., Bridges, T., Creutzig, F., Decker, J., Fox-Lent, C., Kröger, W., Lambert, J. H., Levermann, A., Montreuil, B., Nathwani, J., et al. (2014). Changing the Resilience Paradigm. *Nature Climate Change 4*, 407.

Lintott, J. (1996). Environmental Accounting: Useful to Whom and For What? *Ecological Economics 16*, 179–190.

Liu, G. (2011). *Measuring the Stock of Human Capital for Comparative Analysis: An Application of the Lifetime Income Approach to Selected Countries* (Paris: OECD).

Lovelock, J. (1979). *Gaia: A New Look at Life on Earth* (Oxford: Oxford University Press).

Lu, Y., Nakicenovic, N., Visbeck, M., and Stevance, A.-S. (2015). Policy: Five Priorities for the UN Sustainable Development Goals. *Nature 520*, 432–433.

Lucas, R. E. (2003). Macroeconomic Priorities. *The American Economic Review 93*, 1–14.

Luhmann, M., Hofmann, W., Eid, M., and Lucas, R. E. (2012). Subjective Well-being and Adaptation to Life Events: A Meta-analysis. *Journal of Personality and Social Psychology 102*, 592–615.

Malakoff, D. (2017). A Matter of Fact. *Science 355*, 562.

Malthus, T. R. (1798). *An Essay on the Principle of Population* (London: J. Johnson).

Maluck, J., and Donner, R. V. (2015). A Network of Networks Perspective on Global Trade. *PLOS ONE 10*, e0133310.

Manski, C. F. (2015). Communicating Uncertainty in Official Economic Statistics: An Appraisal Fifty Years after Morgenstern. *Journal of Economic Literature 53*, 631–653.

Margo, R. A. (2011). The Economic History of the American Economic Review: A Century's Explosion of Economics Research. *American Economic Review 101*, 9–35.

Marques, A., Rodrigues, J., Lenzen, M., and Domingos, T. (2012). Income-based Environmental Responsibility. *Ecological Economics 84*, 57–65.

Martin, B. R. (2016). Twenty Challenges for Innovation Studies. *Science and Public Policy 43*, 432–450.

Martínez-Alier, J., Pascual, U., Vivien, F.-D., and Zaccai, E. (2010). Sustainable Degrowth: Mapping the Context, Criticisms and Future Prospects of an Emergent Paradigm. *Ecological Economics 69*, 1741–1747.

Maslow, A. (1954). *Motivation and Personality* (New York: Harper & Brothers).

Masood, E. (2016). *The Great Invention: The Story of GDP and the Making and Unmaking of the Modern World*. (New York: Pegasus Books).

Massey, D. S. (1990). Social Structure, Household Strategies, and the Cumulative Causation of Migration. *Population Index 56*, 3–26.

Massey, D. S., Arango, J., Hugo, G., Kouaouci, A., Pellegrino, A., and Taylor, J. E. (1993). Theories of International Migration: A Review and Appraisal. *Population and Development Review 19*, 431–466.

Max-Neef, M. (1992). Development and Human Needs. In P. Ekins and M. Max-Neef (Eds.) *Real Life Economics* (London: Routledge), pp. 197–213.

Max-Neef, M. A., Elizalde, A., and Hopenhayn, M. (1991). *Human Scale Development: Conception, Application and Further Reflections* (New York: Apex Press).

Mazzucato, M. (2013). *The Entrepreneurial State: Debunking Public vs. Private Sector Myths* (London: Anthem Press).

Mazzucato, M. (2018). *The Value of Everything: Making and Taking the Global Economy* (London: Allen Lane Penguin Books).

McCabe, K., and Houser, D. (2008). *Neuroeconomics* (Bingley: Emerald Group Publishing Limited).

McCulla, S. H., Moses, K. E., and Moulton, B. R. (2015). The National Income and Product Accounts and the System of National Accounts 2008: Comparison and Research Plans. *Survey of Current Business, June 2015*, 1–17.

Meadows, D. H., Meadows, D. L., Randers, J., and Behrens III, W. W. (1972). *The Limits to Growth* (New York: Universe Books).

Merciai, S., and Schmidt, J. (2018). Methodology for the Construction of Global Multi-Regional Hybrid Supply and Use Tables for the EXIOBASE v3 Database. *Journal of Industrial Ecology* 22, 516–531.

Mervis, J. (2017). Data for All? *Science 355*, 573.

Michalos, A. C., Smale, B., Labonté, R., Muharjarine, N., Scott, K., Moore, K., Swystun, L., Holden, B., Bernardin, H., Dunning, B., et al. (2011). *The Canadian Index of Wellbeing: Technical Report 1.0* (Waterloo, ON: Canadian Index of Wellbeing and University of Waterloo).

Michel, B., Hambÿe, C., and Hertveldt, B. (2018). The Role of Exporters and Domestic Producers in GVCs: Evidence for Belgium based on Extended National Supply-and-Use Tables Integrated into a Global Multiregional Input–Output Table. National Bureau of Economic Research Working Paper Series *No. 25155*.

Milanovic, B. (2016). *Global Inequality: A New Approach for the Age of Globalization* (Cambridge, MA: Belknap Press).

Milo, R., Shen-Orr, S., Itzkovitz, S., Kashtan, N., Chklovskii, D., and Alon, U. (2002). Network Motifs: Simple Building Blocks of Complex Networks. *Science 298*, 824.

Mirowski, P. (1991). *More Heat than Light: Economics as Social Physics, Physics as Nature's Economics* (Cambridge: Cambridge University Press).

Mirowski, P. (2002). *Machine Dreams: Economics Becomes a Cyborg Science* (Cambridge: Cambridge University Press).

Mitchell, L., Frank, M. R., Harris, K. D., Dodds, P. S., and Danforth, C. M. (2013). The Geography of Happiness: Connecting Twitter Sentiment and Expression, Demographics, and Objective Characteristics of Place. *PLOS ONE 8*, e64417.

Mora, C., Tittensor, D. P., Adl, S., Simpson, A. G. B., and Worm, B. (2011). How Many Species Are There on Earth and in the Ocean? *PLOS Biology 9*, e1001127.

Morgenstern, O. (1950). *On the Accuracy of Economic Observations* (Princeton, NJ: Princeton University Press).

Moyer, B. C. (2016). Updated Security and Release Procedures. Memorandum for all employees. Washington, DC: Bureau of Economic Analysis.

Naeem, S., Chazdon, R., Duffy, J. E., Prager, C., and Worm, B. (2016). Biodiversity and Human Well-being: An Essential Link for Sustainable Development. *Proceedings of the Royal Society B: Biological Sciences* 283 (http://dx.doi.org/10.1098/rspb.2016.2091).

Nahapiet, J., and Ghoshal, S. (1998). Social Capital, Intellectual Capital, and the Organizational Advantage. *The Academy of Management Review 23*, 242–266.

Nannestad, P. (2008). What Have We Learned About Generalized Trust, If Anything? *Annual Review of Political Science.* 11, 413–436.

NEF (2006). *The Happy Planet Index: An Index of Human Well-being and Environmental Impact* (London: The New Economics Foundation).

Nelson, R. R., and Consoli, D. (2010). An Evolutionary Theory of Household Consumption Behavior. *Journal of Evolutionary Economics 20*, 665–687.

Nelson, R. R., and Winter, S. G. (1982). *An Evolutionary Theory of Economic Change* (Cambridge, MA: The Belknap Press of Harvard Univeristy Press).

Nelson, G. C., Bennett, E., Berhe, A. A., Cassman, K., DeFries, R., Dietz, T., Dobermann, A., Dobson, A., Janetos, A., Levy, M., et al. (2006). Anthropogenic Drivers of Ecosystem Change: an Overview. *Ecology and Society 11*, 29 (www.ecologyandsociety.org/vol11/iss2/art29/).

Newman, M. E. J. (2003). The Structure and Function of Complex Networks. *SIAM Review 45*, 167–256.

Ng, Y.-K. (1997). A Case for Happiness, Cardinalism, and Interpersonal Comparability. *The Economic Journal 107*, 1848–1858.

Ng, Y.-K. (2003). From Preference to Happiness: Towards a More Complete Welfare Economics. *Social Choice and Welfare 20*, 307–350.

Ng, I. C. L., and Tseng, L.-M. (2008). Learning to Be Sociable: The Evolution of Homo Economicus. *The American Journal of Economics and Sociology 67*, 265–286.

Nordhaus, W. D., and Tobin, J. (1972). *Is Growth Obsolete? In Economic Growth*, (Cambridge, MA: National Bureau of Economic Research (NBER)).

Nordhaus, W. D., Landefeld, J. S., Jorgenson, D. W., and Conference on Research in Income and Wealth (2006). *A New Architecture for the U.S. National Accounts* (Chicago, IL: University of Chicago Press).

Norgaard, R. B. (2010). Ecosystem Services: From Eye-opening Metaphor to Complexity Blinder. *Ecological Economics 69*, 1219–1227.

North, D. C. (1991). Institutions. *The Journal of Economic Perspectives 5*, 97–112.

Nourry, M. (2008). Measuring Sustainable Development: Some Empirical Evidence for France from Eight Alternative Indicators. *Ecological Economics 67*, 441–456.

Nussbaum, M. C. (2000). *Women and Human Development: The Capabilities Approach* (Cambridge: Cambridge University Press).

OECD (2001a). *The Well-being of Nations: The Role of Human and Social Capital* (Paris: Organisation for Economic Co-operation and Development (OECD)).

OECD (2001b). *Measuring Capital: Measurement of Capital Stocks, Consumption of Fixed Capital and Capital Services* (Paris: Organisation for Economic Co-operation and Development (OECD)).

OECD (2013). *Guidelines on Measuring Subjective Well-being* (Paris: Organisation for Economic Co-operation and Development (OECD)).

OECD (2015). *The Future of Productivity* (Paris: Organisation for Economic Co-operation and Development (OECD)).

OECD (2017). *Policy Coherence for Sustainable Development 2017: Eradicating Poverty and Promoting Prosperity* (Paris: Organisation for Economic Co-operation and Development (OECD)).

Osberg, L., and Sharpe, A. (1998). *An Index of Economic Well-being for Canada* (Ottawa: Ontariom Canada).

Paine, R. T. (1966). Food Web Complexity and Species Diversity. *The American Naturalist 100*, 65–75.

Parris, T. M., and Kates, R. W. (2003). Characterizing and Measuring Sustainable Development. *Annual Review of Environmental Resources 28*, 559–586.

Pearce, D. (2002). An Intellectual History of Environmental Economics. *Annual Review of Energy and the Environment 27*, 57–81.

Pearce, D. W., and Atkinson, G. D. (1993). Capital Theory and the Measurement of Sustainable Development: An Indicator of "Weak" Sustainability. *Ecological Economics 8*, 103–108.

Peters, G. P. (2008). From Production-based to Consumption-based National Emission Inventories. *Ecological Economics 65*, 13–23.

Peters, G. P., Minx, J. C., Weber, C. L., and Edenhofer, O. (2011). Growth in Emission Transfers via International Trade from 1990 to 2008. *Proceedings of the National Academy of Sciences 108*, 8903–8908.

Pfister, C. (2010). The "1950s Syndrome" and the Transition from a Slow-Going to a Rapid Loss of Global Sustainability. In *The Turning Points of Environmental History* (Pittsburgh, PA: University of Pittsburgh Press), pp. 90–118.

Philipsen, D. (2015). *The Little Big Number: How GDP Came to Rule the World and What to Do about It* (Princeton, NJ: Princeton University Press).

Piketty, T. (2014). *Capital in the Twenty-First Century* (Cambridge, MA: Harvard University Press).

Piketty, T., Saez, E., and Zucman, G. (2016). *Distributional National Accounts: Methods and Estimates for the United States*. National Bureau of Economic Research Working Paper Series No. 22945.

Pimm, S. L., and Raven, P. (2000). Biodiversity: Extinction by Numbers. *Nature 403*, 843–845.

Polenske, K. R. (2004). Leontief's "Magnificent Machine" and Other Contributions to Applied Economics. In E. Dietzenbacher and M. L. Lahr (Eds.) *Wassily Leontief and Input–Output Economics* (Cambridge: Cambridge University Press), pp. 9–29.

Portes, A. (1998). Social Capital: Its Origins and Applications in Modern Sociology. *Annual Review of Sociology 24*, 1–24.

Pradhan, M., Sahn, D. E., and Younger, S. D. (2003). Decomposing World Health Inequality. *Journal of Health Economics 22*, 271–293.

Prescott-Allen, R. (2001). *The Wellbeing of Nations: A Country-by-Country Index of Quality of Life and the Environment* (Washington, DC: Island Press).

Pretty, J., and Ward, H. (2001). Social Capital and the Environment. *World Development 29*, 209–227.

Putnam, R. D. (2000). *Bowling Alone: The Collapse and Revival of American Community* (New York: Simon & Schuster).

Raworth, K. (2017). *Doughnut Economics: Seven Ways to Think Like a 21st-Centruy Economist* (London: Penguin Random House).

Rayo, L., and Becker, G. S. (2007a). Evolutionary Efficiency and Happiness. *Journal of Political Economy 115*, 302–337.

Rayo, L., and Becker, G. S. (2007b). Habits, Peers, and Happiness: An Evolutionary Perspective. *The American Economic Review 97*, 487–491.

Redclift, M. (2005). Sustainable Development (1987–2005): An Oxymoron Comes of Age. *Sustainable Development 13*, 212–227.

Redmond, W. H. (2001). Exploring Limits to Material Desire: The Influence of Preferences vs. *Plans on Consumption Spending. Journal of Economic Issues 35*, 575–589.

Rees, W. E. (2017). Ecological Footprints and Appropriated Carrying Capacity: What Urban Economics Leaves Out. *Urbanisation 2*, 66–77.

Robeyns, I. (2005). The Capability Approach: A Theoretical Survey. *Journal of Human Development 6*, 93–117.

Robeyns, I. (2006). The Capability Approach in Practice. *Journal of Political Philosophy 14*, 351–376.

Rockstrom, J., Steffen, W., Noone, K., Persson, A., Chapin, F.S ., Lambin, E. F., Lenton, T. M., Scheffer, M., Folke, C., Schellnhuber, H. J., et al. (2009). A Safe Operating Space for Humanity. *Nature 461*, 472–475.

Rodrik, D. (2011). *The Globalisation Paradox: Democracy and the Future of the World Economy* (New York: W. W. Norton and Company).

Rodrik, D. (2015). *Economics Rules: Why Economic Works, When it Fails and How to Tell the Difference* (Oxford: Oxford University Press).

Røpke, I. (2004). The Early History of Modern Ecological Economics. *Ecological Economics 50*, 293–314.

Rosser, J. B. (1999). On the Complexities of Complex Economic Dynamics. *The Journal of Economic Perspectives 13*, 169–192.

Ruggles, N., and Ruggles, R. (1973). A Proposal for a System of Economic and Social Accounts. In *The Measurement of Economic and Social Performance* (Cambridge, MA: NBER), pp. 111–160.

Rutledge, R. B., Skandali, N., Dayan, P., and Dolan, R. J. (2014). A Computational and Neural Model of Momentary Subjective Well-being. *Proceedings of the National Academy of Sciences 111*, 12252–12257.

Sachs, J., Schmidt-Traub, G., Kroll,C., Durand-Delacre, D., and Teksoz, K (2017). *SDG Index and Dashboards Report 2017* (New York: Bertelsmann Stiftung and Sustainable Development Solutions Network (SDSN)).

Sala, O. E., Chapin III, F. S., Armesto, J. J., Berlow, E., Bloomfield, J., Dirzo, R., Huber-Sanwald, E., Huenneke, L. F., Jackson, R. B., Kinzig, A., et al. (2000). Global Biodiversity Scenarios for the Year 2100. *Science 287*, 1770.

Sandmo, A. (2015). The Early History of Environmental Economics. *Review of Environmental Economics and Policy 9*, 43–63.

Sapienza, P., and Zingales, L. (2013). Economic Experts versus Average Americans. *The American Economic Review 103*, 636–642.

Saracco, F., Di Clemente, R., Gabrielli, A., and Squartini, T. (2016). Detecting Early Signs of the 2007–2008 Crisis in the World Trade. *Scientific Reports 6*, 30286.

Scheffer, M., Carpenter, S., Foley, J. A., Folke, C., and Walker, B. (2001). Catastrophic Shifts in Ecosystems. *Nature 413*, 591.

Scheffers, B. R., De Meester, L., Bridge, T. C. L., Hoffmann, A. A., Pandolfi, J. M., Corlett, R. T., Butchart, S. H. M., Pearce-Kelly, P., Kovacs, K. M., Dudgeon, D., et al. (2016). The Broad Footprint of Climate Change from Genes to Biomes to People. *Science 354* (10.1126/science.aaf7671).

Schmelzer, M. (2016). *The Hegemony of Growth The OECD and the Making of the Economic Growth Paradigm* (Cambridge: Cambridge University Press).

Schoenaker, N., Hoekstra, R., and Smits, J. P. (2015). Comparison of Measurement Systems for Sustainable Development at the National Level. *Sustainable Development 23*, 285–300.

Schultz, T. W. (1961). Investment in Human Capital. *The American Economic Review 51*, 1–17.

Schumpeter, J. A. (1939). *Business Cycles. A Theoretical, Historical and Statistical Analysis of the Capitalist Process* (New York: McGraw-Hill).

Schumpeter, J. A. (1942). *Capitalism, Socialism and Democracy* (New York: Harper and Row).

Schuster, P. (2016). The End of Moore's law: Living Without an Exponential Increase in the Efficiency of Computational Facilities. *Complexity 21*, 6–9.

Schwartz, B. (2004). *The Paradox of Choice: Why More is Less. How the Culture of Abundance Robs Us of Satisfaction* (New York: Harper Perennial).

SCP (1974). *Sociaal en Cultureel Rapport 1974* (Rijswijk: Sociaal en Cultureel Planbureau).

Sen, A. (1985). *Commodities and Capabilities* (Amsterdam: North-Holland).

Sen, A. (1999). *Development as Freedom* (New York: Anchor Books).

Sen, A. (2013). The Ends and Means of Sustainability. *Journal of Human Development and Capabilities 14*, 6–20.

Serrano, M. Á., and Boguñá, M. (2003). Topology of the World Trade Web. *Physical Review E 68*, 015101.

Shah, A. K., Shafir, E., and Mullainathan, S. (2015). Scarcity Frames Value. *Psychological Science 26*, 402–412.

Shy, O. (2011). A Short Survey of Network Economics. *Review of Industrial Organization 38*, 119–149.

Silk, L. (1976) *The Economists* (New York: Basic Books).

Simon, H. A. (1991). Organizations and Markets. *The Journal of Economic Perspectives 5*, 25–44.

Sirgy, M. J. (2011). Theoretical Perspectives Guiding QOL Indicator Projects. *Social Indicators Research 103*, 1–22.

Sirgy, M. J., Michalos, A. C., Ferriss, A. L., Easterlin, R. A., Patrick, D., and Pavot, W. (2006). The Quality-of-Life (QOL) Research Movement: Past, Present, and Future. *Social Indicators Research 76*, 343–466.

Sirgy, M. J., Gurel-Atay, E., Webb, D., Cicic, M., Husic-Mehmedovic, M., Ekici, A., Herrmann, A., Hegazy, I., Lee, D.-J., and Johar, J. S. (2013). Is Materialism All That Bad? Effects on Satisfaction with Material Life, Life Satisfaction, and Economic Motivation. *Social Indicators Research 110*, 349–366.

Skidelsky, R. (2010). The Relevance of Keynes. *Cambridge Journal of Economics 35*, 1–13.

Slesnick, D. T. (1998). Empirical Approaches to the Measurement of Welfare. *Journal of Economic Literature 36*, 2108–2165.

Smith, A. (1776). *An Inquiry into the Nature and Causes of the Wealth of Nations* (London: W. Strahan and T. Cadell).

Smith, P., Davis, S. J., Creutzig, F., Fuss, S., Minx, J., Gabrielle, B., Kato, E., Jackson, R. B., Cowie, A., Kriegler, E., et al. (2016). Biophysical and Economic Limits to Negative CO2 Emissions. *Nature Climate Change 6*, 42–50.

Smits, J. P., Hoekstra, R., and Schoenaker, N. (2014). The e-Frame Convergence Report: Taking Stock of the Measurement Systems for Sustainable Development and the Opportunities for Harmonisation. Deliverable D2.5, 19 June.

Sobel, J. (2002). Can We Trust Social Capital? *Journal of Economic Literature 40*, 139–154.

Solow, R. (2008). The State of Macroeconomics. *The Journal of Economic Perspectives 22*, 243–246.

Solow, R. M. (1956). A Contribution to the Theory of Economic Growth. *The Quarterly Journal of Economics 70*, 65–94.

Srinivasan, U. T., Carey, S. P., Hallstein, E., Higgins, P. A. T., Kerr, A. C., Koteen, L. E., Smith, A. B., Watson, R., Harte, J., and Norgaard, R. B. (2008). The Debt of Nations and the Distribution of Ecological Impacts from Human Activities. *Proceedings of the National Academy of Sciences 105*, 1768–1773.

Statistics Netherlands (2017). *National Accounts of the Netherlands 2016* (The Hague: Statistics Netherlands).

Steffen, W., Crutzen, P. J., and McNeill, J. R. (2007). The Anthropocene: Are Humans Now Overwhelming the Great Forces of Nature. *AMBIO: A Journal of the Human Environment 36*, 614–621.

Stern, D. I. (2004). The Rise and Fall of the Environmental Kuznets Curve. *World Development 32*, 1419–1439.

Stern, S., Wares, A., Orzell, S., and O'Sullivan, P. (2014). *Social Progress Index 2014: Methodological Report* (Washington, DC: Social Progress Imperative).

Steurer, R., and Hametner, M. (2013). Objectives and Indicators in Sustainable Development Strategies: Similarities and Variances across Europe. *Sustainable Development 21*, 224–241.

Stiglitz, J. E. (2003). *Globalization and its Discontents* (New York: W. W. Norton).

Stiglitz, J. E. (2013). *The Price of Inequality: How Today's Divided Society Endangers Our Future* (New York: W. W. Norton).

Stiglitz, J. E., Sen, A., and Fitoussi, J.-P. (2009). Report by the Commission on the Measurement of Economic Performance and Social Progress (https://ec.europa.eu/eurostat/documents/118025/118123/Fitoussi+Commission+report).

Stone, R. (1942). The National Income, Output and Expenditure of the United States of America, 1929–41. *The Economic Journal 52*, 154–175.

Stone, R. (1971). *Demographic Accounting and Model-Building* (Paris: Organisation for Economic Co-operation and Development (OECD)).

Stone, R. (1975). *Towards a System of Social and Demographic Statistics* (New York: United Nations).

Strack, F., Martin, L. L., and Schwarz, N. (1988). Priming and Communication: Social Determinants of Information Use in Judgments of Life Satisfaction. *European Journal of Social Psychology 18*, 429–442.

Strogatz, S. H. (2001). Exploring Complex Networks. *Nature 410*, 268–276.

Studenski, P. (1958). *The Income of Nations: Theory, Measurement, and Analysis: Past and Present; A Study in Applied Economics and Statistics* (New York: New York University Press).

Sturgeon, T. J. (2013). Global Value Chains and Economic Globalization – Towards a New Measurement Framework (Report to Eurostat). Industrial Performance Center, Massachusetts Institute of Technology.

Suh, S. (2005). Theory of Materials and Energy Flow Analysis in Ecology and Economics. *Ecological Modelling 189*, 251–269.

Talberth, J., and Weisdorf, M. (2017). Genuine Progress Indicator 2.0: Pilot Accounts for the US, Maryland, and City of Baltimore 2012–2014. *Ecological Economics 142*, 1–11.

TEEB (2010). *The Economics of Ecosystems and Biodiversity: Ecological and Economic Foundations* (London: Earthscan).

Thaler, R. H. (2000). From Homo Economicus to Homo Sapiens. *The Journal of Economic Perspectives 14*, 133–141.

Thaler, R. H. (2015). *Misbehaving: The Making of Behavioural Economics* (New York: W. W. Norton and Company).

The Economist (2011). Exports to Mars. *The Economist*, 12 November.

The Economist (2015). Death and Transfiguration. *The Economist*, 19 September.

The Guardian (2016). We've Hit Peak Home Furnishings, Says Ikea Boss: Company's Head of Sustainability Says Consumption of Many Familiar Goods Is at Its Limit. *The Guardian*, 18 January.

Thurow, L. C. (1977). Economics 1977. *Daedalus 106*, 79–94.

Timmer, M. P., Erumban, A. A., Los, B., Stehrer, R., and de Vries, G. J. (2014). Slicing Up Global Value Chains. *The Journal of Economic Perspectives 28*, 99–118.

Timmer, M. P., Miroudot, S., and de Vries, G. J. (2018). Functional Specialisation in Trade. *Journal of Economic Geography* 1–30 (https://doi.org/10.1093/jeg/lby056).

Tinbergen, J., and Hueting, R. (1991). *GNP and Market Prices: Wrong Signals for Sustainable Economic Success That Mask Environmental Destruction* (Washington, DC: World Bank).

Trentmann, F. (2016). *Empire of Things: How we Became a World of Consumers, from the Fifteenth Century to the Twenty-First* (London: Allen Lane Penguin Books).

Tsai, W., and Sumantra, G. (1998). Social Capital and Value Creation: The Role of Intrafirm Networks. *Academy of Management Journal 41*, 464–476.

Tukker, A., and Dietzenbacher, E. (2013). Global Multiregional Input-Output Frameworks: An Introduction and Outlook. *Economic Systems Research 25*, 1–19.

Tversky, A., and Kahneman, D. (1992). Advances in Prospect Theory: Cumulative Representation of Uncertainty. *Journal of Risk and Uncertainty 5*, 297–323.

Tylianakis, J. M., and Morris, R. J. (2016). Ecological Networks Across Environmental Gradients. *Annual Review of Ecology, Evolution, and Systematics 48*, 25–48.

UN (1947). *Measurement of National Income and the Construction of Social Accounts* (Geneva: United Nations).

UN (1952). *Statistical Papers. Series H: Statistics of National Income and Expenditure* (New York: United Nations Statistical Office, United Nations Statistical Division, United Nations Department of Economic Affairs, United Nations Department of Economic and Social Affairs, United Nations Department of Economic and Social Development, United Nations Department of International Economic and Social Affairs, United Nations Secretariat).

UN (1953). *A System of National Accounts and Supporting Tables. Report Prepared by a Group of National Income Experts Appointed by the Secretary General* (New York: United Nations).

UN (1957). *Yearbook of National Accounts Statistics* (New York: United Nations Statistical Office, United Nations Statistical Division, United Nations Department of Economic Affairs, United Nations Department of Economic and Social Affairs, United Nations Department of Economic and Social Development, United Nations Department of International Economic and Social Affairs, United Nations Secretariat).

UN (1968a). *Yearbook of National Accounts Statistics.* Volume 1: Individual country data (New York: United Nations Statistical Office, United Nations Statistical Division, United Nations Department of Economic Affairs, United Nations Department of Economic and Social Affairs, United Nations Department of Economic and Social Development, United Nations Department of International Economic and Social Affairs, United Nations Secretariat).

UN (1968b). *A System of National Accounts* (New York: Department of Economic and Social Affairs, Statistical Office of the United Nations).

UN (1982). *National Accounts Statistics: Main Aggregates and Detailed Tables* (New York: United Nations Statistical Office, United Nations Statistical Division, United Nations Department of Economic Affairs, United Nations Department of Economic and Social Affairs, United Nations Department of Economic and Social Development, United Nations Department of International Economic and Social Affairs, United Nations Secretariat).

UN (1989). *Handbook on Social Indicators* (New York: United Nations).

UN (1992). *Agenda 21* (New York: United Nations Conference on Environment & Development).

UN (1993). *Integrated Environmental and Economic Accounting* (New York: United Nations).

UN (1996). *Indicators of Sustainable Development Framework and Methodologies* (New York: United Nations Sales Publication).

UN (2012). The Future We Want. Resolution adopted by the General Assembly on 27 July 2012. New York: United Nations General Assembly.

UN (2015). Transforming Our World: The 2030 Agenda for Sustainable Development. Resolution adopted by the General Assembly on 25 September 2015. New York: United Nations General Assembly.

UN (2016). *Global Sustainable Development Report 2016* (New York: Department of Economic and Social Affairs).

UN (2017). *Resolution adopted by the General Assembly on 6 July 2017. 71/313. Work of the Statistical Commission pertaining to the 2030 Agenda for Sustainable Development* (New York: United Nations).

UN, EC, IMF, OECD, and World Bank (2003). Integrated Environmental and Economic Accounting 2003. Handbook of National Accounting. Final draft circulated for information prior to official editing.

UN, EC, FAO, IMF, OECD, and World Bank (2014). *System of Environmental-Economic Accounting 2012- Central Framework* (New York: United Nations, European Commission, Food and Agriculture Organization of the United Nations, International Monetary Fund, Organisation for Economic Co-operation and Development and the World Bank).

UNDESA (2008). *Principles and Recommendations for Population and Housing Censuses Revision 2* (New York: Department of Economic and Social Affairs Statistics Division).

UNDESA (2015). *World Population Prospects: The 2015 Revision, Methodology of the United Nations Population Estimates and Projections,* (New York: United Nations, Department of Economic and Social Affairs, Population Division).

UNDP (1990). *Human Development Report: Work for Human Development* (New York: Oxford University Press).

UNDP (2015). *Human Development Report: Work for Human Development* (New York: United Nations Development Programme).

UNECE (2015). *Guide to Measuring Global Production* (Geneva: United Nations Economic Commission for Europe).

UNECE (2016). *Guide on Measuring Human Capital* (New York: United Nations Economic Commission for Europe).

UNECE, OECD, and Eurostat (2008). *Measuring Sustainable Development: Report of the Joint UNECE/OECD/Eurostat Working Group on Statistics for Sustainable Development* (Geneva: United Nations Economic Commission for Europes, Organisation for Economic Co-operation and Development and Eurostat).

UNECE, OECD, and Eurostat (2014). *Conference of European Statisticians Recommendations on Measuring Sustainable Development* (New York: United Nations Economic Commission for Europes, Organisation for Economic Co-operation and Development and Eurostat).

UNU-IHDP and UNEP (2012). *Inclusive Wealth Report 2012: Measuring Progress toward Sustainability* (Cambridge: Cambridge University Press).

UNU-IHDP and UNEP (2014). *Inclusive Wealth Report 2014: Measuring Progress toward Sustainability* (Cambridge: Cambridge University Press).

Van de Kerk, G., and Manuel, A. R. (2008). A Comprehensive Index for a Sustainable Society: The SSI – the Sustainable Society Index. *Ecological Economics 66*, 228–242.

Van den Bergh, J. C. J. M. (2009). The GDP Paradox. *Journal of Economic Psychology 30*, 117–135.

Van den Bergh, J. C. J. M. (2017). A Third Option for Climate Policy within Potential Limits to Growth. *Nature Climate Change 7*, 107–112.

Van den Bergh, J. C. J. M. (2018). *Human Evolution beyond Biology and Culture: Evolutionary Social, Environmental and Policy Sciences* (Cambridge: Cambridge University Press).

Vanoli, A. (2005). *A History of National Accounting* (Amsterdam: IOS Press).

Van Zanden, J. L., Baten, J., d'Ercole, M. M., Rijpma, A., Smith, C., and Timmer, M. (2014). *How Was Life?* (Paris: OECD Publishing).

Vavreck, L. (2009). *The Message Matters: The Economy and Presidential Campaigns* (Princeton, NJ: Princeton University Press).

Veenhoven, R. (1996). Happy Life-Expectancy. *Social Indicators Research 39*, 1–58.

Veenhoven, R. (2017). World Database of Happiness (https://worlddatabaseofhappiness.eur.nl/).

Vemuri, A. W., and Costanza, R. (2006). The Role of Human, Social, Built, and Natural Capital in Explaining Life Satisfaction at the Country Level: Toward a National Well-Being Index (NWI). *Ecological Economics 58*, 119–133.

Victor, P. (1972). *Pollution, Economy and Environment* (Toronto: University of Toronto Press).

Victor, P. (2010). Questioning Economic Growth. *Nature 468*, 370–371.

Vitali, S., and Battiston, S. (2014). The Community Structure of the Global Corporate Network. *PLOS ONE 9*, e104655.

Vitali, S., Glattfelder, J. B., and Battiston, S. (2011). The Network of Global Corporate Control. *PLOS ONE 6*, e25995.

Vitousek, P. M., Ehrlich, P. R., Ehrlich, A. H., and Matson, P. A. (1986). Human Appropriation of the Products of Photosynthesis. *BioScience 36*, 368–373.

Vitousek, P. M., Mooney, H. A., Lubchenco, J., and Melillo, J. M. (1997). Human Domination of Earth's Ecosystems. *Science 277*, 494.

Volkery, A., Swanson, D., Jacob, K., Bregha, F., and Pintér, L. (2006). Coordination, Challenges, and Innovations in 19 National Sustainable Development Strategies. *World Development 34*, 2047–2063.

Wackernagel, M. (1994). *Ecological Footprint and Appropriated Carrying Capacity: A Tool for Planning Toward Sustainability* (Vancouver: The University of British Columbia).

Wallis, J. J., and North, D. C. (1988). Should Transaction Costs be Subtracted from Gross National Product? *The Journal of Economic History 48*, 651–654.

Ward, M. (2004). *Quantifying the World: UN Ideas and Statistics* (Bloomington: Indiana University Press).

Warr, B., and Ayres, R. U. (2012). Useful Work and Information as Drivers of Economic Growth. *Ecological Economics 73*, 93–102.

Warr, B., Ayres, R., Eisenmenger, N., Krausmann, F., and Schandl, H. (2010). Energy Use and Economic Development: A Comparative Analysis of Useful Work Supply in Austria, Japan, the United Kingdom and the US during 100 Years of Economic Growth. *Ecological Economics 69*, 1904–1917.

WCED (1987). *Our Common Future – Report of the World Commission on Environment and Development* (Oxford: World Commission on Environment and Development, Oxford University Press).

Weintraub, E. R. (2002). *How Economics Became a Mathematical Science* (Durham, NC: Duke University Press).

Weitzman, M. L. (1976). On the Welfare Significance of National Product in a Dynamic Economy. *The Quarterly Journal of Economics 90*, 156–162.

Weitzman, M. L. (1998). Why the Far-Distant Future Should Be Discounted at Its Lowest Possible Rate. *Journal of Environmental Economics and Management 36*, 201–208.

Whitby, A. (Ed.) (2014). BRAINPOoL Final Report: Beyond GDP – From Measurement to Politics and Policy. Deliverable 5.2, 31 March 2014.

WHO (1948). *Preamble to the Constitution of the World Health Organization* (New York: World Health Organization).

Wikiprogress.org (2017). Wikiprogress – Well-being and Sustainability Initiatives (http://wikiprogress.org/).

Williams, R. J., and Martinez, N. D. (2000). Simple Rules Yield Complex Food Webs. *Nature 404*, 180–183.

Williams, J. R., Masuda, Y. J., and Tallis, H. (2016). A Measure Whose Time has Come: Formalizing Time Poverty. *Social Indicators Research 128*, 265–283.

Wilson, E. O. (1998). *Consilience: The Unity of Knowledge* (New York: Knopf.).

Wilson, J., Tyedmers, P., and Pelot, R. (2007). Contrasting and Comparing Sustainable Development Indicator Metrics. *Ecological Indicators 7*, 299–314.

Wilting, H. C., Schipper, A. M., Bakkenes, M., Meijer, J. R., and Huijbregts, M. A. J. (2017). Quantifying Biodiversity Losses Due to Human Consumption: A Global-Scale Footprint Analysis. *Environmental Science and Technology 51*, 3298–3306.

Woolcock, M. (1998). Social Capital and Economic Development: Toward a Theoretical Synthesis and Policy Framework. *Theory and Society 27*, 151–208.

World Bank (2006). *Where is the Wealth of Nations? Measuring Capital for the 21st Century* (Washington, DC: The World Bank).

World Bank (2010). *The Changing Wealth of Nations* (Washington, DC: The World Bank).

Wößmann, L. (2003). Specifying Human Capital. *Journal of Economic Surveys 17*, 239–270.

WWF (1998). *Living Planet Report: Overconsumption is Driving the Rapid Decline of the World's Natural Environments* (Gland, Switzerland: World Wildlife Fund).

Yang, C., Dietzenbacher, E., Pei, J., Chen, X., Zhu, K., and Tang, Z. (2015). Processing Trade Biases: The Measurement of Vertical Specialisation in China. *Economic Systems Research 27*, 60–76.

Zhou, P., and Wang, M. (2016). Carbon Dioxide Emissions Allocation: A Review. *Ecological Economics 125*, 47–59.

Zwijnenburg, J. (2017). *Unequal Distributions? A Study on Differences between the Compilation of Household Distributional Results according to DINA and EGDNA Methodology* (Paris: OECD).

Zwijnenburg, J., Bournot, S., and Giovannelli, F. (2016). *OECD Expert Group on Disparities in a National Accounts Framework – Results from the 2015 Exercise* (Paris: OECD).

Index

Printed in the United States
By Bookmasters